FINE LINES

FINE LINES

THE BEST OF **Ms.** FICTION

Edited and with an Introduction by
RUTH SULLIVAN

CHARLES SCRIBNER'S SONS
New York

Copyright © 1981 Ms. Foundation for Education and Communication, Inc.

1982 Paperback edition first published by Charles Scribner's Sons

Library of Congress Cataloging in Publication Data
Main entry under title:

Fine lines.

  Contents: Bodies / Hilma Wolitzer—Life without
Martin / Jane Shapiro—Not a very nice story /
Doris Lessing—[etc.]
    1. Short stories, American—Women authors.
  2. Short stories, English—Women authors.
  I. Sullivan, Ruth.   II. Ms.
  PS647.W6F5   813'.01'089287   81–8857
  ISBN 0–684–17143–0 (cloth)   AACR2
  ISBN 0–684–17650–5 (paper)

1 3 5 7 9 11 13 15 17 19   F/P   20 18 16 14 12 10 8 6 4 2

Printed in the United States of America

ACKNOWLEDGMENTS

The stories included here represent thousands of stories evaluated over the past nine years by the following members of the *Ms.* staff: Ingeborg Day, Joanne Edgar, Nina Finkelstein, Donna Handly, Suzanne Braun Levine, Susan McHenry, Robin Morgan, Catherine O'Haire, Joan Philpott, Letty Cottin Pogrebin, Marcia Rockwood, Phyllis Rosser, Gloria Steinem, Ellen Sweet, Mary Thom, and Alice Walker.

CONTENTS

Contents

INTRODUCTION

When *Ms.* magazine appeared in 1972, its pages became a magnet for the newly honest, often provocative writing of women. The hundreds of poems and stories *Ms.* received each week were proof that the process of becoming a woman had become a central theme of contemporary literature. As Simone de Beauvoir wrote, women have been created by men and defined as the Other. But when women no longer accept this definition, there is a momentary loss of self—and the process of self-creation is a painful one. The female protagonist in much recent fiction is fighting against both society's definition and her own internalized values.

"Everything of importance about my life," writes Louise Bogan in *Journey Around My Room,* "is in my poetry, except the raw and vulgar facts." A hallmark of the new writing by women is the fine line between the life and the work. Elinor Langer distinguishes good literature from the confessional writings associated with the first outpourings of women's lives in consciousness raising: "In confession the self runs rampant; in autobiography, the writer uses the self to inspect the world." And as women inspect the world, they open up new areas of subject matter that haven't been written about before—friendships among women, sexuality between women, aging, mother–daughter relationships, maternity, the crisis of divorce, sex as women experience it, and, especially in the writing of black women, a shattering of stereotypes. Women's stories reclaim female experience or name it for the first time.

A new voice emerges in these stories—strong, self-confident, often self-mocking. It sounds both new and instantly recognizable. In the writing represented in this collection, women are no longer mining old angers, but rather are exploring the whole range of human emotion and experience.

So the stories here are anything but predictable or doctrinaire. In fact, some work playfully against the old definition of "female literature," while others confound the new stereotype of "feminist writing." Lessing writes against the prevailing notion of the very private "female sensibility"; her social and political vision is larger than the private consciousness would allow. She chooses an omniscient, detached, and cynical narrator to tell "Not a Very Nice Story." The story itself demonstrates a profound distrust of emotion. The point about adultery, realizes the unromantic Muriel, is not the lovemaking, not the sex, but the "spilling of emotion afterward, the anguish, the guilt . . . the *belief* that great emotion had been felt."

The question of whether feminism frees women to write exactly what they think or constricts them with new limitations is answered humorously by Margaret Drabble in a story that she says could not have been told five years ago: "The opposite case, for political reasons, would have to be made." But now her heroine, Kathy Jones, an otherwise typical feminist "success story," can admit that she would rather, at that particular moment, have a man admire her legs than her mind, would rather he lust after her than talk to her. The point about liberation is the power to choose, even though that choice—as in Kathy Jones's case—may be the conventional one.

While Lessing and Drabble are consciously using traditional forms or expectations to say something new, other writers are experimenting with totally new fictive forms. Science fiction, explains one of its best practitioners, Joanna Russ, is a perfect vehicle to explore assumptions about innate values and natural social arrangements. The futuristic fantasy Sally Gearhart uses to celebrate women's ancient powers of intuition and nurturance in "Krueva and the Pony" takes the idea of a female subculture to the extreme of an all-female universe where women live in loving harmony with other sentient beings. Meghan Collins takes an old form, the fairy tale, but tells it from the witch's point of view to suggest woman's mystical connection to nature. And Joyce Thompson's "Ice Flowers" can be read as a subtle variation on the mad housewife genre: the young wife communes with the passionate, nightside of her being through the Heathcliff-like creature who howls each night beneath her bedroom window.

In attitude toward their subjects, these writers run against traditional assumptions as well. Fanny Howe challenges the romanticizing of the maternal instinct in "The Right Thing." Margaret Atwood defies an earlier trend by *not* glorifying the victim, Betty. The story is saved from being predictable by focusing on the mystery of the trivialized, subservient woman and not on the men who abuse her. The sympathy with / repulsion for the "victim" haunts us at the same time as it reminds us of our childhood responses to some of our mother's friends.

New perspectives emerge from the way women are reclaiming their childhood experiences. Mary Gordon's "The Thorn," told from a very young child's point of view, reveals the profound burden of parental love. Although the representative story of childhood happens here to be about a father and daughter, a more urgent theme in recent writing is the mother–daughter bond that Adrienne Rich describes as "fraught with the deepest mutuality and the most profound estrangement." Whether it's Virginia Woolf trying to put her own mother in perspective through the portrait of Mrs. Ramsey in *To the Lighthouse,* or Alice Munro writing recently, "This whole journey [of writing] has been to reach my mother, to mark her off, to illumine, to celebrate, to get rid of her," women have been trying to write out their mothers. Critic Elizabeth Janeway proposes that in women's fiction the passage from daughterhood to motherhood, whether actual or symbolic, is replacing the rite of marriage in male literature as the symbol of maturity. Women's experience tells us that this is the more radical change.

Lessing's *Golden Notebook* opens on two women engaged in that "intimate conversation that passed for gossip." Although such talk was dismissed by men as mere chatter, women were creating their own social history over those kitchen tables, but only recently has what they were saying to one another been heard. Depictions of camaraderie so prevalent in fiction about men have been absent from stories about women. Mary Heaton Vorse's "Quiet Woman," written in 1907 and only recently retrieved, is a first tentative, awkward and strangely moving vignette of two women who like each other. Vorse was tuned into the unspoken between women; she was also amazingly prescient in depicting the ruthlessness of the intimacy that coexists with the magnetism between men and women. When the quiet woman finds her voice to speak to the younger of things she had kept hidden even from herself, it is an act that is only now being defined as female heroism.

By contrast, the friendship in "The Barking" lies in what the women *don't* tell each other. On the surface, the story is the gradual revelation of the true character of a man through the lies two women tell each other to protect both him and themselves. Though the only relationship allowed them by a rigid

Viennese society is that of mother-in-law and daughter-in-law and their topic of conversation remains the prescribed one of the son, Leo, the two women break through to a genuine kindness toward each other. Ingeborg Bachmann subtly portrays this affection as a vital undercurrent that is never acknowledged between them.

A more tenuous and fragile relationship exists in Alice Walker's view of an interracial friendship that survived the civil rights movement. Writing out of what she calls the "twin affliction" of race and sex, Walker here raises difficult questions about sisterhood. "Advancing Luna and Ida B. Wells" reflects what Gloria Steinem has described as a second stage of feminism: "after the first flush of feminist understanding that women, no matter how diverse, share the common dilemmas of sexual caste, the second stage . . . is measuring the diversity and understanding what chasms there are to bridge." In Walker's story, the rape of the white woman Luna by a black man comes between the friends, and their bond as women cannot transcend either the history of white privilege or the power that Luna's—or any white woman's—word on rape still has over an entire people. Like the vase that Luna gives the narrator, friendship between black and white women remains flawed, though perhaps more precious because of what it has survived. Though this is a conclusion the narrator would rather not face, at the end of her quest she realizes that sisterhood and innocence cannot coexist and that from this "real" knowledge there is no turning back.

In "Requiem for Willie Lee," a middle-class black woman reaches out to identify with another member of a powerless group, in this case a victim of racism, the rage-filled Willie Lee. "Since all the Willie Lees have been erased from history," writes black critic Mary Helen Washington, "it is the most profound act of recognition to see them. To see these invisible ones means confronting the terror of one's own invisibility." Embracing the dying man, the narrator acknowledges her tie to him and shows compassion for the thwarted need for love that had been twisted into violence. In its own way this is a love story, albeit an uncommon one.

Other uncommon love stories in this collection range from Lynda Schor's wry and satirical account of a male–female relationship that cannot transcend political differences to Hilma Wolitzer's stunning story of love transcending "bodies"—"that place where all human misery can be traced." Schor's voice, rejecting the old amenities, is candid about her sexual needs and her lover's privilege. Like many recent stories of a woman's epiphany, this one turns on the sudden recognition of her connection with another woman—her lover's all-capable, invisible housekeeper.

Women's politics started with their own bodies, but in Wolitzer's "Bodies" the heroine can afford, at no loss to herself, to look at a man's body and feel *his* vulnerability. The story itself transcends sexual politics by showing how to risk loving even though it seems we will never know one another. Once the rhetorical points have been made, perhaps it is for fiction to go on to explore the psychological and human nuances. In a story like "Life Without Martin," an amusing and very topical glimpse of a marriage coming apart, or about to, the reader can identify emotionally with the texture of change, the missed connections and flashes of tenderness. Fiction is as complex and untidy, as lumpy and layered as the actual relationships between men and women.

The task of all fiction is to make the world whole. Once the feminist perception split the familiar world open, women writers faced the challenge of reintegrating the world from their own perspective. Perhaps because they have less faith in the mental categories that men use to organize their perceptions, women experience and reflect back a more fluid reality and give it immediacy and significance. The result is a revolution both in content—for example, the domestic dailiness of women's lives is offered as a serious subject for fiction—and in technique, for example, the effort by some writers to eliminate literary devices that distanced the reader from the story. Women's fiction re-presents the world.

Women found in fiction a haven, a place where truth telling became possible, and not because a writer hides behind a character, but because in creating fiction one has access to the unconscious and to a different kind of truth. The fiction women have written in the last decade is a record of personal discovery, a document of our collective conscious; to read it is to see where we have been. But because fiction frees the imagination to project all kinds of worlds and lives, this collection suggests a vision of women's future as well. "In non-fiction, I write about what I know," says Barbara Grizzuti Harrison, who is working on her first novel. "But what I write about in fiction is what I don't know I know." We can look forward to what she and other writers will discover, create, reveal.

—RUTH SULLIVAN

BODIES

Hilma Wolitzer

Hilma Wolitzer, born in Brooklyn, New York, in 1930, decided at age eighteen that earning twenty-eight dollars a week was more attractive than earning a degree. She married early, had two children, and did not write her first story until she was thirty-five. Six months later, "Today a Woman Went Mad in the Supermarket" was published by the Saturday Evening Post. Since then her stories have appeared in numerous periodicals and anthologies and she has written three novels—Ending (1974), In The Flesh (1977), and Hearts (1980), as well as three young adult novels. Wolitzer has taught at the Bread Loaf Writers' Conference and the Bennington Summer Writing Workshop. She has been named the Bread Loaf Scholar in Fiction and awarded Guggenheim and National Endowment for the Arts fellowships, and the Great Lakes Colleges Association Best New Writer award.

Wolitzer sometimes regrets her late start as a writer but expresses relief that she didn't follow the dictum to "write only about what you know," since her years of being "just a housewife" would have brought on terminal writer's block. Her books are about troubling matters that she has not experienced firsthand—the death by cancer of a thirty-two-year-old man; a woman whose husband leaves her for another woman—and yet in her novels, as in the story "Bodies," she writes about what she obviously knows well: the secrets of the human heart and what it is capable of in moments of crisis. In one of the rarer love stories of our time, Wolitzer here embraces the male body in all its beauty and indecency.

MICHAEL AND SHARON FORTUNE are too young to have ever seen Lenny Bruce in performance, but they have vintage editions of Bruce's records, on which he denies vulgarity in anything sexual. There are no dirty words. And there are no dirty acts, except for the insidious ones of social injustice.

At the end of one record there's something about a flasher, a man who opens his raincoat and displays a bunch of lilacs instead of a penis. Like the trick of a gentle magician, Sharon thought the first time she heard it, and the visual image has stayed with her. Because she is an artist, all words convert finally into pictures; even her dreams are a silent, colorful banner of events.

Michael interviews elderly welfare applicants, and Sharon believes he is a vessel for language, a Steinberg figure composed of the hard-luck stories of strangers and his own urgent, unspoken words.

He's only the second lover she's ever had. The first was a prose poet named Beau Carpenter, and she met Michael on the rebound from that affair. The difference between the two men astounded her. Beau had been so authoritative, and she such a willing follower. She would wait in the wings of their bed for her cue to enter, apprentice to a master in a complicated acrobatic act. Not that Michael was passive. But he always allowed her a fair healthy share of aggression, and sometimes Sharon was surprised to find herself raucously sexual.

With Beau, she had affected silence because he required it. After two years of marriage to Michael, she still questioned him as if *she* were the social worker, and he had come to her for aid. He'd had the worst childhood she could imagine. And he spoke about it, when asked, with an almost detached calm. The family had lived in the Midwest. His mother was the breadwinner, a practical nurse who traveled around, staying in other people's houses to care for newborn infants. His father, once a Linotype operator, was house-bound with severe emphysema. The rooms were clogged with his breathing. Michael was their only child, an easy target for his father's maniacal revenge on the world.

When Michael was about four or five years old, he told her, his father held his hands over the open gas jets on the stove until his palms were scorched, until they cooked and blistered, a lesson on the dangers of playing with matches.

Sharon had cried out in an agony of compassion, "I'd like to *kill* him!"

"Too late," Michael said. "He's already dead."

"Well, what did your mother do about it?"

"She wasn't there. I guess she was out on a case."

"But she must have seen your hands when she came home."

Michael shrugged. "I don't remember," he said. "Maybe they were healed by then, I don't know. She came back every few weeks, dying for sleep, and headed for bed."

"Terrible," Sharon said, and he thought she meant for his mother.

"Yeah. She used to wake up and she couldn't remember where she was. She'd forget sometimes if a baby was a boy or a girl until she diapered it again."

"You must have hated your father."

"Yes."

Sharon stared at him. "Michael, why are you smiling?" she asked.

His mother died suddenly, of a stroke, and Michael flew to Dayton to take care of the funeral. While he was there, he rented a car and then decided to drive it all the way home. When the phone rang that night, she thought it was Michael, sleepless and lonely, calling from a motel room. But it was their friend Dick Schaffner.

She was working, finishing the last in a series of political cartoons. She clamped the receiver between her chin and her shoulder and continued to work. Then she said, "What? *What?*" as if the connection had been broken or her hearing had failed, so that Dick was forced to shout the details at her. As she listened, she scribbled nervous markings all over her drawing, ruining it.

Dick told her to try and keep things in perspective, that it was pretty complicated, in a legal sense. "And it's not even supposed to be really sexual, you know," he said.

Of *course* she knew, and felt both tenderness and irritation at his affectionate condescension.

But despite everything, she clung to the idea that it *was* sexual, part of the whole damn business of bodies to which all human misery can probably be traced. What else is it if a man takes his prick out in a public place and invites a strange woman to look at it?

She was alternately cold with shock and blazing with humiliation. She had been this way once before, when Beau left her for that other woman. The analogy was all wrong, but she felt stubbornly logical. *This* was a kind of jilting, too. She had become as ludicrous as those poor writers of letters to newspaper columnists:

Dear Abby,

Is love blind? My husband (I'll call him Joe) is a wonderful lover and a good provider. He is also a swell father and an outstanding member of the community. Imagine my shock, Abby, when I discovered last week that he's been carrying on for years with:

                A. My mother! or:
                B. The mailman! or:
                C. A German shepherd! or:
                D. All of the above!

Abby, do I let him know I'm on to his little game, or do I just count my blessings and keep my big mouth shut?

Sign me,
Myopic Mabel from Missoula

Now Sharon is flying to Ohio because she urgently wants to go, and because Dick said that the presence of an attractive supportive wife is invaluable in cases like this. He added wistfully that if she were pregnant or could conjure up a kid or two for the trip, it would even be better. Would she like to rent one of his? His office would make travel arrangements for her, and he would follow on a later flight and meet her there.

Sharon wishes that Dick was beside her now, holding her hand in one of his bear's paws and shuffling through official papers with the other. Instead, she has the aisle seat next to a man with tortuously styled hair who is drinking a Scotch sour and staring out the window as if he were communing with Saint-Exupéry. Sharon has refused a drink; in a couple of hours she will be in a motel room where she can smoke one of the joints she has hidden in a cigarette pack, and be soothed.

Across the aisle an elderly woman, dressed resolutely in black

—dress, scarf, stockings, shoes—is asleep. Italian, probably, or maybe Greek. She looks like a billboard for death. Why is it always the women in those places who are assigned the work of perpetual mourning?

After Beau left her, Sharon had plunged into mourning, too. Not inaccurately, or even unkindly, he predicted a full, formal year of grieving for her. She'd wondered if this was based on his own past experience or whether it was an absolute standard for female behavior in that kind of situation. That's how dumb and innocent she was in those days. But obediently she began to grieve, to start to get it over with. In a few weeks, she was able to think about him again. It wasn't that grief had become less, but that it had become different, moving up into the intellect, away from the body, from those aching places, the shoulders and the fingertips.

She is trying to focus on Michael, and ironically it's his body she thinks of first, or about bodies in general, a commuter's crowd of them in which his appears looking reasonable, if mortal. Cautiously, she imagines him clothed: the singing corduroy of his trousers as he walks, that yellow shirt. Sharon remembers the work of the cartoonist after whom she first fashioned herself stylistically, and who undressed everyone in the mind's eye of his characters. She does that sometimes, too, in life. Not for the sake of humor, though, or even for democracy: there is no democracy, anyway. Sharon is tall and the woman Beau went off with is not, et cetera, et cetera.

But she is unable to undress Michael now, must keep him protectively, lawfully covered. Instead she considers what has happened, what might happen next. The night before, after she had recovered a little, she called Dick back. Her voice was tremulous and uncertain, but her questions were not. "Why didn't he call me, too? Did he say, did he actually *say* that he did it?"

Dick sighed deeply and Sharon realized that it was very late and that he was probably in bed beside Anna. "We didn't go into it, Sharon," he said. "It's never a good idea, on the telephone. And he was allowed only one brief call, like in the movies. You know how that goes; they always call their mouthpiece."

"But why can't he be released until the arraignment? Isn't that what usually happens?" She hesitated and her voice fell into a hoarse whisper. "He doesn't have a record or anything, does he?"

"No, babe, no. Of course not. It's just that his timing was lousy for this particular place. There's been a series of assorted complaints over the past month or so. So they've invented a few extra charges to hold him on."

"That's not fair!" she cried.

"Fair!" Dick said. "Are you kidding? What does fair have to do with anything? Don't worry, Sharon. Come on. We'll get them to drop them all. We'll get the best local counsel. Everything will be okay."

"Did he explain that he was only driving through? Did he tell them about his mother?"

"Yeah, he explained everything. But the natives are restless. And suspicious. They've *all* just buried their mother. And they don't know our Mikey the way we do."

But now Sharon didn't know him either. "What kind of complaints?" she asked.

"What?"

"You said before—assorted complaints."

"Oh. An attempted rape in the Laundromat. Kids talking about a guy who hangs around the schoolyard."

"Oh, God, it wasn't a child, was it?" Sharon has always been sternly moralistic about what adults do to children. She might even have to cast the first stone herself. She remembered a drawing she did for a newspaper decrying inadequate security in city schools, after a child had been molested in a stairwell. Her version of the molester lurked in shadows, a grotesque, subhuman figure.

But Dick reassured her. "No, no. I *told* you. A grown woman."

He said it in the condoning way one says "consenting adults."
"In the parking lot of a supermarket."

"She could be lying, couldn't she? Or hallucinating?"

"Sure," Dick said, but his tone was palliative, and the details
finally stunned her into silence.

"Are you okay?" Dick asked. "Listen, do you want me to bring
Anna over to spend the rest of the night?"

And then Anna took the phone and asked a few gentle questions in a sleepy voice.

"No, I'm fine," Sharon said. "Really." And she did feel better,
not only because there wasn't a child involved, but because the
situation was becoming less real again. Men, *other* men, did that
sort of thing in subway passages, or in dark alleyways. The parking lot of a supermarket seemed foolishly domestic for such an
unnatural gesture.

Yet suddenly she pictured Michael unfolding to his height
from the car. He was stopping for cigarettes, probably, on the
way to a motel. And she pictured the woman, also, mid-thirties,
darkly pretty, wheeling one of those recalcitrant shopping carts,
or juggling too many grocery bags and trying to find the car keys,
and thinking of dinner and what to do about her elderly widowed
father, and recalling a fleeting lust for her minister, and then
seeing Michael.

Public nudity still surprises Sharon. When she was sixteen,
she took a life drawing class. She was late for the first session and
arrived after the model was arranged in her pose on the platform.
How flagrant her nakedness seemed; she loomed so large Sharon
could not fit her onto the newsprint page. Sometimes her feet
were missing, sometimes her head. After several poses, the model
put on a robe and wandered among the easels smoking a cigarette.
Sharon felt embarrassed and apologetic, as if she were witness-
ing the aftermath of the Primal Scene. And she knew again the
frustration of not knowing anything, with the underlying fear
that it was not due to her youth, but to some fatal flaw that would

keep her from the world's mysteries forever. She smoked one of the model's cigarettes and said pretentious things about form and space. Later the bare breasts stared at her with contempt.

The plane dips slightly and Sharon presses back against a wave of vertigo. The man in the window seat looks at her inquiringly, and she shakes her head and shuts her eyes.

Oh, consider passion for a moment! Dick has assured her that Michael's is not a crime of passion. And once she couldn't wait to agree with Beau that it all begins in the head and then sends its orders rushing down through the nerves and into the blood-stream, arousing the troops, those mercenaries. But when he told her that the first thing he admired about her was her eyesight, she was bewildered, wanting only to be wanted in more conventional ways. Why not admire her blondness, which was everywhere, or her buttocks, which were worthy of praise?

But soon she learned to feel cherished and, covering each eye in turn, read aloud to him the small print of a sign on the other side of the Williamsburg Bridge. Acting further in kind, she told him that his feet pleased her. Vision and stride. An uncommon attraction, but stirringly original.

All right, she decides, forget passion. It's really comfort she's trying to think of in bodily terms, anyway. How each of us starts out bravely alone, lover and beloved at once, and works toward the ultimate collaboration, that other serious presence in the darkness. Is it that she always fails in this connection, or that Michael is hopelessly wounded, inconsolable?

When the flight attendant comes down the aisle offering news-papers, Sharon takes one. But she cannot concentrate on the headlines, on the larger, shared tragedies of floods, famine, and politics. She reads a small article on an inside page. It says that scientists have discovered that the bones of fat people are especially dense and sturdy. As she reads it, she thinks of Michael and his thinness. She imagines his bones (a murderous urge and a longing), and they are as delicate and as porous as coral, yet unable to resist the loping curve of his posture. His breastbone is an archer's bow.

Early that morning, Sharon had awakened abruptly and in a panic. "I can't, I *can't*," she said, not sure what she meant, but feeling more desperate for distraction than for interpretation. Thought was treacherous. Getting out of bed might require major effort. To delay it she took a magazine from the nightstand and opened it at random to an interview with Sartre, by Simone de Beauvoir. He said, "We yield our bodies to everyone, even beyond the realm of sexual relations, by looking, by touching."

Tell that to the judge, she thinks now, wishing she could be convinced of it herself. Maybe she will be when she is seventy, like Sartre.

Her seatmate gets up to go to the bathroom. His legs brush over Sharon's and he murmurs, "Excuse me," but he winks.

When he returns, she rises to let him pass.

"Business or pleasure?" he asks, and she looks at him blankly.

"In Columbus," he says.

"I'm meeting my husband there. Not really there, further east, on the outskirts. His mother just died," she adds, and is horrified to realize she is smiling.

He smiles back. "What does your husband do?"

Do? He's in zippers. He pops flies. He shows his choice goods to discriminating shoppers.

"He's a social worker," she says, "with the city's welfare system."

The man continues to smile, not registering her answer. He's had a second drink, and maybe still another from a flask in the john, and she can see that he has a buzz on. He leans back in his seat and faces her intimately, as if they are sharing a bed pillow. He is wearing the kind of suit she most dislikes, with very large lapels and contrasting piping, and he has exaggerated sideburns. He looks like a member of a barbershop quartet, or like Captain Kangaroo. Yet she understands that he imagines himself attractive to her, sexy.

She goes through the mind process that removes his offending clothing, a piece at a time. Off with the jacket, with the busy tie. Off with the shiny synthetic shirt that clutches his bull neck in a stranglehold. She drops his trousers and they fall to his ankles, clanking keys and loose change everywhere. Impatiently, she pulls off his stacked-heel shoes, his socks, his patterned under-shorts, even the chains that protect his slack and hairy chest from evil with amulets from three separate cultures. But when he sits there at last, heavy-eyed with seduction and whiskey, the seat belt strapped across his puckered navel, just above his nodding cock, his body is as absurd to her as his clothing. Quickly, she dresses him again and turns away.

Michael always undressed without shyness or seduction, a practical business before bath or bed, as if he were unconscious of how well he was made, or of his easy athletic grace. And Sharon resisted what she considers a crude tendency toward voyeurism. He isn't the first man she's ever seen, though, and maybe he won't be the last.

Once it was her goal in life. Father and grandfather dead before memory, she lived in a household of females: grand-mother, aunt, mother, older sister. They undressed openly, too, offering Sharon the various stages of her future, and she was interested, but of course she wasn't satisfied. Word was out.

She had seen statues of men at the Brooklyn Museum, budding in marble, bloodless and chaste. Their eyes were absent, too. At the circumcision of a neighbor's infant when Sharon was four, someone turned her face to the wall at the last minute. "Don't look," the woman said, a good beginning for a fairy tale with moral significance if Sharon had not been consistently obedient, had not shielded those twenty-twenty eyes and counted until it was over. But just before the ritual, she watched closely and saw that the baby's parts were still wrinkled from passage, and she heard him cry piteously, as if he were intolerably burdened.

And she had a male dog for a while during childhood. He was a small mixed breed with a coarse brown coat and an affectionate nature. She called him Prince. She would take him into bed in the morning and stroke his belly and ears, and he would loll, sighing. Once, while she petted him, a thin red tube emerged from that hair-tipped pinch of flesh with the startling clarity of her sister's first lipstick. Sharon picked him up quickly and roughly and put him on the floor. "Bad dog!" she scolded, uncoached, and Prince growled at her.

The first naked man she saw was a friend's father, after Sharon slept at their house one night in the summertime. He must have been about thirty-five or forty years old. Sharon opened the door to her friend's parents' bedroom in the morning. There was that particular early stillness, the clockwork pause before life resumes. The mother was asleep, face down in the bedclothes, and the father was just getting up. He stood, in profile to Sharon, stretching his arms overhead, and then sat down on the edge of the bed, holding a pair of shorts in one hand. He seemed to be daydreaming.

He was a depressed man. Years later he committed suicide. In those days, though, he was only eccentric and moody, given to ironic remarks that were hurtful to others. Sharon was afraid of him in an instinctive way; he had never been cruel to her, had hardly noticed her.

But in that quick and brilliant moment—she is sure she remembers sunlight in the bedroom—she saw his melancholy in the droop of his genitals, and felt a rush of knowledge and of anguish.

She hurries from the plane as if she is going to be met by friends or loved ones. Other passengers *are* greeted and she moves past their pleasured cries and embraces to an exit from the terminal and a taxi.

She gives the driver the name of the motel and sits back.

"Well, hello, *hello!*" he says, and bending one sunburned and tattooed arm onto the window ledge, he pulls away from the curb like a madman.

In the past, Sharon has been amused by this kind of silly attention from men, the construction worker syndrome of whistles, catcalls, and general showing off. It was a kind of harmless, universal foreplay. But now it seems like such primitive behavior, one step beyond chest-thumping. She feels annoyed—worse—imposed upon. Who asked for this?

The cab driver sings, leans on the horn needlessly, and watches Sharon in the rearview mirror so that he has to brake sharply for a squirrel that decides to cross the road. "Fucker," he mutters, and goes forward again, but more slowly this time, his spirit tamed.

The motel is the same one Michael went to, after, and where he was arrested. Dick has made reservations, but it is not a sadistic choice. The rented Chevy is still parked there, and the place is clean and convenient to the jail where Michael is being held. Early tomorrow, she and Dick will go there together for the only visitation permitted before arraignment.

The motel manager's face gives nothing away when she claims her reservation. Behind him, a door opens briefly and she can see a living room and two small children watching television, before it closes again. She signs the registration slip and has an urge to ask to see the one Michael must have signed the day before. How does a man feel after such an act? Frightened? Breathless with exhilaration? So deeply affected, perhaps, that his handwriting is irrevocably altered. And there is the keener secret fantasy that it will be another man's signature altogether, one of those wonderful minor news stories about mistaken identity. Families of men killed in the war and sent home in sealed coffins must suffer that possibility over and over again.

But she asks for nothing but the key to her room and the one to the car.

The room is shabbily genteel and telescopically smaller than the one depicted on the postcards for sale in the motel office. There are twin beds with green covers, and matching drapes that transform the last of an Ohio sunset into a Martian luminescence.

Dick's flight won't be in until seven thirty, and he has instructed her to stay put, not to drive to the airport to meet him.

He will come directly to the motel and they can go out for dinner and talk about the next day.

There are almost two hours ahead during which she will be alone in this place and she contemplates them with increasing nervousness. She rejects the idea of smoking pot, losing confidence in its shamanistic powers to thwart loneliness. She knows intuitively that this is a dangerous time of day when, for some people, blood sugar plummets, and fatigue is a marauder. If records were to be checked, she is sure there would be a disproportionate number of suicides, automobile accidents, and violent crimes committed just before dusk. Brooders begin to gather evidence for their brooding. Insomniacs think of scary darkness, depressives of death.

Sharon opens the drapes and her room faces a small swimming pool surrounded by a locked cyclone fence. A few children run crazily around it, shrieking and hurling scraps of paper at one another that blow back into their own faces. She wonders what Michael is doing at this moment and thinks how awkward it will be to see him in that place, with this new knowledge between them. She feels that changes are taking place inside her, as mysterious and involuntary as metabolism and circulation. What if she experiences a complete failure of love, even of charity? She closes the drapes, making the room green again, and lies down on the bed nearest the window. Now she regrets not having brought along something to read, even the complimentary magazine from the seat pocket in the plane.

On the night table next to her, a pictorial breakfast menu from the motel's coffee shop is propped against an ashtray. Glorified color photos of eggs and sausage, of waffles and pancakes, looking more like Oldenburg sculptures of food than like real food, are advertised at irregular prices, as if they had been marked down: $1.79 for The Sunrise Special, $2.05 for Old Mac-Donald's Choice. She reads a printed message from the maid thanking her for being such a wonderful guest, and it is hand signed in a childishly broad scrawl: *Sincerely, Wanda.*

Sharon looks at her watch and then holds it to her ear to confirm its function. With her splendid vision she can read the sign on the back of the door at least eight feet away from the bed. Checkout time, she learns, is at 11 A.M., and the fire exits are posted.

In the drawer of the night table there is a thin phone book for the local area, and the mandatory Bible. She opens the phone book to see if there is anyone listed with the same name as Michael or herself. If there is, she decides, she will take that as a good omen for tomorrow. There isn't, but she finds a Richard Schaffner and someone with a spelling variation of her father's name living on Sharon Court. *That* could mean something, couldn't it? She wonders about the woman who saw Michael in the parking lot the day before, and if she is listed in the telephone book, too. Sharon imagines calling the number just to hear her voice, and then hanging up again without speaking.

Michael had called her a few hours after his mother's funeral. He sounded fine at first and then his voice became softer and fainter as if he were traveling swiftly away on a boat or a train, and twice she had to ask him to speak louder. He said that a few neighbors had come to the chapel, and the woman his mother lived with, another practical nurse, had gone to the cemetery with him. She wore her uniform and those rubber-soled shoes. She said that his mother had died from the babies, from sleeping in those small rooms they gave you, and the babies used up all the air. She complained bitterly about eating tainted luncheon meat while the family ate lamb chops, about having only a tiny corner of a closet in which to hang her uniforms, next to stored luggage, ironing boards, and folded bridge tables.

She was crazy. She said she dreamed of poisoning babies or drowning them and what was she supposed to do now that his mother wouldn't be sharing the rent on their apartment; she couldn't afford it, and that young couples didn't even wait six weeks postpartum anymore; she could hear them going at it through the walls all night.

When he left, she walked outside with him, her shoes squeaking. He gave her some money that she tucked into her pocket without even looking at it, and she kept walking alongside the car and talking to him as he drove slowly away. He was afraid she would fall under the wheels.

"I should have come with you," Sharon said. "You should have let me."

"No," he insisted. "It's all right. I handled it. You had a deadline, anyway—"

"But I wanted to," she said, which wasn't really true. "Someone else could have taken this assignment."

"Well, it's fine, it's all settled now. I'm on my way," he told her. "I'll be home soon."

The telephone book slides to the floor and Sharon opens the Bible to Ecclesiastes and reads, "Sorrow *is* better than laughter: for by the sadness of the countenance the heart is made better."

When Beau was packing his books, she watched him silently for a while, still reflexively aiming to please. Then she said, in her new, diminished voice, "And what did you admire about *her*, first?"

One of his hands rested on a volume of Donne; with the other he took off his glasses and rubbed his eyes. "The usual," he said. "Hair, breasts, skin."

She closes the Bible and puts it back into the night-table drawer. Her hand goes to her heart, to her breast, and then up to the dependable pulse of her throat.

Last year, when her aunt had her breast removed, Sharon went to the hospital to visit her. And they did not talk about the breast, as if it were a mutual friend who had done something offensive and was suddenly in disfavor. They talked about Sharon and Michael instead, and her aunt confessed shyly that she had never liked the other fellow, that poet Sharon used to go out with, and that she was relieved when Sharon and Michael were safely married. And Sharon had begun to brag, exaggerating Michael's virtues. She told her aunt that it was she who had broken with

Beau and that he had begged and pleaded for another chance. She took extraordinary pleasure in her aunt's approval, in the lying itself, and in her own intact flesh later that night.

There is a knocking at the door and she realizes she has been asleep. It is past eight o'clock. Dick comes into the room and hugs her. His large mustache scrapes her face and his embrace is amazingly solid.

They drive to a restaurant in the rented car, and Sharon's appetite is much better than she expected. In fact, she eats everything on her plate and some of Dick's dinner, too. He's confident things will work out well the next day. They share a full bottle of Chablis, and Sharon feels an aura of celebration. Dick has done some research. He's been reading up on the subject and has even called a couple of shrinks he knows. A single, isolated episode of exhibitionism, he tells her, especially following a trauma like the death of one's mother, doesn't have to be pathological in origin. Did she know that in a great percentage of recent cases, the offender is seated in a car? There is reasonable consideration about his wish to be apprehended through license-plate identification. And did she know that indecent exposure occurs most frequently in the spring?

"A young man's fancy?" she says, and is further loosened by Dick's laughter. Oh, oh, she thinks.

Back at the motel, she asks him to come to her room to talk some more.

He looks at her speculatively and then follows her inside. "Only for a few minutes," he says. "I want to be sparkling in the morning. So you won't be sorry you didn't bring F. Lee Bailey instead."

She takes the package of cigarettes from her purse and empties it carefully onto one of the beds. She selects the joints and shows them to Dick.

"Oy," he says, clapping his forehead. "Do you want to get us busted, too?" Then he takes matches from his pocket and lights one.

It is potent stuff, as promised, or perhaps the wine has eased the way. They become high quickly. Sharon feels uncommonly happy and hopeful. But even as she considers this blissful new state, she senses a sobering one approaching from a great distance, like a storm.

What if I come down too quickly? she thinks. What if Dick's optimism is artificially induced, too? She tries to remember if he was this cheerful and reassuring before dinner. What if he wants to make love to me? And she knows that it is her own desire she contemplates.

Dick takes off his jacket and falls into a chair, lifting his feet onto the bed. He is barrel-chested, growing a little paunchy.

Sharon is touched by what she sees as the body's first small concession to aging. She takes off her shoes and lies down on the bed, her feet almost touching Dick's.

"Freud gave up sex at forty," Dick says. "My friend Marshall says he was probably screwing his own sister-in-law."

They both laugh.

"Wow," Sharon says, and they laugh again.

Dick tells her a joke about a woman who goes to a psychiatrist because she has repeated dreams about long, pointed objects. "You know, like swords, pencils, arrows. 'That's very simple, dear lady,' the psychiatrist says. 'You are obsessed by phallic symbols.' 'By what?' the woman asks. 'By symbols of the phallus,' the psychiatrist tells her. 'Huh?' the woman says and he can see she doesn't get it. He decides to do something really drastic. So, he gets up and opens his fly. 'There,' he says. '*That's* a phallus!' 'Ohhhh,' says the woman, 'like a penis, only smaller.'" Neither of them laughs.

"I love Anna," Sharon says. "I really do."

"Me, too," Dick says. He stands, picks up his jacket, and leaning precariously over her, kisses her sweetly on the mouth.

After he leaves, Sharon feels restless and she lies awake for a long time. She thinks of an editor she knows who insists she remembers being born. She claims to have understood instantly her mother's profound sorrow at learning her baby was a girl.

Sharon thinks it is only hysteria induced by the editor's own disappointment in her life as a woman, and she argued that such early memory isn't possible, before language, before the ability to form concepts.

"Listen," the other woman said. "Dreaming begins *in utero*."

What a notion—a small, crouched and floating dreamer! The image has always appealed to Sharon, and thinking of it now, she floats, too, then starts to feel drowsy, the way Beau did whenever she wanted to talk in bed.

Floating. Once, when he was coming, Michael called out, "Oh, Sharon, your legs are holding me like arms!"

She meets Dick in the coffee shop for breakfast. "How do you feel?" he asks, and it is not a perfunctory question. He wants to know.

"Afraid of how I feel," Sharon answers. "Maybe more angry than sympathetic. Not loving enough, not *Christian*. Michael had such a rotten childhood, didn't he? I mean, his parents should have been arrested. It's a miracle that he's such a good person, really, isn't it? I'm like an evil-minded child in church, trying hard to have holy thoughts. And I feel so selfish now, as if the only crimes that matter are the ones committed against me."

She is exhausted, self-conscious. It was like a courtroom speech, or one made on a deathbed. "And I'm a little nauseous, besides," she adds.

Dick signals the waitress for the check.

At the car, he takes the driver's seat. Leaving the motor running, he gets out and goes into the motel office. When he comes back, he hands her a morning newspaper.

On the front page, there is a photograph of a baby who was born with his heart on the outside of his chest. Not the first recorded case, but still a medical phenomenon. Temporary surgical repair has been done to keep the baby alive until the cavity enlarges enough to hold the heart. Skin taken from his little legs and back has been used to build a thin wall against that terrible beating.

On the way to the jail, Sharon rubs her cold hands and thinks about men and how they always wear their parts on the surface of their bodies, indecently exposed and vulnerable, an appendage of their joy and their despair. She realizes that she has never regretted being female, the keeper of the gates. If she were given another shot at it, she wouldn't choose a different animal form, either, not even the bird's with its feathered grace and alleged freedom. And she would never be a man for anything.

The jail looks like a schoolhouse. There is a flag flapping outside, and on the corner a policeman, middle-aged and portly, like the friendly ones in children's primers, directs traffic.

They are taken to a room with a square table and four hard chairs in it. The door is left open, so that they hear the footsteps when a guard approaches with Michael, and she looks up and sees him immediately. He is attempting to smile, and about to weep.

Dick remains seated as Sharon stands and goes to Michael. When he puts his hands on her, she can feel the burning of his palms, and she goes into him, pressing the place where the lilacs bloom.

LIFE WITHOUT MARTIN

Jane Shapiro

Jane Shapiro, whose grandfather was a newspaperman and whose mother wrote poetry and fiction while raising five children, has almost always kept a journal, but she did not begin to write professionally until she was thirty. She dropped out of Middlebury College in 1962, married, had two children, and, while her children were still young, went to night school at N.Y.U. to finish her B.A. She has written articles for the New York Times and a number of national magazines. For the Village Voice she wrote a series of profiles of people she describes as "obsessive," such as marathon swimmer Diana Nyad and movie director Mel Brooks. She thinks the interviewer's attempts at immersion in her subject's world, her efforts to get inside someone else's head, have been useful preparation for the writing of fiction.

"Life Without Martin," Shapiro's first published story, was nominated for the One Hundred Best Short Stories of 1979. In her novel-in-progress she is continuing to explore the theme of the "uneasy equilibrium" in a long marriage.

Jane Shapiro lives in Princeton, New Jersey, and New York City, with her two teen-aged children, in another sort of uneasy equilibrium.

SOME CHUBBY PEOPLE had gathered on a panel on television, talking together about our overweight society. Although I am of average size, this seemed to speak to me.

The host gazed all around him with respectful glances, appearing peaceful and happy to be flanked by a panel of people so dramatically bigger than himself. "I have with me tonight," he said, "six people who know how to put away the groceries! And they're going to tell you about it, after this word." Soon there was a long and sensible discussion about learning to like ourselves, to feel good about ourselves, and to really know that we are adequate people, even though we inevitably will have the occasional munchy attack. The second camera picked up the one slender woman, who piped up and laughed and seized hunks of air and wrestled them to her mouth and nose; she was describing her own crazy face-stuffing, still a vivid memory though long in the past. This woman knew how to exaggerate. She had lumbered around her studio apartment, strolling, chewing. Unerringly, she linked all of it to her former self-hatred. Describing the transformation to beautiful slimness, she grew even livelier, then started to seem overwrought. Meanwhile the several larger panelists were thoughtful, playful, conscious of paradox, full of wisdom; they leaned in their chairs, serene and staring.

At the set, I was eating a bag of potato chips, at least as slowly as recommended—savoring, even sniffing, delicately chewing, chip by chip. I lingered over the details of size, configuration, and relative brownness, holding each chip up in the glare, noting each chip's uniqueness, enjoying each chip to the hilt. Tears gathered behind my eyes and nose, obscuring some potato flavor though not salt. I was thinking how Martin had flown the coop.

Things had been bad. Months of misunderstanding and discord had left us jumpy, dejected, hideously bored. Throughout the time of growing dissatisfaction, we had been watching "Marriage Manual" on television, where troubled partners sat on a couch and let two psychologists lean near them and look right into their private marriage with all its missed connections and terrible contracts. Every Sunday night at ten, Doctors Lydia Kemp and Ernie Mollendorf inclined in the direction of the troubled partners, smiled bittersweet smiles of understanding, and talked turkey.

Martin and I slumped side by side in our beanbag chairs, sullen and demoralized, breathing through our mouths. We wanted to be those couples, old and young, whose marital problems were so transparent, who had Lydia Kemp and her sideman Dr. Ernie to steadily gaze at them until they looked life in the face and, haltingly but with growing confidence, two moving as one, changed direction. "Marriage Manual" touched our deep longing, but we had come to see bad faith everywhere at home. How do such accidents happen? Martin has sense, and also abilities to burn, trained into his brains and eyes and fingers. He has a resonant voice, fancy yet flowing. If Martin would turn to me sweetly, I thought, I could tell him how often I have viewed him with admiration and desire. The beanbag would rustle, I would bend like grasses. Each of us was waiting for the other to speak, but each was prevented by mysterious forces. Actually there have been several good years.

"Let's be creative," I had said to Martin, cheerfully. "Now's the moment, man!" I shouted, projecting. I heard my voice, angry, stirring, and basically optimistic. "Look, Martin," I said, "give yourself a change, face the facts: right now the outlook is bleak."

"Beyond belief," Martin said, turning pale and looking out the window. He bitterly squinted; squirrels crossed his eyes. His head was filled with the news about how vicious and misguided a woman I had become.

Later I told Martin outright to go away for a few days and think it over, which caused him to grin with rage and start running through the house. From this point on, he began acting wild, and endearing himself to me: silence has been the worst; when he gets enthusiastic, I perk up. This late in the game, however, I kept my counsel.

He rushed up and down the stairs carrying out his suits and ties with tender hands, and pantomiming ecstatic relief. I looked out an upstairs window; his car was stuffed with pinstripes and tweeds. "I ain't impressed!" he shrieked from the driveway, before getting in and smashing the car into reverse, and I became drawn to him with fresh, unfamiliar wholeheartedness just as he bucked out of view.

The kids wanted to know why Martin was gone. Zachary cracked his shoulders while I talked. Zachary thinks I overstep boundaries of taste and appropriateness and am generally overaggressive and touchy in the marital relationship, and his school friends have encouraged him in his twisted idea of the types of women the world has room for. I took a ride, and when I got home Nora, my former little baby girl, was standing up in the middle of the kitchen waiting for me. When she heard me, she turned and began to talk, and began wetly to cry, and she tossed her head back and forth in impatience and frustration and deep unhappiness, and tears flew out of her eyes all around her, straight out to the sides. "You blew it!" Nora shouted, as I paused on the threshold. "Big expert, always yelling, you can't even stay married?" she asked sensibly.

"Marty and I are still married," I said. "We just have some thinking to do."

"Right, in separate houses! *Thanks a lot!*" Nora cried, miserably gurgling.

The night was long, and full of incident. I woke in drifting haze, looked at the glowing center of the clockface, fell into blackness while the sky was fading to gray. In between, against my better judgment, my feet walked around the bed.

In the early morning the cat has the habit of walking on the roof, scratching at my window. At four thirty I heard his little cries next to my ear; at five he was screaming and throwing his body against the screen. I am trying to train him out of this, so I don't let him in up there. At six I walked down and opened the front door, and a boulder fell out of the sky in front of my face and crashed to the walk. It was the cat, leaping off into darkness, landing on white feet. He immediately walked past me into the house and began to purr. On the way back to bed, I bent and spoke to his back. "Oh, Kibbie! I've carried things too far," I said, into fur.

All morning I drifted in sunlight. The air swam with light, I was littering the bed, sprawled as if dead under quilts, tenderly remembering my own qualities. Circumstances have not brought me out. Secretly I am soft; the yielding me has always been hanging around waiting for the moment to go on, stuck in the wings, long past stage fright. I dreamed, or recalled, Martin saying, mournfully, in baby talk, "Last night in the night I twied to hug you tight."

"Look," I cried. *"Don't try it again!"*

Nora had left me notes while I slept: "To Liz, hi! Anonomiss." And: "Dear Mom, the vacume cleaner man called. He said he will be 'in touch.'"

I called up a few friends and barked into the phone, with energy and cheer. In the afternoon I went to the discount clothing store, to further improve my mood. Although I had been busy since noon, underneath I was still and sinking. I plunged into the mall as if into the swirling sea.

People were moving along in there, through swells of music, strolling in their coats under the roof in controlled air, resisting Latin rhythms while dreaming of a new life around the corner. The store had bought out an entire failing boutique and would go as high as sixty percent off on selected items. I pushed past racks like a woman on an errand of mercy, fixed on summer clothes, although it was forty-five degrees and dropping. Summer, of course, had been the scene of previous happiness.

In T-shirts, I ran my fingers down the cotton and poly sleeves, while the tiny children of slim and young mothers circled the cruise wear in packs; other shoppers paused nearby, idling their motors; gloomy employees uncrated new bargains from the People's Republic of China, a cold, vast, and incomprehensible land they would never see. I stood in the dressing room watching myself stand around in jeans outfits, marked way down, while on either side of me other women shifted their weight in identical garments. The women intently eyed their own flanks, then looked for long minutes over their shoulders at their own backs, preparatory to going home to husbands. Probably such women were naturals at marriage, possessing as they did calmness, humor, and perspective, deep and unnamed reserves of irony.

In half an hour anxiety had risen up in me, but I wrenched myself into forgetfulness, showing the mirror my stuff, kicking higher than the other ladies. The Indian cotton shirts evoked thoughts of a veranda, my face and arms stinging with sunburn, me all aglow. Men tossed me fascinated glances like fish to a seal, which I snapped up.

At home I drank two cups of tea and lay down with my packages next to me on the bed, and went to sleep again. All afternoon I struggled to the surface, looked at the sunlight, slipped under again. I got up, drank coffee, went back to bed. Against such sleepiness, caffeine was powerless. I was dreaming about my fuzzy winter coat. I am seated in a restaurant, gripped by my banquette in an embrace both confidential and firm; I extend my arms across the table, the captain turns back my sleeves.

When I remembered Nora at piano, I lurched up and into my bathrobe, rushed to the car, and drove right over the newspaper and downtown. Outside the piano teacher's house my friend Marilyn was escorting her son down the sidewalk, holding on to him by his piano books. I love Marilyn, who has been witty through many missteps and twists and turns, and dauntless in her loyalty, and whose efficiency is well known.

I rolled down the window and leaned out, struggling to awaken. "Please! Look at this!" I called to Marilyn, who moved toward me through dark wispy areas. Clumps of my own hair obscured my view. "I'm totally under water!" I said.

Marilyn leaned into my car window and looked at my feet. "All right, so you're not dressed."

"No, I can't wake up! I can't emerge!"

"No, it's fine, you're just in your bathrobe, go back home," she said, giving me a firm look of warm approval.

At home, Nora was wearing many pieces of delicate jewelry, wire pinkie rings, silver bracelets, and tiny lockets on chains, with her sweater and skirt, and lolling in both beanbags watching a makeup man on TV changing a woman into somebody else. In real life six hundred dollars would buy one hour of talent from this saucy boy. "You were late, so I left," Nora said. She followed me to the kitchen. "Can Alison and Cindy come over?" she said, staring into the refrigerator. Alison spends every afternoon at Cindy's house because it's her father's turn for custody, and he works. Her father has custody for four months, then her father moves out and her mother moves in for the next four months, then for four months they supervise together, from separate bedrooms. A terrible fearfulness came over me; still I slumped in my bathrobe. I felt as if just hearing this could make matters worse. "How rotten for the parent who's off," I said.

"Not really. Anyway, Alison's mom's in South America till March."

"She went to South America until March?" I cried. *"Why? How?"*

Nora's jewelry glittered in refrigerator light. Still she leaned my way, cold cuts and milk cartons her backdrop. "Alison's mom's boyfriend is shooting in South America. When Alison's mom comes back, Alison might get her ears pierced."

"Oh, Nora," I said, tears springing to my eyes.

"You think that's bad?" she said. "How do you think Daddy feels?"

How Daddy feels had increasingly been coming to mind. Martin called Marilyn and left the number where he could be reached; somehow this made me feel Martin was securely established elsewhere and would never return. In two days of thinking it over, he had decided it wasn't worth it.

On Saturday I jumped up, full of energy, and started taking action. One thing I did supposed that Martin would return: I called Cape Cod Realty and rented a house for two weeks for next June, with two bedrooms, one with double bed. On the other hand, I repotted my dieffenbachia, struggling with big pots, trailing black strings of earth around the kitchen. It's something I usually don't do alone; once a year in years past Martin has helped me, and it was always a good day.

Then I got the kids together and drove them to see the matches at the indoor tennis association. Loitering in the lobby between walls of glass, with the small sharp women in tennis dresses darting by, I was bulky and preoccupied as in dreamy babyhood. Actually I was thinking about how I once learned about the love of men and women from a book. A few times a week I read my sex education book, which told me that when a man and a woman loved each other very much they got married, and that then as part of their love the husband placed his penis in the wife's vagina. For years I thought about them, the loving couple, standing up there close together at the altar, with organ music floating all around and white sunlight piercing the stained glass: he in his tuxedo, she in her wedding dress, whose wide skirt concealed that they were consummating their love. I had treasured the story of sexual intercourse, that wonderful dark commingling at the friendly moment of marriage.

I figured if Martin didn't get in touch by Sunday I would call the number and make it clear that we needed to get our plans straight.

Back at the house, Martin's car was in the driveway. The kids ran into the house, came out again, and began playing a game of freezing in place, standing around on the grass looking like lawn ornaments. "Not interested in going inside?" Nora said to me, through grinning clenched teeth.

Inside, Martin was in the kitchen stepping all around on the linoleum as if before a jury, talking on the phone. Teddy Lewis had called four times to ask if our roof leaks or our refrigerator is running.

"Come on, don't call us any more," Martin was saying. "We're trying to do some work here now. It was funny and cute and I'm not gonna get mad at you, but come on now, really. No. Don't ask me any more funny questions."

Zachary came in and stood next to Martin and looked at him. Zachary said, "Teddy can't make crank calls for shit. Teddy is the stupidest kid. He can't even make a crank call." I was breathing shallow breaths, and quietly, because of my sudden happiness. I was very taken with the corkscrew phone cord dangling in loops against Martin's leg as well as with the way he'll give any telephoner the time of day.

Martin said affably into the phone: "No, that's all, you call somebody else now." He waggled his fingers at me. I love Martin; if he gets off the phone I'll tell him so. While he talked he reached behind himself on the counter and pulled out a large menu and waved it at me. Martin had been to a restaurant during the last few days and when he got off the phone he was going to read aloud and comment upon the entire menu in a careful edgy manner, with much French and self-congratulatory lip smacking and overweening attention to detail.

"Too much, man! Too much!" I'll holler, and then Martin's jaw will clamp and he'll blink with rage, and Martin will either stay around to hear the rest of my remarks, or he won't.

NOT A VERY NICE STORY

Doris Lessing

Born in Iran in 1919 to British parents, Doris Lessing grew up on a farm in southern Rhodesia. A year after arriving in London in 1950, she published her first novel, The Grass Is Singing. Since then she has written several successful plays and twenty-five books, most notably The Golden Notebook (1962) and the five-volume series The Children of Violence (1952–1969), and has created two of the most fully realized female protagonists in literature, Martha Quest and Anna Wulf. Wulf is an intellectual, Marxist activist and artist, as well as mother and lover, whose personality is so fragmented that she keeps four notebooks to contain it. Her plight as an independent woman, incomplete without love yet inevitably undermined by it, remains contemporary and painfully accurate.

Lessing's social vision darkened in Briefing for a Descent Into Hell (1971) and Memoirs of a Survivor (1974) as she bore witness to the breakdown of civilization and depicted a world on the brink of nuclear destruction. But even in her most recent space fictions, the series Canopus in Argos: Archives, she continues to explore the interplay between dominance and need in the relations between men and women.

"Not a Very Nice Story" is a sardonic look at a rather unusual foursome. Ever the iconoclast, Lessing has written a love story that is antisentimental and "not very nice." A masterpiece in detachment, it is typical of her cynicism about the modern need to "feel deeply."

THIS STORY IS DIFFICULT TO TELL. Where to put the emphasis? Whose perspective to use? For to tell it from the point of view of the lovers (but that was certainly not their word for themselves—from the viewpoint then of the guilty couple), it is as if a life were to be described through the eyes of some person who scarcely appeared in it; as if a cousin from Canada had visited, let's say, a farmer in Cornwall half a dozen unimportant times, and then wrote as if these meetings had been the history of the farm and the family. Or it is as if a stretch of years were to be understood in terms of the extra day in Leap Year.

To put it conventionally is simple: two marriages, both as happy as marriages are, both exemplary from society's point of view, contained a shocking flaw, a secret cancer, a hidden vice.

But this hidden horror did not rot the marriages, and seemed hardly to matter at all: the story can't be told as the two betrayed ones saw it; they didn't see it. They saw nothing. There would be nothing to tell.

Now, all this was true for something like twenty years; then something happened which changed the situation. To be precise, what happened was the death of one of the four people concerned. But at any moment during those twenty years, what has been said would have been true: conventional morality would judge these marriages to have a secret face, all lies and lust; from the adulterers' point of view, what they did was not much more important than sharing a taste for eating chocolate after the doctor has said no.

After that death, however, the shift of emphasis: the long unimportance of the twenty years of chocolate eating could be seen as a prelude to something very different; could be seen as heartless frivolity or callousness redeemed providentially by responsibility. But suppose the death had not occurred?

It is hard to avoid the thought that all these various ways of looking at the thing are nonsense. . . .

Frederick Jones married Althea; Henry Smith married Muriel, at the same time, that is, in 1947. Both men, both women, had been much involved in the war, sometimes dangerously. But now it was over, they knew that it had been the way it had gone on and on that had affected them most. It had been endless.

There is no need to say much about their emotions when they married. Frederick and Althea, Henry and Muriel, felt exactly as they might be expected to feel, being their sort of people— middle-class, liberal, rather literary—and in their circumstances, which emotionally consisted of hungers of all kinds, but particularly for security, affection, warmth, these hungers having been heightened beyond normal during the long war. They were all four aware of their condition, were able to see themselves with the wryly tolerant eye of their kind. For they at all times knew to a fraction of a degree the state of their emotional pulse, and were much given to intelligent discussions about their individual psychologies.

Yet in spite of views about themselves which their own parents would have regarded as intolerable to live with, their plans and aims for themselves were similar to those of their parents at the same age. Both couples wished and expected that their marriages would be the bedrock of their lives, that they would have children and bring them up well. And it turned out as they wanted. They also expected that they would be faithful to each other.

At the time these marriages took place, the couples had not met. Both Doctor Smith and Doctor Jones, separately, had had the idea of going into partnership and possibly founding a clinic in a poor area. Both had been made idealists by the war, even socialists of a nonideological sort. They advertised, made contact by letter, liked each other, and bought a practice in a country town in the west of England where there would be many poor people to look after, as well as the rich.

Houses were bought, not far from each other. While the two men were already friends, with confidence in their being able to work together, the wives had not met. It was agreed that it was high time this event should take place. An occasion was to be made of it. The four were to meet for dinner in a pub five miles outside the little town. That they should all get on well was known by them to be important. In fact, both women had made small humorous complaints that if their "getting on" was really considered so important, then why had their meeting been left so late?—this was the real reason for the special dinner.

As the two cars drove up to the country inn, the same state of affairs prevailed in each. There was bad humor. The women felt they were being patronized, the men felt that the women were probably right but were being unreasonable in making a fuss when after all the main thing was to get settled in work and in their homes. All four were looking forward to that dinner—the inn was known for its food—while for their different reasons they

resented being there at all. They arrived in each other's presence
vivid with variegated emotions. The women at once knew they
liked each other—but after all, they might very well have not
liked each other!—and made common cause about the men. The
four went into the bar where they were an animated and com-
bative group.

By the time they moved into the dining room, ill humor had
vanished. There they sat, with their wine and good food. They
were attracting attention, because they were obviously dressed
up for a special occasion, but chiefly because of their own consciousness of well-being. This was the peak of their lives; the long
tedium of the war was over; the men were still in their early
thirties, the women in their twenties. They were feeling as if at
last their real lives were starting. They were all good looking.
The men were of the same type: jokes had been made about that
already. They were both dark, largely built, with the authority
of doctors, "comfortable," as the wives said. And the women were
pretty. They soon established (like showing each other their
passports or references of decency and reliability) that they
shared views on life—tough, but rewarding; God—dead; children—to be brought up with the right blend of permissiveness
and discipline; society—to be cured by common sense and mild
firmness but without extremes of any sort.

Everything was well for them; everything would get better.

They sat a long time over their food, their wine, and their
happiness, and left only when the pub closed, passing into a cold,
clear night, frost on the ground. It happened that conversations
between Frederick Jones and Muriel Smith, Althea Jones and
Henry Smith were in progress, and the couples, so arranged,
stood by their respective cars.

"Come back to us for a nightcap," said Henry, assisting his
colleague's wife in beside him, and drove off home.

Frederick and Muriel, not one word having been said, watched
them go, then turned to each other and embraced. This embrace
can best be described as being the inevitable continuation of

their conversation. Frederick then drove a few hundred yards into a small wood, where the frost shone on the grass, stopped the car, flung down his coat, and then he and Muriel made love—no, that's not right—had sex, with vigor and relish and enjoyment, while nothing lay between them and their nakedness and some degrees of frost but a layer of tweed. They then dressed, got back into the car, and went back to town, where Frederick drove Muriel to her own home, came in with her for the promised nightcap, and took his own wife home.

Both married couples made extensive love that night, as the atmosphere all evening had promised they would.

Muriel and Frederick did not examine their behavior as much as such compulsive examiners of behavior might have been expected to do. The point was, the incident was out of character, unlike them, so very much *not* what they believed in, that they didn't know what to think about it, let alone what to feel. Muriel had always set her face against the one-night stand. Trivial, she had said it was—the word *sordid* was overemphatic. Frederick, both professionally and personally, had a lot to say about the unsatisfactory nature of casual sexual relationships. In his consulting room he would show carefully measured disapproval for the results—venereal disease or pregnancy—of such relations. It was not a moral judgment he was making, he always said; no, it was a hygienic one. He had been heard to use the word *messy*. Both these people had gone in, one could say on principle, for the serious affair, the deep involvement. Even in wartime, neither had had casual sex.

So while it was hardly possible that such extraordinary behavior could be forgotten, neither thought about it: the incident could not be included in their view of themselves.

And besides, there was so much to do, starting the new practice, arranging the new homes.

Besides, too, both couples were so pleased with each other, and had such a lot of love to make.

About six weeks after that evening at the pub, Frederick had to drop in to Henry and Muriel's to pick up something, and found Muriel alone. Again, not one word having been said, they went to the bedroom and—but I think the appropriate word here is *screwed*. Thoroughly and at length.

They parted; and again unable to understand themselves, let the opportunity to think about what had happened slide away.

The thing was too absurd! They could not say, for instance, that during that famous evening at the pub, when they first met, that they had eyed each other with incipient desire, or had sent out messages of need or intent. They had not done more than to say to themselves, as one does: I'd like to make love with that man/woman if I wasn't well suited already. They certainly could not have said that during the intervening six weeks they had dreamed of each other, finding their actual partners unsatisfactory. Far from it.

For if these, Muriel and Frederick, were natural sexual partners, then so were Frederick and Althea, Henry and Muriel.

If we now move on ten years and look back, as the guilty couple, Frederick and Muriel then did—or rather, as both couples did, ten years being a natural time or place for such compulsive self-examiners to make profit-and-loss accounts—it is only in an effort to give the right emphasis to the thing.

For it is really hard to get the perspective right. Suppose that I had, in fact, described the emotions of the two very emotional courtships, the emotional and satisfying affairs that preceded marriage, the exciting discoveries of marriage and the depths and harmonies both couples found, and had then said, simply: On many occasions two of these four people committed adultery, without forethought or afterthought, and these adulterous episodes, though extremely enjoyable, had no effect whatever on the marriages—thus making them sound something like small bits of grit in mouthfuls of honey. Well, but even the best of marriages can hardly be described as honey. Perhaps it is that word *adultery*—too weighty? Redolent of divorces and French farce? Yet it is still in use, very much so: it is a word that people think, and not only in the law courts.

Perhaps, to get the right emphasis, insofar as those sexual episodes were having an effect on the marriages, one might as well not mention them at all. But not to mention them is just as impossible—apart from what happened in the end, the end of the story. For surely it is absolutely outside what we all know to be psychologically possible for the partners of happy marriages, both of them founded on truth and love and total commitment, to have casual sex with close mutual friends—thus betraying their marriages, their relationships, themselves—and for these betrayals to have no effect on them at all.

No guilt? No private disquiet? What was felt when gazing into their loving partners' eyes, with everything open and frank between them, Frederick, Muriel, had to think: How can I treat my trusting partner like this?

They had no such thoughts. For ten years the marriages had prospered side by side. The Joneses had produced three children, the Smiths two. The young doctors worked hard, as doctors do. In the two comfortable gardened houses, the two attractive young wives worked as hard as wives and mothers do. And all that time the marriages were being assessed by very different standards, which had nothing to do with those trivial and inelegant acts of sex—which continued whenever circumstances allowed, quite often, though neither guilty partner searched for occasions—all that time the four people continued to take their emotional pulses, as was their training: the marriages were satisfactory; no, not so satisfactory; yes, very good again. It was better in the second year than in the first, but less good in the third than in the fourth. The children brought the couples closer together in some ways, but not in others—and so on. Frederick was glad he had married delightful and sexy little Althea; and she was glad she had married Frederick, whose calm strength was her admirable complement. And Henry was pleased with Muriel, so vivacious,

fearless and self-sufficing; and Muriel was similarly glad she had
chosen Henry, whose quietly humorous mode of dealing with life
always absorbed any temporary disquiets she might be suffering.

All four, of course, would sometimes wonder if they should
have married at all, in the way everyone does; and all four would
discuss with themselves and with each other, or as a foursome,
the ghastliness of marriage as an institution and how it should
be abolished and something else put in its place. Sometimes, in
the grip of a passing attraction for someone else, all four might
regret that their choices were now narrowed down to one. (At
such times neither Frederick nor Muriel thought of each other,
they took each other for granted, since they were always available to each other, like marriage partners.) In short, and to be
done with it, at the end of ten years, and during the soul searching and bookkeeping that went on then, both couples could look
back on marriages that had in every way fulfilled what they had
expected, even in the way of "taking the rough with the smooth."
For where is the pleasure in sweet-without-sour? In spite of, because of, sexually exciting times and chilly times, of temporary
hostilities and harmonies, of absences and illnesses, of yearning,
briefly, for others—because of all this they had enjoyed a decade
of profoundly emotional experience. In joy or in pain, they could
not complain about flatness, or absence of sensation. And after
all, emotion is the thing, we can none of us get enough of it.

What transports the couples had suffered! What tears the two
women had wept! What long delicious nights spent on prolonged
sexual pleasure! What quarrels and crises and dramas! What
depth of experience everywhere! And now the five children,
each one an emotion in itself, each one an extension of emotion,
claiming the future for similar pleasurable or at least sensational
rivers of feeling.

It was round about the eleventh year that there came a moment
of danger to them all. Althea fell in love with a young doctor
who had come to help in the practice while the two senior doctors took leave. The two families usually took holidays together,

but this time the men went off tramping in Scotland, leaving the women and children.

Althea confided in Muriel. It was not a question of leaving her Frederick: certainly not. She could bear to hurt neither him nor the children. But she was suffering horribly, from desire and all kinds of suddenly discovered deprivations, for the sake of the young man with whom she had slept half a dozen times furtively—horrible word!—when the children were playing in the garden or were asleep at night. Her whole life seemed a desert of dust and ashes. She could not bear the future. What was the point of living?

The two young women sat talking in Althea's kitchen.

They were at either end of the breakfast table around which so many jolly occasions had been shared by them all. Althea was weeping.

Perhaps this is the place to describe these two women. Althea was a small, round dark creature, who always smelled delightful, and who was described by her husband as the most eminently satisfactory blend of femininity and common sense. As for Muriel, she was a strong, large-boned woman, fair, with the kind of skin that tans quickly, so that she always looked very healthy. Her clothes were of the kind called casual, and she took a lot of trouble over them. Both women, of course, often yearned to be like the other.

These two different women sat stirring coffee cups as they had done a hundred times, while the five children shouted, competed, and loved in the garden, and Althea wept, because she said this was a watershed in her marriage, like eating the apple in Eden. If she told her beloved husband that she was—temporarily, she did so hope and believe—besottedly in love with this young doctor, then it must be the end of everything between them. But if she didn't tell him, then it was betrayal. Whatever she did would have terrible results. *Not* telling Frederick seemed to her worse even than the infidelity itself. She had never, ever concealed anything from him. Perfect frankness and sincerity had been their rule—no, not a rule, they had never had to lay down rules for behavior that came so excellently and simply out of their love and trust. She could not imagine keeping anything from Frederick. And she was sure he told her everything. She could not bear it, would certainly leave him at once, if she knew that he had ever lied to her. No, she would not mind infidelity of a certain kind—how could she mind?—now that she forfeited any rights in the matter! But lies, deceptions, furtiveness—no, that would be the end, the end of everything.

Althea and Muriel stayed together, while one woman wept and talked and the other listened, stopping only when the children came in, for all that day, and all the next, and for several after that. For Muriel was understanding that it was the words and tears that were the point, not what was said: soon the energy of suffering, the tension of conflict, would have spent itself, making it all seem less important. But Muriel was determined not to listen for one minute more than was necessary. And soon she was able to advise Althea, the tears having abated, not to tell her Fred anything at all; she would just have to learn to live with a lie.

And now of course she had to think, really to think, whether she liked it or not, about the way she had been making love— or sex—in a frivolous, and some people might say sordid, way with her best friend's husband. She was being made to think. Most definitely she did not want to think: it was extraordinary, the strength of her instinct *not* to examine that area of her life.

However, examining it, or, rather, touching lightly on it, she was able to congratulate herself or, rather, both herself and dear Fred, that never had they in the presence of their spouses enjoyed that most awful of betrayals, enjoyment of their complicity while their said spouses remained oblivious. She could not remember ever, when together, their so much as looking at each other in an invitation to make love, or sex; she was positive they had never once allowed their eyes to signal: these poor fools don't know our secret. For certainly they had never felt like this.

They had not ever, not once, made plans to meet alone. They might have fallen into each other's arms the moment the opportunity offered, as if no other behavior was possible to them, but they did not engineer opportunities. And, having arrived in each other's arms, all laughter and pleasure, there was never a feeling of having gone one better than Althea and Henry, of doing them down in any way. And, having separated, they did not think about what had happened, nor consider their partners: it was as if these occasions belonged to another plane altogether. That trivial, or sordid and unimportant; that friendly, good-natured and entirely enjoyable plane that lay beside, or above, or within these two so satisfactory marriages.

It occurred to Muriel that its nature, its essence, was lack of emotion. Her feeling for Frederick, what Frederick felt for her, was all calm sense and pleasure, with not so much as a twinge of that yearning anguish we call being in love.

And, thinking about it all, as these long sessions with weeping and miserable (enjoyably miserable?) Althea had made her do, she understood, and became determined to hold on to, her belief that her instinct, or compulsion, never to examine, brood, or make emotional profit-and-loss accounts about if the sex she had with Frederick was healthy. For as soon as she did put weight on that area, start to measure and weigh, all sorts of sensations hitherto foreign to this relationship began to gabble, gobble and insist and demand. Guilt, for one.

She came to a conclusion. It was so seditious of any idea held in common by these four and their kind that she had to look at it, as it were, sideways. It was this: that very likely the falling in love with the young doctor was not at all as Althea was seeing it—as anyone was likely to see it—the point was not the periods of making love—love, not sex!—which of course had been all rapture, though muted, inevitably, with their particular brand of wry and civilized understanding, but it was the spilling of emotion afterward, the anguish, the guilt. Emotion was the point. Great emotion had been felt, had been suffered. Althea had suffered, was suffering abominably. Everyone had got it wrong: the real motive for such affairs was the need to suffer the pain and the yearning afterward.

The two marriages continued to grow like trees, sheltering the children who flourished beneath them.

Soon, they had been married fifteen years.

There occurred another crisis, much worse.

Its prelude was this. Due to a set of circumstances not important—Althea had to visit a sick mother and took the children; Henry was away, the Jones children sent to visit a grandmother—Frederick and Muriel spent two weeks alone with each other. Ostensibly, they were in their separate homes, but they were five minutes' drive from each other, and not even in a gossipy, inbred little English town could neighbors see anything wrong in two people being together a lot who were with each other constantly year in and out.

It was a time of relaxation. Of enjoyment. Of quiet. They spent nights in the same bed—for the first time. They took long intimate meals together alone—for the first time. They had seldom been alone together, when they came to think of it. It was extraordinary how communal it was, the life of the Joneses and the Smiths.

Their relationship, instead of being the fleeting, or flighty thing it had been, rolls in the hay (literally) or in the snow, an hour on the drawing-room carpet, or a quick touch-up in a telephone booth, was suddenly all dignity, privacy, and leisure.

And now Frederick showed a disposition to responsible feeling—love was the word he insisted on using, while Muriel nervously implored him not to be solemn. He pointed out that he was betraying his beloved Althea, that she was betraying her darling Henry, and that this was what they had been doing for years and years, and without a twinge of guilt or a moment's reluctance.

And without, Muriel pointed out, *feeling*.

Ah, yes, she was right, how awful, he was really beginning to feel that . . .

For God's sake, she cried, stop it, don't spoil everything, can't you see the dogs of destruction are sniffing at our door? Stop it, darling Fred, I won't have you using words like love, no, no, that is our redeeming point, our strength—we haven't been in love, we have never agonized over each other, desired each other, missed each other, wanted each other; we have not ever "felt" anything for each other. . . .

Frederick allowed it to be seen that he found this view of them too cool, if not heartless.

But, she pointed out, what they had done was to help each other in every way, to be strong pillars in a foursome, to rejoice at the birth of each other's children, to share ideas and read books recommended by the other. They had enjoyed random and delightful and irresponsible sex without a twang of conscience when they could—had, in short, lived—for fifteen years in close harmony.

Fred called her a sensible woman.

During that fortnight love was imminent on at least a dozen occasions. She resisted.

But there was no doubt, and Muriel saw this with an irritation made strong by self-knowledge—for of course she would have adored to be "in love" with Frederick, to anguish and weep and lie awake—that Frederick, by the time his wife came back, was feeling thoroughly deprived. His Muriel had deprived him. Of emotional experience.

Ah, emotion, emotion, let us bathe in thee!

For instance, the television, that mirror of us all:

A man has crashed his car, and his wife and three children have burned to death.

"And what did you feel when this happened?" asks the bland, but humanly concerned, young interviewer. "Tell us, what did you *feel?*"

Or, two astronauts have just survived thirty-six hours when every second might have meant their deaths.

"What did you feel? Please tell us, what did you feel?"

Or, a woman's two children have spent all night exposed on a mountain top but were rescued alive.

"What did you feel?" cries the interviewer. "What did you feel while you were waiting?"

An old woman has been rescued from a burning building by a passerby, but for some minutes had every reason to think that her end had come.

"What did you feel? You thought your number was up, you said that, didn't you? What did you feel when you thought that?"

What do you think I felt? You silly nit, you jackal, what would you have felt in my place? Doesn't everybody watching this program know perfectly well what I felt? So why ask me when you know already?

Why, madam?—of course it is because feeling is our substitute for tortured slaves and dying gladiators. We have to feel sad, anxious, worried, joyful, agonized, delighted. I feel. You feel. They felt. I felt. We were feeling . . . if we don't feel, then how can we believe that anything is happening to us at all?

And since none of us feel as much as we have been trained to believe that we ought to feel in order to prove ourselves profound and sincere people, then luckily here is the television where we can see other people feeling for us. So tell me, madam, what did you *feel* while you stood there believing that you were going to be burned to death? Meanwhile, the viewers will be chanting our creed: we feel, therefore we are.

Althea came back, the children came back, life went on, and Frederick almost at once fell violently in love with a girl of twenty who had applied to be a receptionist in the surgery. And Muriel felt exactly the same, but on the emotional plane, as a virtuously frigid wife felt—so we are told—when her husband went to a prostitute: "If I had only given him what he wanted, he wouldn't have gone to *her!*"

For she knew that her Frederick would not have fallen in love with the girl if she had allowed him to be in love with her. He had had an allowance of "love" to be used up, because he had not understood—he had only said that he did—that he was wanting to fall in love: He needed the condition of being in love, needed to feel all that. Or, as Muriel muttered (but only very privately, and to herself), he needed to suffer. She should have allowed him to suffer. It is clear that everybody needs it.

And now there was this crisis, a nasty one, which rocked all four of them. Althea was unhappy, because her marriage was at stake: Frederick was talking of a divorce. And of course she was remembering her lapse with the young doctor four years before, and the living lie she had so ably maintained since. And Frederick was suicidal, because he was not so stupid as not to know that to leave a wife he adored, and was happy with, for the sake of a girl of twenty was—stupid. He was past forty-five. But he had never loved before, he said. He actually said this, and to Henry, who told Muriel.

Henry, who so far had not contributed a crisis, now revealed that he had suffered similarly some years before, but "it had not seemed important." He confessed this to Muriel, who felt some irritation. For one thing, she felt she had never really appreciated Henry as he deserved, because the way he said "it had not seemed important" surely should commend itself to her. Yet it did not; she felt in some ridiculous way belittled because he made light of what had been—surely?—a deep experience. And if it had not, why not? And then, she felt she had been betrayed; that she was able to say to herself she was being absurd did not help. In short, suddenly Muriel was in a bad way. More about Frederick than about Henry. Deprived in a flash of years of sanity, she submerged under waves of jealousy of the young girl, of deprivation—but of what? what? she was in fact deprived of nothing!—of sexual longing, and of emotional loneliness. Her Henry, she had always known, was a cold fish. Their happiness had been a half-thing. Her own potential had always been in cold storage.

And so she raged and suffered, for the sake of Frederick, her real love—so she felt now. Her only love. How could she have been so mad as not to enjoy being really in love, two weeks of love. How could she not have seen, all those years, where the truth lay. How could she . . .

That was what she felt. What she *thought* was, and knew, that she was mad. Everything she felt now had nothing, but nothing to do with her long relationship with Frederick, which was pleasant as a good healthy diet and as unremarkable, and nothing to do with her marriage with Henry, whom she loved deeply, and who made her happy, and whose humorous and civilized company she enjoyed more than anyone's.

Frederick brought his great love to an end. Or, to put it accurately, it was brought to an end: the girl married. For a while he sulked; he could not forgive life for his being nearly fifty. Althea helped him come back to himself, and to their life together.

Muriel and Henry reestablished their loving equilibrium.

Muriel and Frederick for a long time did not, when they found themselves together, make sex. That phase had ended, so they told each other, when they had a discussion: they had never had a discussion of this sort before, and the fact that they were having one seemed proof indeed that they had finished with each other. It happened that this talk was taking place in his car, he having picked her up from some fete given to raise funds for the local hospital. Althea had not been able to attend. The children, once enjoyers of such affairs, were getting too old for them. Muriel was attending on behalf of them all, and Frederick was giving her a lift home. Frederick stopped the car on the edge of a small wood, which was now damp and brown with winter: this desolation seemed a mirror of their own dimmed and aging state. Suddenly, no word having been spoken, they were in an embrace, and shortly thereafter, on top of his coat and under hers in a clump of young birches whose shining winter branches dropped large, tingling, lively drops tasting of wet bark onto their naked cheeks and arms.

But, the psychologically oriented reader will be demanding, what about those children? Adolescent by now, surely?

Quite right. The four had become background figures for the dramas of the young ones' adolescence; their passions were reflections of their children's; and part of their self-knowledge had to be that Frederick's need to be in love and the associated traumas were sparked off by the adults being continually stimulated by their five attractive offspring, all of whom were of course perpetually in love or in hate.

It goes without saying, too, that the parents felt even more guilty and inadequate because they worried that their lapses—past, present, and imaginary—might have contributed to the stormy miseries of the children. Which we all know too well to have to go through again—but what violence! what quarrels! what anguish! Adolescence is like this. The Jones and Smith youngsters were behaving exactly as they were expected to. Oh, the dramas and the rebellions, the leavings of home and the sullen returns; oh, the threats of drug-taking, then the drug-taking and the return to caution; the near-pregnancies, the droppings out and in, the ups and downs at schools, the screamed accusations at the parents for their total stupidity, backwardness, thickheadedness, and responsibility for all the ills in the world.

But just as the script prescribes crisis, so it prescribes the end of crisis. Those five attractive young people, with benefits of sound middle-class background and its institutions, with their good education, with their intelligent and concerned parents—what could go wrong? Nothing did. They did well enough at school and were soon to go to the university. Could they have any other future beyond being variations on the theme of their parents?

Twenty years had passed.

There came an opportunity for the two doctors to join a large doctors' combine in London. It was in a working-class area, but the senior doctors had consulting rooms in Harley Street. Doctors Smith and Jones had continued idealistic, conditionally socialist, and were shocked by the thought that they might also succumb to what they thought of as a Jekyll-and-Hyde existence.

The two families decided to buy a very large house in North London, and to divide it. That way they would all have much more space than if they each had a house. And the children were more like brothers and sisters and should not be separated by anything as arbitrary as a move to a new home.

Soon after the move to London, Henry died. There was no reason for him to die in his fifties. He had thought of himself as healthy. But he had always smoked heavily, he was rather plump, and he had always worked very hard. These were reasons enough, it was thought, for him to have a stroke and for Muriel to be a widow in her forties.

Muriel stayed in the shared house with her two children, a boy of eighteen and a girl of fourteen. After discussing it thoroughly with Althea, Frederick made arrangements to help support Muriel, to be a father to the children, to support this other family as he was sure Henry would have done for Althea and the three children if it had been Frederick who had had the stroke. As it might have been: Frederick's habits and constitution were similar to Henry's. Frederick was secretly frightened, made resolutions to eat less, smoke less, work less, worry less: but he was doing more of everything because Henry had gone.

In order to support his greater responsibilities, Frederick attended two days a week and a morning in Harley Street—Muriel acted as his receptionist there, and for the two other doctors who shared his set of rooms. He also worked hard in the combine's clinics, making up by evening sessions and night visiting for time spent in Moneyland. So Frederick and Muriel were now working together, as well as seeing each other constantly in the much-shared family life. Muriel was more with Frederick than Althea was.

And now that Muriel was a widow, and the opportunities were

more, the sex life of the two had become as stable as good married sex.

Muriel, thinking about it, had decided that it was probable Frederick had deliberately "stepped up" his sexual life with her because he knew she must be feeling sexually deprived. This was very likely the kind of sexually friendly consideration that would happen in a polygamous marriage. What made her come to this conclusion was that now they would often cuddle as married people do, for instance staying an hour or so after time in the Harley Street rooms, their arms around each other, discussing the day's problems, or perhaps driving off onto Hampstead Heath to discuss the children, sharing warmth and affection—like married people.

For Fred could hardly be missing this sort of affection, far from it, and that he was giving it to her must be the result of a conscious decision, of kindness.

They sometimes did say to each other that what they all had together—but only they two knew it—was a polygamous marriage.

When in company, and people were discussing marriage, the marriage problems of Western man—the problems caused by the emancipation of women, monogamy, fidelity, whether one should "tell" or not—these two tended to remain silent or to make indifferent remarks that sounded in spite of themselves impatient—as people do when entertaining inadmissible thoughts.

Both of them, the man and the woman, had found themselves thinking, had even heard themselves exclaiming aloud as the result of such thoughts: "What a lot of rubbish, what lies!"— meaning, no less, these intelligent and sensible ideas we all do have about the famous Western problematical marriage.

Muriel had only understood that she was married to Frederick when she started to think about marrying again: but it was not likely that anyone would want to marry a forty-five-year-old woman with children at their most demanding and difficult time. She could not imagine marrying again: for it would mean the end of her marriage with Frederick. This was probably how they would all go on, into their old age, or until one of them died.

This was Muriel's thinking on the situation.

Frederick: Muriel was right—he had indeed thought carefully about his old friend's loneliness. She would probably not marry again. She was not, after all, of the generation where there were more men than women. And there was something too independent and touch-me-not about her. Her silences were challenging. Her green eyes were frank. A tall, rangy woman with bronze hair—she dyed it—people noticed her, and called her beautiful or striking: of her, people used the strong adjectives. The older she got, the dryer and cooler became her way of talking. Enemies called her unkind, or masculine; friends, witty. *He* enjoyed these qualities, but would he if they were not the other half, as it were, of Althea? Whom people tended to call "little." So did he. Dear little Althea.

He would give Muriel as much warmth, as much sex as he could, without, of course, giving any less to his wife. For years his relations with Muriel had been all jam, nothing to pay, a bonus. Now he felt her as part of his sudden increase in responsibility when Henry died, part of what he must give to the two children. He was fond of Muriel—indeed, he was sure he loved her. He knew he loved the children almost as well as his own. It was an ungrudging giving of himself—but there was something else in him, another worm was at work. For what was strongest in Frederick now neither his wife nor Muriel knew anything about. It was his longing for the girl Frances—now married with children. Neither of his women had understood how deep that had gone. He had not understood it himself at the time.

Now, years later, it seemed to him that his life was divided between dark, or perhaps a clear flat gray, and light—Frances. Between everything heavy, plodding, difficult, and everything delicious—Frances. Nothing in his actual life fed delight or sprang from it: somewhere else was a sweetness and ease which he had known once, when he had loved Frances.

By now he did know that Frances, a lovely but quite ordinary girl, must be a stand-in for something else. It must be so. No small human being could possibly support the weight of such a force and a fierceness of longing, of want, of need. From time to time, when he straightened himself morally, and physically—for it was like a physical anguish, from a pain that swept all through him—or when he woke up in the morning, out of a dream that was all pain of loss, to see Althea's sleeping face a few inches away on the other pillow, he had to tell himself this: It is not possible that I am suffering all this, year after year, because of a girl I was in love with for a few crazy months.

Yet that was how it felt. On one side was the life he actually led; on the other, "Frances."

His intelligence told him everything it ought, such as that if he had been fool enough to leave Althea for Frances, or if Frances had been fool enough to marry him, that in a very short time Frances would have been a dear, known face on a shared pillow, and that what Frances had represented would have moved its quarters elsewhere.

But that was not what he felt. Although he worked so hard— it was virtually two jobs that he had now, one with the poor and the ignorant, for whom he remained concerned, and one with the rich—although he maintained with the most tender love and consideration the emotional and physical needs of the two women; although he was a good and tactful father for five children—he felt he had nothing, lacked everything.

Althea: We move into the shoes or behind the eyes of, the innocent party.

These three people had all taken on loads with the death of Henry. With Muriel working, Althea's was to run all the large house, to do the shopping, to cook, to be always available for the children. She did not mind it; she had never wanted a career.

But it was hard work, and soon she felt herself to be all drudgery and domesticity, and just at the time when, with the children older, she had looked forward to less. But this strain was nothing compared to the real one, which was that she had cared very much about being so attractive, and cherished for it. Cherished no less, she demanded even more of her vanishing looks. She could not bear to think that soon she would be elderly, soon Frederick would not want her. Comparing her tragic sessions in front of her mirror, and her feelings of inadequacy, with her husband's affection, she knew that she was unreasonable. Well, it was probably the "change."

She read many medical books and consulted another doctor— not one her husband knew—and got pills and came to regard her emotional state, all of it, everything she thought and felt, as a symptom without validity.

For she knew that her relationship with her husband was warm, good—wonderful. While other people's marriages frayed and cracked and fell apart, hers, she knew, was solid.

But when she looked at her life, when she looked back, she, too, divided what she saw into two. For her, the sunlit time lay on the other side of the affair with the young doctor. It was not the physical thing she regretted, no; it was that she had not told her husband. Time had done nothing at all to soften her guilt about it. Frederick and she had known a time of perfection, of complete trust and belief. Then she, Althea, had chosen to destroy it. It was her fault that he had fallen so much in love with the girl Frances. Oh, he was likely to fall in love with someone at some point—of course, everyone did, hadn't she? But so violently? That could only have been because of some deep lack between them. And she knew what it was: she had told him lies, had not trusted him.

She was left now with much more than she deserved. If she had to share him now—a little, with Muriel—then it was what she deserved. Besides, if she, Althea, had been left a widow, then she would have leaned as heavily on Henry. On who else?

Sometimes Althea had wild moments when she decided to tell Frederick about the young doctor; but that would be absurd, out of proportion. To talk about it now would surely be to destroy what they still had. To say: for more than a decade now I have been lying to you—she could not imagine herself actually doing it.

Sometimes she listened to other people talking about their marriages, and it seemed to her that they were able to take infidelities much more lightly. Lies, too. Althea kept telling herself that there was something very wrong in her, that she kept brooding about it, worrying, grieving.

For instance, there were these people who went in for wife swapping. They thought nothing of making love in heaps and in bunches, all together. Some of them said their marriages were strengthened—perhaps they were. Perhaps if she and her Fred had shared each other with other couples . . . who, Muriel and Henry?—no, surely that could be too dangerous, too close? Surely they—the wife swappers—made a rule not to get involved too close to home? But that was not the point at all, the point was the lying, the deception.

The fact was, the only person in the world who knew all the truth about her was Muriel. Muriel had known about the young doctor, and knew about the years of lying. How odd that was, for your woman friend to be closer than your own husband! It was *intolerable*. Unbearable. Althea found it horrible to say to herself: I trust Muriel more than I do Frederick; my behavior has proved that I do.

Of course she had sometimes had her thoughts about Frederick and Muriel. She had recently been jealous—a little, not much. This was because Muriel was working with Frederick now.

Often, when the three of them were together, Althea would look at those two, her husband, her closest friend, and think: Of course, if I died, they would marry. This was not envy, but her way of coming to terms with it. She even thought—though this was the sort of thing Muriel said, the kind of thing people expected from Muriel: This is a sort of group marriage, I suppose.

But Althea did not suspect a sexual tie. Not that he hadn't often said he found Muriel attractive. But one always could sense that sort of thing. Of course, in all those years there must have been something: a kiss or two? A little more, perhaps, after a party or something like that? But not much more, these two would never deceive her. She could trust Muriel with anything; her old friend was a well into which confidences vanished and were forgotten; Muriel never gossiped, never condemned. She was the soul—if one could use that old-fashioned word—of honor. As for Frederick, when he had fallen in love, not only his wife, but the whole world had known of it: he was not a man who could, or who wanted to, conceal his feelings. But the real thing was this: the three of them had made, and now lived inside, an edifice of kindliness and responsibility and decency; it was simply not possible that this could harbor deception. It was inconceivable. So much so that Althea did not think about it: it was not sexual jealousy that she felt.

But she felt something else that she was ashamed of, that she had to wrestle with, in silence and in secrecy. It was this: she could not stop herself thinking that if Henry could die without warning, apparently in full health, then why not Frederick?

Althea was by nature a fussy and attentive wife, but Frederick did not like this in her. She longed to say: Take it easy, work less, worry less—relax. She knew he believed that he ought to be doing all this; duty ordained otherwise.

Often she would wake in the night out of dreams full of terror: if Frederick was on call, she would see the bed empty beside her, and think that this was what she could expect from the future. Then she would go to the stairs to see if Muriel's light was still on: it often was, and then Althea would descend the stairs to Muriel's kitchen, where they would drink tea or cocoa until Frederick came back. Muriel did not ask what drove Althea down the stairs so often at night, but she was always gay and consoling—kind. She was kind. Well, they were all kind people.

Sometimes, on those rare evenings when they could all be

together, without pressures from Frederick's work, Althea, having cleared the table and come to join those two people, her husband—a large worried-looking man in spectacles sitting by a lamp and piles of medical magazines, engaged in his futile task of keeping up with each new discovery—and a lean, rather restless, woman who was probably helping one of the youngsters with homework, or a psychological problem—sometimes Althea would see that room without its center, without Frederick. She and Muriel were alone in the room with the children. Yes, that is how it would all end, two aging women, with the children—who would soon have grown up and gone. Between one blink of an eye and another, a man could vanish, as Henry had done.

In the long evenings when Frederick was at the clinic, or on call, and it was as if the whole house and its occupants waited for him to come back, then Althea could not stop herself from looking across the living room at Muriel with the thought: *Coming events cast their shadow before. Can't you feel it?*

But Muriel would look up, smile, laugh, offer to make tea for them all, or would say that she heard Frederick's car and she was tired and would take herself to bed—for she was tactful, and never stayed on in the evenings past the time she was wanted.

But this is our future, Althea would think. Their future, hers and Muriel's, was each other.

She knew it. But it was neurotic to think like this and she must try to suppress it.

LOUISE'S BROWNIES
Lynda Schor

Lynda Schor, who lives in New York with her three children, has published short stories in a number of anthologies and magazines including Redbook, the Village Voice, and Fiction, as well as a definitive article on the penis that appeared in Playboy in 1980. Her work has been criticized by male writers as self-indulgent and pornographic, its ugliness unseemly for a lady writer. Schor is interested in the inglorious body and in sex, which she sees as underlying everything, but these critics miss the point.

Her two collections, Appetites (1977) and True Love and Real Romance (1979) are partly surreal satires and partly stories about contemporary relationships. In the latter, the male protagonists change from story to story, but the female character, Lynda, remains the same. A frazzled mother of three children, night-school student, writer, she keeps trying to get it together, but her best is never quite good enough. As one critic aptly describes her, "She's not mad exactly—it's just that you could never mistake her for anyone else, except maybe yourself."

In "Louise's Brownies" Lynda, who has long since known that the personal is political, recognizes that the political is also personal and that her needs are at odds with her lover's appetites. Relationships between men and women look bleak here, as in most of Schor's stories.

THE CLEAN SHEETS feel so cool. I have nothing on but my Lamston's bikinis, which used to be white but are brownish gray because I can never learn how to do the laundry like on TV, plus my socks, which come up to the middle of my calves, and are bright green with orange apples woven in. I'm staring through the glass door, and across the long expanse of terrace, at the blue beaded lights of the Queensboro Bridge. A door opens near the bed, lighting the dimly lit room for a moment, revealing a full-length mirror in which is reflected the sparkling large space of Alan's private bathroom, the fluorescent bathroom light shooting sparks of whiteness off the tile and enamel fixtures, and is suddenly obscured by Alan's long body, which is in the doorway for a moment, dark, with all the light behind it, then light, as he shuts the door behind him. We lie next to each other on the red-white-and-blue percale sheets that his mother bought for him with her discount at B. Altman. I take a glass filled with wine off the night table, sit up higher, and sip it. It's dry and cold, filled with reflections from the only lamp that's lit, which move around inside the glass as I shake it gently around to watch the different shades of soft gold, bright yellow, and pale maize. Alan, sitting on the edge of the bed, dips his hand into a dish of hard smooth beige cookies.

"Have one of these gingerbread cookies Louise baked." He picks up his wineglass after rubbing his fingers together in a circular motion against each other to rid them of a pale clinging powder from the cookies.

"Is the wine good?"

"It's yummy." He looks down at my body, which is again reclining. The only thing he's wearing is his tortoiseshell eyeglasses. I can see his dimple deepen above the edge of his black beard.

"You're a funny girl. You sure have funny socks," he says, referring to my magnificent kelly-green foot coverings.

"I don't think these are funny socks at all. I think yours are funny, those black, sleazy, short Jewish socks."

"Well, I got them on sale at Delancey Street."

"Then they really are Jewish socks." He smiles. I take his set of Flair pens from his desk. A whole box of them, beautiful colors. I pick out magenta first, and begin to draw a tiny flower on his upper thigh as he lies there smiling, content.

Later, when I waken and turn on the lamp, I find that Alan's tattoo I had painted has transferred its image into three blurred flowers near the indentation at the top of my thigh. Alan wakes. I can see the whole city through the terrace doors, yet, perhaps because the door is closed, there is an irrelevant silence, unless it is due to the hour. We dress in silence, too, my teeth clenched with the sensation of cold I feel when looking outside, searching all the underedges of the bed for my socks and underpants, strewn in total disregard for where they would land, and my shirt and slacks, which were, in contrast, placed neatly over a chair. I open the bedroom door and descend the small flight of cold hardwood stairs, carrying my platform shoes so I won't wake his three children, who're asleep in the downstairs bedrooms. Alan is still upstairs in his bathroom and I use one of the children's bathrooms, where, in this overabundance of baths, one shower is completely preempted by four enormous turtles, bits of chop-meat fat still lurking about the edges of their water. I'm standing by the large window next to the couch while Alan ties the shoelaces of his gray Hush Puppies. It's dark except for the faraway light in the kitchen. I can see a man and woman in robes, sitting at a table, through the window of the high rise across the street. Aside from that, everything is dark. Looking across the downstairs terrace, I can see a small portion of the East River, roaring and tumbling wild and cold. For a moment I get a feeling of space and adventure, watching the turbulence, then suddenly I shiver deeply with perception again, of the cold outside, which has nothing to do with the warmth inside.

I walk to the large hall closet where Alan is taking out my coat. I put out my hand to take it, when suddenly, as usual, he opens it like a matador with a cape, flipping it swiftly in such a way that suddenly facing me is the torn two-tone faded purplish mauve lining (perhaps once worn by Joan Crawford), and I half turn to accept the coat with one shoulder, as it always makes me feel strange to have someone put on my coat for me. Alan puts three crumpled dollars into my hand for the taxi. Two-seventy-five, plus tip. I always add another quarter or two to the driver's tip. I say, "Is that all I was worth?" He smiles a rubber-band smile as if, not sure of my joke, it could snap back at any moment to his usual expression. On the way out the door he asks, "Want some brownies Louise baked?"

In the lobby the doorman is sleeping. I hate going out in the middle of the night in the middle of winter, but I can't stay over because my kids are home in my own apartment. I'm frozen, huddled in my antique fur coat given to me by Irene, because luckily her arms are too long for it. Alan hails a cab. I sit huddled inside waiting for some warmth to pervade my body again, and smile frozen at Alan's tentative good-night smile, which disappears into York Avenue, and the faint pale brown of his new sheepskin coat that his mother got with her discount at B. Altman.

Timothy is in the corner of his room, puffed up to twice his fatness, and red as a beet. He's plastered against the wall, his arm raised, holding his waterproof vinyl cowboy boot. He wants to throw it. Zachary is plastered to my knees, and beginning to twine around them like a snake, making it impossible for me to move further into the room, which is only seven feet wide anyway, so that being in the doorway I'm only a few feet from Timothy against the wall.

"Don't throw that boot," I shout. "What happened?"

"Ggggggggggghhhhhhaaaoooouuuuuuuuggggggeeeeeeeemmmm mmmeeee."

"I can't understand one word if you talk while you're crying. Stop crying and calm down and tell me."

"Zachary and I were playing, Lynda, then hesssaaaaallllllmmm mmvmvmvaaaahhhhhhhhhh."

"What? I didn't hear the rest because you were crying again. Start over." I'm holding him gently around his legs, but he still doesn't put down the boot. Zachary is under the wooden desk.

"Zachary gave me his G.I. Joe for this box from Chiclets, Lynda, so I gave him the whistle, Lynda, plus the box of Chiclets for the G.I. Joe, and then I said he should give me something else, Lynda, because I gave him something else, so he gave me the Jeep too, Lynda, and now he wants them back, Lynda."

"But you have to admit that it isn't a fair trade, Timothy. You're taking advantage of him."

"But last year, Lynda, you bought him that trailer, and you only bought me that set of tiny men, for my birthday."

"That's because you got the bike before your birthday."

"Well, it's not fair, Lynda. I'm not giving back his G.I. Joe, Lynda."

I can see that with all these references and cross references to the past, no logical answer will ever suffice. I could always threaten never to buy them anything again, but I know I won't stick to it. I remind Timothy of our blanket solution: "I thought I told you never to trade with him again because he's younger and always wants to trade back. If you insist on trading with him, then do it for a while, and when he wants to trade back, do it."

Alexandra is swinging from the edge of the sleeping loft with all the agility of a spider monkey. She says, "Timo takes advantage of Zachary. He trades him all this junk for good stuff." I don't feel like reminding her about the little piece of wool that she just gave Zach for his new looseleaf notebook with the new paper in it. Accidentally her foot, still wearing the boot with the studs and ecology signs on it that her father got for her on 12th Street and Avenue B, but which I gave him the money for, hits Timothy in the mouth. He whacks her with his cowboy boot, screaming and crying, Alex shouting, "It was an accident, it was an accident, it was an accident!"

"It was not, Alex, you hit me with your shoe, you kicked me in the mouth, Alex."

"Mommmmmmmyy," Alex is screaming, still hanging off the sleeping loft by one hand, trying to protect herself with the other from the blows of the heavy vinyl boot. The doorbell rings. Oh, God, is it eight o'clock already? I wonder how I can go out and leave them in this condition. I unlock the door. It's Alan, his smile towering out in the dim light of the dusty hallway, the filthy gray marble stairs and yellow ochre lead-poison paint glowing sickeningly in the special light of the low-wattage bulbs, a unique quality of most of the buildings I've lived in, framed behind him.

"Hi," he says, his smile broadening. As I open the door, the bookshelf, hiding the hole over the doorway, falls from the wall, injuring no one—*Pale Fire* and 24 *One-Act Plays,* and others, crashing together like opposing waves at the seashore.

"Hi," I say, extricating myself from a hello kiss to run back into the room where part of me wishes the kids to fight it out by themselves and part wants to get it all straightened out immediately so that I can leave, feeling the sensation of some kind of order. Now, down from the loft, Alex is actively beating Timothy.

"Well, he hit me with the shoe."

"But you started it."

"But it was an accident, and he really hit me."

Timothy is screaming now. Zach is still under the desk, relieved that the focus is off him. He's holding his G.I. Joe, which he's retrieved, and trying to get Timothy to take it, perhaps to pacify him so that he ceases that incredible screaming. Alan is standing there half watching through the large doorway, which is framed in large heavy yellow vinyl curtains, as if he's watching a play, because he's not part of it. He's partly mesmerized by the steady drip emanating from the hole in the ceiling over the radiator, where the damp beams are exposed, some wet plaster suppurating around the opening like the edges of a wound, drops of water dripping through and around the plants, making soft plops on the clothes from three loads of laundry that are drying on the radiator because my line fell down yesterday with all the clothes on it, which had to be rewashed, each droplet on the clothes framed with a fine ragged white outline of plaster dust.

I tell Alex to get out of the room and practice her guitar. Long sleepy wails are still emanating from Timothy's mouth, his pink wet face looks like a Spaulding that's fallen into a puddle. I look at Alan. He looks at me deeply, and says, "Hi," again, his eyes trying to extract a happy hello for himself as one extracts a suitcase of valuables from an earthquake. I smile inappropriately like a schizophrenic. I'm almost ready to go. Alex reappears in the front room, which is two feet from her room, where the fallen books are all over the floor. Alan is waiting for me on the studio couch which is really a high riser covered with an Indian spread.

"You just went out last night," says Alex. "You can't go out tonight. You always go out."

"It's almost bedtime anyway. Why do I have to sit here and keep you company while you sleep? Besides, you went to Emily's last weekend, why can't I go out too?"

"But you just went out. You go out every night."

"No I don't. I did go out a lot this week, but so what? Two nights are for school."

"You can't go out."

"Two years ago my kids were just like that," says Alan. He makes me feel better, knowing it isn't just me. I end up promising not to go out quite so much, which isn't my idea of a good solution.

"This term's almost over. Then I won't be out so much," I say. They each kiss me many times, each not wanting the other to have more kisses, in a combination ritualistic, manipulative good-bye, forcing me, as if in a game, to repeat, again and again, a gesture that becomes more and more meaningless, as a way of venting their anger at my leaving, and I kiss them again and again, feeling more and more spiteful, until I shout "Enough!" Somehow I feel manipulated into leaving with a sour parting instead of a neat, pleasant one, the way I'd like. I hear the click of the lock behind me as we descend the stairs, my platform shoes making a familiar clunking noise on the worn, dirty gray stone steps of the hallway.

When we get back, I run in to check the kids with my usual sense of doom, but they're each asleep on their own loft beds; there's order, aside from an enormous mess of papers and orange peels, their semidried deep orange against the turquoise of my deluxe Rya, and the tiny orange pits nestling in the extra-long fibers. I go to the bathroom, first wiping the plaster and the water off the seat from the leak in the ceiling which has been fixed six times and is leaking again, so that no one bothers to plaster the hole again. I often imagine that the people who live in the apartment above can peer through into my bathroom and watch me in there, but I know that's not true. All I can see are pipes. The light isn't working. It probably just needs a bulb, but it can't be reached without a ladder, even by my standing on the edge of the high old-fashioned bathtub, as the ceilings are eleven feet high, even though the bathroom is three feet by four feet. By the time I come out of the bathroom, Alan's already undressed, an unsubtle noncoquettish quality of speed inherent in the expression of his desire. He's standing beside a pile of his clothes, his penis beckoning to me with its slightly upturned angle, erect already, even though I hadn't been in the room at all until that moment. We kiss, and then I shut the door to Alex's room, as it's very close to mine and mine doesn't have a door that shuts, as it's also the living room, and is connected with the kitchen and a small dining room by enormous doorways that are almost as large as the rooms themselves. By the time I'm finished, which is about two seconds, Alan is gone. Then I see his face peering down at me from the edge of my sleeping loft, which was built by my husband before we separated. I smile.

"You sure are horny for a professor." I take off my slacks and socks, which are magenta with an orange ice-cream cone woven in on the sides, and climb the ladder to the loft bed with my shirt on. Lately it bothers me the way men look at me when I'm completely naked. Not the way you look at a person. Alan is helping me remove my shirt, when I notice a cockroach walking slowly along the molding ten feet above the ground, but directly above my bed. I pick up my white diaphragm case and smash it. Alan just looks. At 4:30, when he gets ready to go home to his kids, I lean over the edge of the loft bed and watch him get dressed. This time he shakes out his clothes before putting them on.

* * *

I'm at a day-care rally. A public hearing. I don't know what a public hearing is, but it seems to be a bunch of people who all want the same thing, who meet to tell why, while the adversaries never show up. We've just learned about the new fee scale proposed by Rockefeller for the city day-care centers. It's Tuesday night and last night I had a class and tomorrow night I have a class. Before I left the house Alex said, "You can't go out, you always go out." I know, but I really feel committed to work through this problem. What would I have done without day care? I'd be upstairs in the psych ward of St. Vincent's. President Nixon would like a resurgence of the nuclear family by making it impossible for women with children to support themselves or go to work. I realize that under the new fee scale if I ever finish school and get anywhere above a poverty income I will no longer qualify for day-care services. I'm in an uptown school auditorium, facing a table with rows of name tags of politicians, among them Bella Abzug's name, fiddling with my daughter's tape recorder, which her father gave her and which worked until this moment. I want to write an article and want to record all the speeches, but the thing won't work. "Cheap thing, cheap thing," I keep repeating over and over. Everyone agrees that these rules oppress women, force them onto welfare, as they can't afford the new day-care fees, and when they are just about making a subsistence income, they no longer qualify. Jeanette Washington says, "When they fool with our children, it's time to get mad, time to get bad."

I leave the hearing before it's over. It's raining lightly, such tiny drops that they almost don't fall, but hang in the air, blowing this way and that in the cold wind, getting stuck in my hair, and filling it until it's an enormous halo of tumid curls. I'm in a hurry to listen to whether the tape recorder really did work. I do "rewind" until somewhere in the middle, and I can't wait to really hear whether a sound will come from it or not. I hear the teary, almost inaudible woman's voice saying, ". . . and now, because of day care, I've finally been able to work and take care of my child, and now I won't qualify. Day care is all I have, and if they take it away . . ." Her voice breaks. "All I can say is . . . thank you, thank you for day care!"

I'm in my Comparative Anatomy class. I've just thrown my dog-fish shark away in the garbage, inside a plastic bag. Totally dissected, with my Barnes and Noble beginner's dissection kit, it looks like a flaked tuna casserole. The man in my lab who sits behind me quietly arises and goes to get the professor. She follows him to his table and watches questioningly as silently he opens the pericardial cavity, and spreads it where the mid-ventral incision is made, cranially from the abdomen, through the center of the pectoral girdle, and motions with his head for her to look inside. She does, and then laughs.

"What happened to it?"

"I don't know; it's missing. My lab partner must have taken it."

"What would he do with the heart? Voodoo?"

"Well, he's not here tonight, and the heart is gone."

"Use someone else's heart." He looks at me.

"I have none," I say, and go into the sink room, where a volunteer is opening a case of pickled cats. I'm ready for my cat. I choose a black-and-white one that looks exactly like my cat Dorothy at home, except this is wet, smells of formaldehyde, and is stiff as a board, arms and legs out, mouth open and tongue out, in a silent scream. I don't know whether I can start skinning him tonight without first going home and meditating on it for a week. "Oohh, that's disgusting," I say, looking at it through the plastic bag. From the looks I'm getting I see that it's unusual for someone taking Comparative Anatomy to find these pickled cats disgusting. I wonder if this is a bad omen for my grade. Aside from the fact that I've just been informed that the professor wants to see our dogfish sharks, and mine's already in the garbage. Alan comes to pick me up after the class he teaches. We'd made a date to go to his apartment after class because he lives closer to Hunter, but now I really don't feel like it. I'm feeling angry and very pressured. I've been out every night, I have an exam coming up, my house is a mess, I have to go to work tomorrow, and I want to write an article. I don't feel like going to make love with Alan, especially when things are so easy for him and so hard for me. The sight of him makes me angry, but it isn't his fault personally. I explain the whole day-care situation over coffee in a restaurant, trying to pretend there's nothing personal in my anger, which isn't true, but I dissimulate, directing my anger at circumstances. "I'm going home to do an article about it, and I have to study for an exam, and do the dishes . . . and I don't feel well."

"I understand," he says. "Write a good article."

Alan's holding my hand as we float through the warm, moist night, moving east on Sixty-third. Having no windshield wipers on my eyeglasses, I'm looking through myriad minuscule dots of moisture, creating pointillist paintings with my eyes.

"I really like this street," I say.

"Most of these are private houses," says Alan. "These people must be well connected."

"You're well enough connected," I answer, meaning that I think his apartment is quite nice enough, but he thinks I'm jokingly assessing his genitalia. He's holding the book I've given him to read because I want to share it with him, gingerly, as if he'd like to give it back or drop it into the nearest litter basket. A few moments ago at the Fifty-ninth Street station, framed by Bloomingdale's windows, when I gave it to him, like handing him a revelation about myself, he accepted it with reservation. Wiping the moisture off his own eyeglasses with a large white hanky that he's whipped out of his coat pocket, a few puckers in the shape of Chinese silk tie-dye spots where he'd blown his nose, but still bright white, from an excellent laundry, he stares at it earnestly. The frankly rounded upside-down half-moon shape of his upper lip becomes more pronounced. He says, "Why this? Do you really want me to read this?"

"I really do, because I identify with it. I identify with George Jackson."

He reads the copy off the back of the book, his large head with its black curls slightly tilted, a minute reflection from Bloomingdale's on his right temple. "My credo is to seize the pig by the tusks and ride him till his neck breaks. If fortuitous outcome of circumstance allows him to prevail over me—again—then I want to have this carefully worked-up comment prepared. I want something to remain, to torment his ass, to haunt him, to make him know in no uncertain terms that he did incur this nigger's sore disfavor." He looks up at me with horror, head still tilted, his eyes moving over my open antique fur coat, with the wine-colored satin shirt glowing through the opening, my shiny black slacks, with their thin, thin red belt, and my slender small-boned body on my platform pink suede boots, my wild mass of hair around my tiny face, incredulous.

The candelabra, made completely from elks' horns, is lit, the tiny precise flames reflecting on the shiny teak tabletop. Alan's children are at his mother's and mine are with their father, so I'm staying over, and he's making me a dinner. I'm sitting at the table riffling through an old New York Times magazine section, sipping some red wine at the table, already left set for him by Louise. Alan appears and puts on the table an ovenware dish full of steaming meat and noodles. It's a dinner called "casserole" and was previously prepared for him by Louise, who is a better cook than I am. Has he ever considered marrying Louise? While I help him put the dishes into the dishwasher, I say, "Want to see something?" I open my white sailcloth ecology shopping bag and pull out a plastic bag with a semidissected cat in it. "I'm taking it home to work on for the practical. I have to memorize every single artery, the whole venous system, the renal portal system, hepatic portal system, digestive system, urogenital system . . ." I whip the cat out onto the Formica countertop.

There is an immediate smell of formaldehyde, not a passive odor, but one that whips immediately into one's orifices, evoking tears.

"Look at the blood vessels. Aren't they great?" They've been injected with latex, blue for the veins and red for the arteries. "Isn't it beautiful?"

"It's disgusting," he says, wrapping it up quickly. "Once the smell gets into the house, it's impossible to get rid of it," he smiles. Even he thinks it's disgusting, and he's a biologist. One thing I like about Alan is that though he's not crazy himself, he's very indulgent with me. He never tells me how to be. We talk sometimes about how nice acceptance is and how long it takes to be able to have acceptance of the other person, the way they are, in a relationship.

We're sitting on one of the couches, our feet buried in the blue rug, a large round tumbler with a tiny bit of warm brandy fuming in the bottom, a dish of irregularly shaped brownies on the coffee table next to the brandy warmer.

"Have some brownies Louise made," says Alan.

"Do you tell Louise what to cook?" I ask.

"No. She wanted me to at first, but I just let her take over more and more. I really didn't care about those things."

I'm beginning to get a weird feeling. Strange, I identify with Louise, and I'm beginning to feel upset. I roll my golden brandy about the bottom of the glass. The taste doesn't flip me out but its warmth is nice, and so is sitting on the couch, like a boat on a thick blue carpet, which is pleasantly dirty enough so that I don't feel that perhaps all his demands on Louise are too great. I slough off my boots like the old skin of a snake and leave them, the pale pink suede floating in the rug, to go upstairs with Alan to his room, each carrying our brandy glasses like candles in a church procession. I lie on the bed stiffly, feeling a sort of resentment that is disturbing, as I somehow thought, like in a fairy tale, that this was the best relationship ever, so far. I want to continue to feel that way. He takes his box of Flair pens and chooses dark green. Beginning at the top edge of my dark pubic hair, he draws, in sketchy lines, two long green stems, replaces the green with red, with which he makes two large flowers out of my breasts, then returns to green, finishing it off by connecting the stems more perfectly to the flowers, and making large sketchy green leaves. I laugh. I'm impressed. It's pretty creative and shows he was thinking about it during the time we didn't see each other. My smile floats above his black curls as he buries his head into my chest and my nipple, which is a flower.

I'm looking forward to meeting his brother, this morning, whom he hasn't seen in over a year, who's nine years younger and is having marriage problems with his beautiful Californian wife, who remained there, where he teaches economics at college. Alan is feeling hopeful about becoming closer with him, so I'm surprised that when Tim comes, and we're having coffee, Alan talks about the weather. Their greeting was also very cool. I can't believe it, but no one mentions anything important that's happening in their lives. Perhaps it's because I'm there. I'd love to find out about Tim's wife and all about what's troubling them. At my suggestion we go to see the Lucas Samaras show at the Whitney, which I loved, and feeling spiteful, wanting to see their reaction to that madness. As we leave, Alan says to Tim and me, "I forgot to offer you some of Louise's apple brown betty."

Seated around the dark spotless table at the Whitney Cafeteria, I'm tracing the pattern on a doily that was under my three petits fours and my orange coffee with whipped cream, with a blue Flair pen that I have in my purse.

"Hey, that's not my Flair pen," says Alan.

"So I have a different kind of marker. Does that imply un-faithfulness?" Does that make him feel that I have a strange life aside from him, which he can't imagine?

They're talking. Tim says, "There are lots of things wrong with this country. For instance, certainly something should be done with the postal system."

"What?" I say, butting in.

"Yes, the system is terrible," Alan agrees.

"Certainly, with better management of funds and taxes, it could be remedied."

"I can't believe it—of all the things wrong with this country you complain about the postal service? Are you mad? What about socialized medicine? Don't you think everyone has the right to good medical care? What about day care for women?" I've been turning purple, and neither of them answers me. We discuss psychotherapy, which I know Alan doesn't believe in and which I always bring up when I feel like arguing. Alan says, "I don't believe in therapy. It does more harm than good. I'm perfectly satisfied with myself. People should do more about keeping busy than spend all that energy on introspection and self-obsession."

"The fact that you're so satisfied with yourself seems a bit suspect to me," I say. "What about another area such as relationships? Don't you sometimes feel that there's some secret to them that you can't quite put your finger on, that's missing in your own relationships?"

"Yes," he says softly. I appreciate his honesty. Tim gets up from the table without a word. I think he's annoyed with me. We find him later, buying a Lucas Samaras poster. Contrary to being bugged, he liked the show. It's freezing out. We take a cab to Sixty-third Street and I remain in the taxi to go downtown. We all feel very warm toward each other. I really feel affection for Alan and kiss him good-bye. They each hold out two dollars for the fare, and I take the money from both of them; it'll cost at least three dollars to get downtown.

We're in a luncheonette, waiting for the ten-o'clock show of *Cries and Whispers*. The sight of Alan is irritating to me and I don't know why. It makes me feel insane. We're sitting there having coffee, while the black waiter smiles at me above Alan's black hair. His shirt irritates me, his slacks, his socks. I feel terrible. Prejudiced. I wouldn't appreciate his own gaze to rove over my clothing with the same kind of prejudice. He's reading the newspaper we bought in order to find out what's playing and I'm drinking coffee, watching him with my critical gaze. Yet I don't want him to look up, because I don't want to relate to him. We're like an old married couple who're bored with each other. He's reading about a resurgence of the gangs in the South Bronx. He tells me that Louise has lived in the South Bronx since she came here from Jamaica, but now she's moving because things are so bad, like with the Grim Reapers, and stuff. He says, "There's a direct correlation between the decrease in drug addiction and the rise of these street gangs, like the ones we had in the fifties." I wonder if he's advocating drugs. "It's terrible," he says; "what can be done?"

"Nothing, until we change society," I say. I agree, it's terrible, but I think we both see it as terrible from different directions.

"I understand those kids, why they have gangs. I understand their violence stemming from impotence. They know they have no home for any identity or fulfillment or escape from their own poverty-stricken lives. Instead of living like their parents, they choose another way out, they create their own society, where they're all accepted. I used to belong to a gang when I was sixteen," I reveal, in a complicitory tone.

"You did?" he says as he beckons the waiter for more coffee.

"Yes. We had a motorcycle gang in Brooklyn. We all had jackets. Of course it wasn't the girls' gang, we each had a boyfriend. I had a blood pact with mine. We cut our arms and put them together. I was terrified to leave him."

"Really?"

"No, I'm just putting you on. I really belonged to a fake sorority."

"Can I borrow five dollars?" he asks. "I haven't got enough for the movies."

"I'll be glad to pay for myself tonight."

"Don't be silly; lend me the money and I'll pay for you. I have more money than you." I think it over. Is it socialism? I leave an enormous tip for the waiter as Alan gets my coat and helps me put it on, even though I'm trying to grab it away from him. I rush up to the cashier and pay the forty-cent bill.

Later, when we get up to leave the movie theater, still in a daze from *Cries and Whispers,* I pick up Alan's coat from the seat, hold it open, soft lamb lining facing him, and ease it over his shoulders, awkwardly, as he's tall. He doesn't know whether to laugh or what to do about this brand of sarcasm. I feel sorry for him, but I'm powerless to stop. He looks at me searchingly. "That was sure a depressing picture!" I don't want him to think it's the picture that's causing me to be depressed. It isn't.

We're sitting on my studio couch; his eyes keep rolling up toward my sleeping loft and his tongue is hanging out to the floor, but I don't feel like going to bed with him. I'm still feeling angry. At what I'm not sure. So I heat some chili that we had for dinner and put it into two of the new bowls I bought. It sits there in the middle of the bowl, thick, unmoving. I break saltines over it but it remains impervious. I have to press the saltines in really hard.

"What do you use for chili, a fork or a spoon?" I ask.

"A spoon, silly."

For my chili it really doesn't matter.

"This is good chili."

"Louise made it," I say. Again he looks at me with puzzlement. "What's bothering you?" he says.

I think for a while, but I really don't know.

"I don't know."

"I thought we accepted each other."

"I thought so too, but maybe as our relationship advances we can't afford to without ignoring issues which are a large part of our makeup. I can't always be expected to be happy and ready for you when we have a date, to have a good time and then go home and be horny all the time and ready to make love at the right time like a computer."

"Well, at the present time that's the best we can do because of our kids and our work and all. That's how our lives are defined."

All the time he's eating chili. It annoys me because he makes me wait long periods of time for answers or replies, while he chews.

"This is good chili," he says.

"But it's not strong enough."

"I know, it needs more chili powder."

"Well, tell Louise, she made it."

Silence except for the sound of eating.

"I like your red sheet."

"It's not red, it's hot pink." His bowl, empty now except for the track marks of spoon scrapings, from his last fracas with the stubborn stuff, remains. He burps. He's getting nervous that he won't get laid. He's thinking that I'm still angry and he keeps looking up at the loft bed, wondering how he can calm me down within a reasonable amount of time. I notice that, chili gone, his consciousness of the empty dish disappears, he's so used to being served. I want so badly to tell him to get up and put it in the sink, but I almost can't bear being so nasty. I sit there a moment in conflict because keeping silent is bothering me also. I really feel unhappy now, I just can't leave it.

"Does Louise always serve you your dinners?" I ask.

"Yes, sure."

"She actually puts the dishes in front of you and you just sit there?"

"Yes, why?"

"How many hours a week less does she work than you? Or does she work more hours? I've been seeing Louise, and together we're organizing a housekeepers' union." His crescent lip becomes rounder.

"But I've never seen Louise, maybe she doesn't really exist. Perhaps she's just a spirit." I really haven't seen Louise, as she's never there on weekends or at night, unless we're both out. I've only eaten her cooking. He smiles . . . he thinks it's going to be okay, and soon . . . the loft bed.

"Speaking of spirits," he says, "Louise is very cute. She's really very superstitious. When we moved into my apartment and we had all the stuff all around us, and the moving men had driven off, she said, 'And now, Dr. Linart, let's say a prayer for the house.' " He's smiling deeply, his dimple inverts.

"She calls you Doctor?" I ask, incredulous.

"She wants to," he says.

I'm wondering whether he's simply become a political adversary by being a man. In a panic, I run through all my girl friends trying to imagine which ones I might have a sexual relationship with in case I can't be civil to men anymore.

"I'd really like to go up that sleeping loft with you." I think, how come I never cared so much about all these differences before?

"I can't sleep with you tonight," I say. "It's like Angela Davis making it with Rockefeller." I'm feeling thoroughly miserable, have a case of hives, and feel my asthma coming on. He looks at me, puzzled and hurt.

"Do our political differences have to affect our relationship?"

ADVANCING LUNA— AND IDA B. WELLS

Alice Walker

Alice Walker was born in Eatonton, Georgia, in 1944, the eighth child of sharecropper parents. Educated at Spellman College and then Sarah Lawrence, she returned to the South in the early 1960s to work with voter registration. She has published three books of poetry; two novels, The Third Life of Grange Copeland and Meridian; two collections of short stories; a biography of Langston Hughes, and a Zora Neale Hurston reader. She has received numerous awards and grants, notably the Lillian Smith Award, a National Endowment for the Arts Award for Creative Writing, the Rosenthal Award from the National Institute of Arts and Letters, a National Book Award nomination, and Radcliffe Institute and Guggenheim fellowships.

Walker has lectured at the University of Massachusetts, Jackson State, Tougaloo, Wellesley, Yale, and the University of California at Berkeley. Currently she is a contributing editor of Freedomways, a quarterly journal of the black freedom movement, and of Ms. magazine. She lives in California with her daughter, Rebecca, and is completing a collection of essays on black feminist criticism, In Search of Our Mothers' Gardens.

In Interviews with Black Writers, Alice Walker explains that her preoccupation as a writer is "the spiritual survival, the survival whole of my people. But beyond that, I am committed to exploring the oppressions, the insanities, the loyalties and triumphs of black women." By the end of her novel Meridian a larger freedom has been reached. The quest for wholeness in "Advancing Luna—and Ida B. Wells" is less optimistic.

I MET LUNA the summer of 1965 in Atlanta where we both attended a political conference and rally. It was designed to give us the courage, as temporary civil rights workers, to penetrate the small hamlets farther south. I had taken a bus from Sarah Lawrence in New York and gone back to Georgia, my home state, to try my hand at registering voters. It had become obvious from the high spirits and sense of almost divine purpose exhibited by black people that a revolution was going on, and I did not intend to miss it. Especially not this summery, student-studded version of it. And I thought it would be fun to spend some time on my own in the South.

Luna was sitting on the back of a pickup truck, waiting for someone to take her from Faith Baptist, where the rally was held, to whatever gracious black Negro home awaited her. I remember because someone who assumed I would also be traveling by pickup introduced us. I remember her face when I said, "No, no more back of pickup trucks for me. I know Atlanta well enough, I'll walk." She assumed of course (I guess) that I did not wish to ride beside her because she was white, and I was not curious enough about what she might have thought to explain it to her. And yet I was struck by her passivity, her *patience* as she sat on the truck alone and ignored, because someone had told her to wait there quietly until it was time to go.

This look of passively waiting for something changed very little over the years I knew her. It was only four or five years in all that I did. It seems longer, perhaps because we met at such an optimistic time in our lives. John Kennedy and Malcolm X had already been assassinated, but King had not been and Bobby Kennedy had not been. Then, too, the lethal, bizarre elimination by death of this militant or that, exiles, flights to Cuba, shoot-outs between former Movement friends sundered forever by lies planted by the FBI, the gunning down of Mrs. Martin Luther King, Sr., as she played the Lord's Prayer on the piano in her church (was her name Alberta?) were still in the happily unfathomable future.

We believed we could change America because we were young and bright and held ourselves *responsible* for changing it. We did not believe we would fail. That is what lent fervor (revivalist fervor, in fact; we would *revive* America!) to our songs, and lent sweetness to our friendships (in the beginning almost all interracial), and gave a wonderful fillip to our sex (which, too, in the beginning, was almost always interracial).

What first struck me about Luna when we later lived together was that she did not own a bra. This was curious to me, I suppose, because she also did not need one. Her chest was practically flat, her breasts like those of a child. Her face was round, and she suffered from acne. She carried with her always a tube of that

"skin-colored" (if one's skin is pink or eggshell) medication designed to dry up pimples. At the oddest times—waiting for a
light to change, listening to voter registration instructions, talking about her father's new girl friend—she would apply the stuff,
holding in her other hand a small brass mirror the size of her
thumb, which she also carried for just this purpose.

We were assigned to work together in a small, rigidly segre-
gated south Georgia town whose city fathers, incongruously and
years ago, had named it Freehold, Georgia. Luna was slightly
asthmatic, and when overheated or nervous she breathed through
her mouth. She wore her shoulder-length black hair with bangs
to her eyebrows and the rest brushed behind her ears. Her eyes
were brown and rather small. She was attractive, but just barely
and with effort. Had she been the slightest bit overweight, for
instance, she would have gone completely unnoticed and would
have faded into the background where, even in a revolution, fat
people seem destined to go. I have a photograph of her sitting
on the steps of a house in south Georgia. She is wearing tiny
pearl earrings, a dark sleeveless shirt with Peter Pan collar, Ber-
muda shorts, and a pair of those East Indian sandals that seem
to adhere to nothing but a big toe.

The summer of '65 was as hot as any other in that part of the
South. There was an abundance of flies and mosquitoes. Everyone complained about the heat and the flies and the hard work,
but Luna complained less than the rest of us. She walked ten
miles a day with me up and down those straight Georgia high-
ways, stopping at every house that looked black (one could
always tell in 1965) and asking whether anyone needed help
with learning how to vote. The simple mechanics: writing one's
name, or making one's X in the proper column. And then, though
we were required to walk, everywhere, we were empowered to
offer prospective registrants a car in which they might safely ride
down to the county courthouse. And later to the polling places.
Luna, almost overcome by the heat, breathing through her mouth

like a dog, her hair plastered with sweat to her head, kept looking straight ahead and walking as if the walking itself was her reward.

I don't know if we accomplished much that summer. In retrospect, it seems not only minor but irrelevant. A bunch of us, black and white, lived together. The black people who took us in were unfailingly hospitable and kind. I took them for granted in a way that now amazes me. I realize that at each and every house we visited I *assumed* hospitality, I *assumed* kindness. Luna was often startled by my "boldness." If we walked up to a secluded farmhouse and half a dozen dogs ran up barking around our heels and a large black man with a shotgun could be seen whistling to himself under a tree, she would become nervous. I, on the other hand, felt free to yell at this stranger's dogs, slap a couple of them on the nose, and call over to him about his hunting.

That month with Luna of approaching new black people every day taught me something about myself I had always suspected: I thought black people superior people. Not simply superior to white people, because even without thinking about it much I assumed almost everyone was superior to them; but to everyone. Only white people, after all, would blow up a Sunday school class and grin for television over their "victory," i.e. the death of four small black girls. Any atrocity, at any time, was expected from them. On the other hand, it never occurred to me that black people *could* treat Luna and me with anything but warmth and concern. Even their curiosity about the sudden influx into their midst of rather ignorant white and black Northerners was restrained and courteous. I was treated as a relative, Luna as a much welcomed guest.

Luna and I were taken in by a middle-aged couple and their young school-age daughter. The mother worked outside the house in a local canning factory, the father worked in the paper plant in nearby Augusta. Never did they speak of the danger they were in of losing their jobs over keeping us, and never did their small daughter show any fear that her house might be attacked by racists because we were there. Again, I did not expect this family to complain, no matter what happened to them because of us. Having understood the danger, they had assumed the risk. I did not think them particularly brave, merely typical.

I think Luna liked the smallness—only four rooms—of the house. It was in this house that she ridiculed her mother's lack of taste. Her yellow-and-mauve house in Cleveland, the eleven rooms, the heated garage, the new car every year, her father's inability to remain faithful to her mother, their divorce, the fight over the property, even more so than over the children. Her mother kept the house and the children. Her father kept the car and his new girl friend, whom he wanted Luna to meet and "approve." I could hardly imagine anyone disliking her mother so much. Everything Luna hated in her she summed up in three words: "yellow-and-mauve."

I have a second photograph of Luna and a group of us being bullied by a Georgia state trooper. This member of Georgia's finest had followed us out into the deserted countryside to lecture us on how misplaced—in the South—was our energy, when "the Lord knew" the North (where he thought all of us lived, expressing disbelief that most of us were Georgians) was just as bad. (He had a point that I recognized even then, but it did not seem the point where we were.) Luna is looking up at him, her mouth slightly open as always, a somewhat dazed look on her face. I cannot detect fear on any of our faces, though we were all afraid. After all, 1965 was only a year after 1964 when three civil rights workers had been taken deep into a Mississippi forest by local officials and sadistically tortured and murdered. Luna almost always carried a flat black shoulder bag. She is standing with it against her side, her thumb in the strap.

At night we slept in the same bed. We talked about our schools, lovers, girl friends we didn't understand or missed. She dreamed, she said, of going to Goa. I dreamed of going to Africa. My dream came true earlier than hers: an offer of a grant from an unsuspected source reached me one day as I was writing poems under a tree. I left Freehold, Georgia, in the middle of summer, without regrets, and flew from New York to London, to Cairo, to Kenya, and finally Uganda, where I settled among black people with the same assumptions of welcome and kindness I had taken for granted in Georgia. I was taken on rides down the Nile as a matter of course, and accepted all invitations to dinner, where the best local dishes were superbly prepared in my honor. I became, in fact, a lost relative of the people, whose ancestors had foolishly strayed, long ago, to America.

I wrote to Luna at once.

But I did not see her again for almost a year. I had graduated from college, moved into a borrowed apartment in Brooklyn Heights, and was being evicted after a month. Luna, living then in a tenement on East Ninth Street, invited me to share her two-bedroom apartment. If I had seen the apartment before the day I moved in I might never have agreed to do so. Her building was between Avenues B and C and did not have a front door. Junkies, winos, and others often wandered in during the night (and occasionally during the day) to sleep underneath the stairs or to relieve themselves at the back of the first-floor hall.

Luna's apartment was on the third floor. Everything in it was painted white. The contrast between her three rooms and kitchen (with its red bathtub) and the grungy stairway was stunning. Her furniture consisted of two large brass beds inherited from a previous tenant and stripped of paint by Luna, and a long, high-backed church pew which she had managed somehow to bring up from the South. There was a simplicity about the small apartment that I liked. I also liked the notion of extreme contrast, and I do to this day. Outside our front window was the decaying neighborhood, as ugly and ill lit as a battleground. (And allegedly as hostile, though somehow we were never threatened with bodily harm by the Hispanics who were our neighbors, and who seemed, more than anything, *bewildered* by the darkness and filth of their surroundings.) Inside was the church pew, as straight and spare as Abe Lincoln lying down, the white walls as spotless as a monastery's, and a small, unutterably pure patch of blue sky through the window of the back bedroom. (Luna did not believe in curtains, or couldn't afford them, and so we always undressed and bathed with the lights off and the rooms lit with candles, causing rather nun-shaped shadows to be cast on the walls by the long-sleeved high-necked nightgowns we both wore to bed.)

Over a period of weeks, our relationship, always marked by mutual respect, evolved into a warm and comfortable friendship which provided a stability and comfort we both needed at that time. I had taken a job at the Welfare Department during the day, and set up my typewriter permanently in the tiny living room for work after I got home. Luna worked in a kindergarten and in the evenings taught herself Portuguese.

It was while we lived on East Ninth Street that she told me she had been raped during her summer in the South. It is hard for me, even now, to relate my feeling of horror and incredulity. This was some time before Eldridge Cleaver wrote of being a rapist/revolutionary; of "practicing" on black women before moving on to white. It was also, unless I'm mistaken, before LeRoi Jones (as he was then known; now of course Imamu Baraka, which has an even more presumptuous meaning than "the King") wrote his advice to young black male insurrectionaries (women were not told what to do with *their* rebelliousness): "Rape the white girls. Rape their fathers." It was clear that he meant this literally and also as: to rape a white girl *is* to rape her father. It was the misogynous cruelty of this latter meaning that was habitually lost on black men (on men in general, actually), but nearly always perceived and rejected by women of whatever color.

"Details?" I asked.

She shrugged. Gave his name. A name recently in the news, though in very small print.

He was not a Movement star or anyone you would know. We had met once, briefly. I had not liked him, because he was coarse and spoke of black women as "our" women. (In the early Movement, it was pleasant to think of black men wanting to own us as a group; later it became clear that owning us meant exactly *that* to them.) He was physically unattractive, I had thought, with something of the hoodlum about him: a swaggering, unnecessarily mobile walk, small eyes, rough skin, a mouthful of wandering or absent teeth. He was, ironically, among the first persons to shout the slogan everyone later attributed solely to Stokeley Carmichael—Black Power! Stokeley was chosen as the originator of this idea by the media, because he was physically beautiful and photogenic and articulate. Even the name—Freddie Pye—was diminutive, I thought, in an age of giants.

"What did you do?"

"Nothing that required making a noise."

"Why didn't you scream?" I felt I would have screamed my head off.

"You know why."

I did. I had seen a photograph of Emmett Till's body just after it was pulled from the river. I had seen photographs of white folks standing in a circle roasting something that had talked to them in their own language before they tore out its tongue. I knew why, all right.

"What was he trying to prove?"

"I don't know. Do you?"

"Maybe you filled him with unendurable lust," I said.

"I don't think so," she said.

Suddenly I was embarrassed. Then angry. Very, very angry. *How dare she tell me this!* I thought.

Who knows what the black woman thinks of rape? Who has asked her? Who *cares*? Who has even properly acknowledged that *she* and not the white woman in this story is the most likely victim of rape? Whenever interracial rape is mentioned, a black woman's first thought is to protect the lives of her brothers, her father, her sons, her lover. A history of lynching has bred this reflex in her. I feel it as strongly as anyone. While writing a fictional account of such a rape in a novel, I read Ida B. Wells's autobiography three times, as a means of praying to her spirit to forgive me.

My prayer, as I turned the pages, went like this: *Please forgive me. I am a writer.* (This self-revealing statement alone often seems to me sufficient reason to require perpetual forgiveness; since the writer is guilty not only of always wanting to know— like Eve—but also of trying—again like Eve—to find out.)

I cannot write contrary to what life reveals to me. I wish to malign no one. But I must struggle to understand at least my own tangled emotions about interracial rape. I know, Ida B. Wells, you spent your whole life protecting, and trying to protect, black men accused of raping white women, who were lynched by white mobs, or threatened with it. You know, better than I ever will, what it means for a whole people to live under the terror of lynching. Under the slander that their men, where white women are concerned, are creatures of uncontrollable sexual lust. You made it so clear that the black men accused of rape in the past were innocent victims of white criminals that I grew up believing black men literally did not rape white women. At all. Ever. Now it would appear that some of them, the very twisted, the terribly ill, do. What would you have me write about them?

Her answer was: *Write nothing. Nothing at all. It will be used against black men and therefore against all of us. Eldridge Cleaver and LeRoi Jones don't know who they're dealing with. But you remember. You are dealing with people who brought their children to witness the murder of black human beings, falsely accused of rape. People who handed out, as trophies, black fingers and toes. Deny! Deny! Deny!*

And yet, I have pursued it. *Some black men themselves do not seem to know what the meaning of raping someone is. Some have admitted rape in order to denounce it, but others have accepted*

*rape as a part of rebellion, of "paying whitey back." They have
gloried in it.*

They know nothing of America, she says. *And neither, apparently, do you. No matter what you think you know, no matter
what you feel about it, say nothing. And to your dying breath!*

Which, to my mind, is virtually useless advice to give to a
writer.

Freddie Pye was the kind of man I would not have looked at
then, not even once. (Throughout that year I was more or less
into exotica: white ethnics who knew languages were a peculiar
weakness; a half-white hippie singer; also a large Chinese mathe-
matician who was a marvelous dancer and who taught me to
waltz.) There was no question of belief.

But, in retrospect, there was a momentary *suspension* of belief,
a kind of *hope* that perhaps it had not really happened; that
Luna had made up the rape, "as white women have been wont
to do." I soon realized this was unlikely. I was the only person
she had told.

She looked at me as if to say: "I'm glad *that* part of my life is
over." We continued our usual routine. We saw every inter-
minable, foreign, depressing, and poorly illuminated film ever
made. We learned to eat brown rice and yogurt and to tolerate
kasha and odd-tasting teas. My half-black hippie singer friend
(now a well-known reggae singer who says he is from "de
I-lands" and not Sheepshead Bay) was "into" tea and kasha and
Chinese vegetables.

And yet the rape, the knowledge of the rape, out in the open,
admitted, pondered over, was now between us. (And I began to
think that perhaps—whether Luna had been raped or not—it
had always been so; that her power over my life was exactly the
power *her word on rape* had over the lives of black men, over
all black men, whether they were guilty or not, and therefore
over my whole people.)

Before she told me about the rape, I think we had assumed a

lifelong friendship. The kind of friendship one dreams of having with a person one has known in adversity; under heat and mosquitoes and immaturity and the threat of death. We would each travel, we would write to each other from the three edges of the world.

We would continue to have an "international list" of lovers whose amorous talents or lack of talents we would continue (giggling into our dotage) to compare. Our friendship would survive everything, be truer than everything, endure even our respective marriages, children, husbands—assuming we *did,* out of desperation and boredom someday, marry, which did not seem a probability, exactly, but more in the area of an amusing idea.

But now there was a cooling off of our affection for each other. Luna was becoming mildly interested in drugs, because everyone we knew was. I was envious of the open-endedness of her life. The financial backing to it. When she left her job at the kindergarten because she was tired of working, her errant father immediately materialized. He took her to dine on scampi at an expensive restaurant, scolded her for living on East Ninth Street, and looked at me as if to say: "Living in a slum of this magnitude must surely have been your idea." As a cullud, of course.

For me there was the Welfare Department every day, attempting to get the necessary food and shelter to people who would always live amid the dirty streets I knew I must soon leave. I was, after all, a Sarah Lawrence girl "with talent." It would be absurd to rot away in a building that had no front door.

I slept late one Sunday morning with a painter I had met at the Welfare Department. A man who looked for all the world like Gene Autry, the singing cowboy, but who painted wonderful surrealist pictures of birds and ghouls and fruit with *teeth.* The night before, three of us—me, the painter, and "an old Navy buddy" who looked like his twin and who had just arrived in town—had got high on wine and grass.

That morning the Navy buddy snored outside the bedrooms

like a puppy waiting for its master. Luna got up early, made an immense racket getting breakfast, scowled at me as I emerged from my room, and left the apartment, slamming the door so hard she damaged the lock. (Luna had made it a rule to date black men almost exclusively. My insistence on dating, as she termed it, "anyone," was incomprehensible to her, since in a politically diseased society to "sleep with the enemy" was to become "infected" with the enemy's "political germs." There is more than a grain of truth in this, of course, but I was having too much fun to stare at it for long. Still, coming from Luna it was amusing, since she never took into account the risk her own black lovers ran by sleeping with "the white woman," and she had apparently been convinced that a summer of relatively innocuous political work in the South had cured her of any racial, economic, or sexual political disease.)

Luna never told me what irked her so that Sunday morning, yet I remember it as the end of our relationship. It was not, as I at first feared, that she thought my bringing the two men to the apartment was inconsiderate. The way we lived allowed us to *be* inconsiderate from time to time. Our friends were varied, vital, and often strange. Her friends especially were deeper than they should have been into drugs.

The distance between us continued to grow. She talked more of going to Goa. My guilt over my dissolute if pleasurable existence, coupled with my mounting hatred of welfare work, propelled me in two directions. South, or to West Africa. When the time came to choose, I discovered that *my* summer in the South had infected me with the need to return, to try to understand and write about the people I'd merely lived with before.

We never discussed the rape again. We never discussed, really, Freddie Pye or Luna's remaining feelings about what had happened. One night, the last month we lived together, I noticed a man's blue denim jacket thrown across the church pew. The next morning, out of Luna's bedroom walked Freddie Pye. He barely spoke to me—possibly because as a black woman I was expected to be hostile toward his presence in a white woman's bedroom. I was too surprised to exhibit hostility, however, which was only a part of what I felt, after all. He left.

Luna and I did not discuss this. It is odd, I think now, that we didn't. It was as if he were never there, as if he and Luna had not shared the bedroom that night. A month later, Luna went alone to Goa, in her solitary way. She lived on an island and slept, she wrote, on the beach. She mentioned she'd found a lover there who protected her from the local beachcombers and pests.

Several years later, she came to visit me in the South and brought a lovely piece of pottery which my daughter much later dropped and broke, but which I glued back together in such a way that the flaw improves the beauty and fragility of the design.

AFTERWARDS, AFTERWORDS
Second Thoughts

That is the "story." It has an "unresolved" ending. That is because Freddie Pye and Luna are still alive, as am I. However, one evening while talking to a friend I heard myself say that I had, in fact, written *two* endings. One, which follows, I considered appropriate for such a story published in a country truly committed to justice, and the one above, which is the best I can afford to offer a society in which lynching is still reserved, at least subconsciously, as a means of racial control.

I said that if we in fact lived in a society committed to the establishment of justice for everyone ("justice" in this case encompassing equal housing, education, access to work, adequate dental care, et cetera), thereby placing Luna and Freddie Pye in their correct relationship to each other, i.e., that of brother and sister, *compañeros,* then the two of them would be required to struggle together over what his rape of her had meant.

Since my friend is a black man whom I love and who loves me, we spent a considerable amount of time discussing what this particular rape meant to us. Morally wrong, we said, and not to be excused. Shameful; politically corrupt. Yet, as we thought of what might have happened to an indiscriminate number of innocent young black men in Freehold, Georgia, had Luna screamed, it became clear that more than a little of Ida B. Wells's fear of probing the rape issue was running through us, too. The implications of this fear would not let me rest, so that months and years went by with most of the story written but with me incapable, or at least unwilling, to finish or to publish it.

In thinking about it over a period of years, there occurred a number of small changes, refinements, puzzles, in angle. Would these shed a wider light on the continuing subject? I do not know. In any case, I returned to my notes, hereto appended for the use of the reader.

Luna: Ida B. Wells—Discarded Notes

Additional characteristics of Luna: At a time when many in and out of the Movement considered "nigger" and "black" synonymous and indulged in a sincere attempt to fake Southern "hip" speech, Luna resisted. She was the kind of WASP who could not easily imitate another's ethnic style, nor could she even exaggerate her own. She was what she was. A very straight, clear-eyed, coolly observant young woman with no talent for existing outside her own skin.

Imaginary Knowledge

Luna explained the visit from Freddie Pye in this way:
"He called that evening, said he was in town, and did I know the Movement was coming North? I replied that I did know that."
When could he see her? he wanted to know.
"Never," she replied.
He had burst into tears, or something that sounded like tears,

over the phone. He was stranded at wherever the evening's fund-raising event had been held. Not in the place itself, but outside, in the street. The "stars" had left, everyone had left. He was alone. He knew no one else in the city. Had found her number in the phone book. And had no money, no place to stay.

Could he, he asked, crash? He was tired, hungry, broke—and even in the South had had no job, other than the Movement, for months. Et cetera.

When he arrived, she had placed our only steak knife in the waistband of her jeans.

He had asked for a drink of water. She gave him orange juice, some cheese, and a couple of slices of bread. She had told him he might sleep on the church pew and he had lain down with his head on his rolled-up denim jacket. She had retired to her room, locked the door, and tried to sleep. She was amazed to discover herself worrying that the church pew was both too narrow and too hard.

At first he muttered, groaned, and cursed in his sleep. Then he fell off the narrow church pew. He kept rolling off. At two in the morning she unlocked her door, showed him her knife, and invited him to share her bed.

Nothing whatever happened except they talked. At first, only he talked. Not about the rape, but about his life.

"He was a small person physically, remember?" Luna asked me. (She was right. Over the years he had grown big and, yes, burly, in my imagination, and I'm sure in hers.) "That night he seemed tiny. A child. He was still fully dressed, except for the jacket and he, literally, hugged his side of the bed. I hugged mine. The whole bed, in fact, was between us. We were merely hanging to its edges."

At the fund raiser—on Fifth Avenue and Seventy-first Street, as it turned out—his leaders had introduced him as the unskilled, barely literate, former Southern fieldworker that he was. They had pushed him at the rich people gathered there as an example of what "the system" did to "the little people" in the South. They *asked him to tell about the thirty-seven times he had been jailed. The thirty-five times he had been beaten. The one time he had lost consciousness in the "hot" box. They told him not to worry about his grammar. "Which, as you may recall," said Luna, "was horrible." Even so, he had tried to censor his "ain'ts" and his "us'es." He had been painfully aware that he was on exhibit, like Frederick Douglass had been for the Abolitionists. But unlike Douglass he had no oratorical gift, no passionate language, no silver tongue. He knew the rich people and his own leaders perceived he was nothing: a broken man, unschooled, unskilled at anything. . . .*

Yet he had spoken, trembling before so large a crowd of rich, white Northerners—who clearly thought their section of the country would never have the South's racial problems—begging, with the painful stories of his wretched life, for their money.

At the end, all of them—the black leaders, too—had gone. They left him watching the taillights of their cars, recalling the faces of the friends come to pick them up: the women dressed in African print that shone, with elaborately arranged hair, their jewelry sparkling, their perfume exotic. They were so beautiful, yet so strange. He could not imagine that one of them could comprehend his life. He did not ask for a ride, because of that, but also because he had no place to go. Then he had remembered Luna.

Soon Luna would be required to talk. She would mention her confusion over whether, in a black community surrounded by whites with a history of lynching blacks, she had a right to scream as Freddie Pye was raping her. For her, this was the crux of the matter.

And so they would continue talking through the night.

This is another ending, created from whole cloth. If I believed Luna's story about the rape, and I did (had she told anyone else I might have dismissed it), then this reconstruction of what might have happened is as probable an accounting as any is liable to be. Two people have now become "characters."

I have forced them to talk until they reached the stumbling block of the rape, *which they must remove themselves*, before proceeding to a place from which it will be possible to insist on a society in which Luna's word alone on rape can never be used to intimidate an entire people, and in which an innocent black man's protestation of innocence of rape is unprejudicially heard. Until such a society is created, relationships of affection between black men and white women will always be poisoned—from within as from without—by historical fear and the threat of violence, and solidarity among black and white women is only rarely likely to exist.

POSTSCRIPT: HAVANA, CUBA, NOVEMBER 1976

I am in Havana with a group of other black American artists. We have spent the morning apart from our Cuban hosts bringing each other up to date on the kind of work (there are no apolitical artists among us) we are doing in the United States. I have read "Luna."

High above the beautiful city of Havana I sit in the Havana Libre pavilion with the muralist/photographer in our group. He is in his mid-thirties, a handsome, brown, erect individual whom I have known casually for a number of years. During the sixties he designed and painted street murals for both SNCC and the Black Panthers, and in an earlier discussion with Cuban artists he showed impatience with their explanation of why we had seen no murals covering some of the city's rather dingy walls: Cuba, they had said, unlike Mexico, has no mural tradition. "But the point of a revolution," insisted Our Muralist, "is to make new traditions!" And he had pressed his argument with such passion for the *usefulness*, for revolutionary communication, of his craft, that the Cubans were both exasperated and impressed. They drove us around the city for a tour of their huge billboards, all advancing socialist thought and the heroism of men like Lenin, Camilo, and Che Guevara, and said, "These, *these* are our 'murals'!"

While we ate lunch, I asked Our Muralist what he'd thought of "Luna." Especially the appended section.

"Not much," was his reply. "Your view of human weakness is too biblical," he said. "You are unable to conceive of the man without conscience. The man who cares nothing about the state of his soul because he's long since sold it. In short," he said, "you do not understand that some people are simply evil, a disease on the lives of other people, and that to remove the disease altogether is preferable to trying to interpret, contain, or forgive it. Your 'Freddie Pye,'" and he laughed, "was probably raping white women on the instructions of his government."

Oh ho, I thought. Because, of course, for a second, during which I stalled my verbal reply, this comment made both very little and very much sense.

"I am sometimes naïve and sentimental," I offered. I am sometimes both, though frequently by design. Admission in this way is tactical, a stimulant to conversation.

"And shocked at what I've said," he said, and laughed again. "Even though," he continued, "you know by now that blacks could be hired to blow up other blacks, and could be hired *by someone* to shoot down Brother Malcolm, and hired *by someone* to provide a diagram of Fred Hampton's bedroom so the pigs could shoot him easily while he slept, you find it hard to believe a black man could be hired *by someone* to rape white women. But think a minute, and you will see why it is the perfect disruptive act. Enough blacks raping or accused of raping enough white women and any political movement that cuts across racial lines is doomed.

"Larger forces are at work than your story would indicate," he continued. "You're still thinking of lust and rage, moving slowly into aggression and purely racial hatred. But you should be considering money—which the rapist would get, probably from your very own tax dollars, in fact—and a maintaining of the status quo, which those hiring the rapist would achieve. I know all this," he said, "because when I was broke and hungry and selling my blood to buy the food and the paint that allowed me to work, I was offered such 'other work.' "

"But you did not take it."

He frowned. "There you go again. How do you know I didn't take it? It paid, and I was starving."

"You didn't take it," I repeated.

"No," he said. "A black and white 'team' made the offer. I had enough energy left to threaten to throw them out of the room."

"But even if Freddie Pye *had been* hired *by someone* to rape Luna, that still would not explain his second visit."

"Probably nothing will explain that," said Our Muralist. "But assuming Freddie Pye *was* paid to disrupt—by raping a white woman—the black struggle in the South, he may have wised up enough later to comprehend the significance of Luna's decision not to scream."

"So you are saying he *did have* a conscience?" I asked.

"Maybe," he said, but his look clearly implied I would never understand anything about evil, power, or corrupted human beings in the modern world.

But of course he is wrong.

ICE FLOWERS

Joyce Thompson

Born in Seattle, Washington, in 1948, Joyce Thompson has been writing in some form ever since her graduation from Cornell University. She has been a script writer, copywriter for publishing houses, and a "Poet in the Schools" in Massachusetts in 1976 and 1977. Poetry is her first love; she published, with Anne Ballou, a suite of prints and poems, Naked at the Window (1974), and was co-founder in 1974 of the Dark-Horse, Boston's first fiction and poetry tabloid.

Thompson's prose incorporates the impulse and techniques of poetry as well as the lessons learned from writing two film scripts (one the award-winning A Fine and Common Place, 1976). She has published a collection of short stories, 35¢ Thrills, and three novels, The Blue Chair (1977), Merry-Go-Round (1980), and Hothouse, a story about campus politics in the 1960s, which she is revising for reissue. The latest "projects" in her experimentation with new forms are two matched novellas, one almost entirely in dialogue, the other highly textured and romantic.

Joyce Thompson lives in a remote section of the Oregon coast with her husband, filmmaker Paul Steele, their baby daughter, and three step-children. She is trying to balance the demands and rewards of raising a family with those of being a writer. "I will not be silenced," she insists.

"Ice Flowers" can be read as a subtle variation on the mad-housewife genre: as her husband's affections become mechanical, a young wife identifies increasingly with the madman next door, in hope of some understanding, some passion. The story transcends its genre as well in its technical perfection, delicate visual imagery, and in its incantatory language which creates a kind of magical realism.

Being warned that a madman will howl under your windows when the moon is full does not prepare you for it when it happens. Nothing can prepare you for it—that first night when the strange voice penetrates your dreams and you mistake it, at first, for some nightmare voice of your own. You shift under the covers, burrow deep, trying to protect yourself against this renegade inside you, until at last you wake and see the moonlight, and know it is not you.

You get up, finally, and go to the window that lets the moonlight in, because no matter what is there, not to see it is worse than seeing it.

It takes you a while to find him, hidden in the tree trunks

and almost as slender. When you do see him, it is as shape only, a negative exposure on the dark woods that close around your house. His hair is silver, long and wild. It is the realest thing about him. You look for the moon that does this to a man. As you find it, a dark cloud bites down on it and leaves a jagged scar.

He is not talking to you now. He talks to the trees, and to the horses. They have stolen out of the woods and gathered at the paddock fence to listen—three dark shapes and one white, tails twitching nervously, hooves pawing the dark earth.

His voice drops now and he speaks to them privately. Is he talking horse? Horse breath makes clouds in the night. When they turn and gallop off, dismissed, they leave a vapor trail behind them. He speaks again, and now you are sure he is speaking to you.

Being warned that a madman will howl under your window when the full moon comes does not prepare you for the fact that he speaks brilliant nonsense that cuts into your heart.

He turns to go now, and you return to bed. When he reaches the kennel, the dogs explode; their barking shatters the calm. When you get in bed again, your husband stirs enough to reach out a hand to find your thigh and ask, "What is it?"

Once they've started, the dogs do not stop barking easily or all at once. They excite each other, spur each other on. "What scared the dogs?" your husband asks.

"It was him," you whisper. "It was Mr. Hart."

Your husband's name is Tom. His work is a drug that puts him to sleep, exhausted, and a goad that drives him early from your bed. In the morning, you tell him about the visitation. It did not penetrate the pillow he put over his head, did not seep into his dreams. Only the racket of the dogs aroused him; that is the kind of music he, a veterinarian, is wired for. "Next time," he tells you, "wake me up."

You query the neighbors. Hart is older than you guessed, past sixty. Brilliant. Italy. Fast cars. Fast women. Madness. No one knows more. Fourteen years in an asylum, then release. For seven years he has been the nearest neighbor of your house, and you have lived in the house one month, while one moon shrank and grew.

As long as you live here and he lives there, the visits will not stop.

He is not seen by day, though he walks the woods with his dogs and knows, knows everything that happens in your house and in the neighbors'.

He never washes. He is covered with boils.

His dogs have mange.

There is nothing you can do.

He is a well-connected madman. When his people bought him his house, they bought the local police chief, too. Complaints will go unheeded.

Is he ever lucid? you ask them.

No one knows.

It is the first of many visits. Some nights your husband wakes up, too, and mourns his broken sleep. His body and the demands he makes of it are in a race, and there is no slack in his schedule for the howling of madmen. One night he jumps from the bed, wraps himself in his bathrobe, goes to the window and throws it open. The cold rushes in. You get up, too.

"Hart! Mr. Hart!"

And the face, always hidden before, raises up, reveals itself, wreathed by the wild, white hair.

"Oh, Dr. Tanner. Good evening, sir."

It is not much of a revelation; the eyes continue in hiding, two stars shining at the bottom of two deep wells.

"Why don't you go home and go to bed?" your husband says. "It's three in the morning."

"I would if I could, but she . . ." he gestures at the moon, "will not permit it. I have business to transact, with these trees, with these beasts."

"Can't you do it during the day? I need my sleep."

"I never sleep. I seem to have lost the hang of it. And it's so comforting, to do one's business in the dark."

"Well, you have no business here." Your husband's voice is tense, and you put your hand, a hand intending caution and restraint, on his arm.

"Please," you whisper gently, "please don't."

"And my wife. You frighten my wife, coming around like this."

"My respects to your wife. Is she there with you now, young Mrs. Doctor?"

Your flesh prickles. He knows you from the trees.

"She is. And she'd like to go back to bed, if you'd give us some peace and quiet."

"A thousand apologies. I don't wish to disturb you. But you see, I act under compulsion, almost exclusively, when the sky is in such configurations. I intend you no harm. Please tell your wife I wish her good rest, and pleasant dreams."

"Jesus Christ," your husband says. The words freeze visibly. He slams the window shut. "Does he always have to sound like he's playing Hamlet, for Christ's sake?"

"Mrs. Winter says he went to Oxford."

"Good," your husband says. "Fantastic."

You go to bed, and go to sleep in silence.

It affects everything somehow. That voice. The voice slides between you and your husband, pushes you, ever so slightly at first, apart. He comes home to you later and less passionate, speaks less and less. It is not your fault a madman howls under your window at night, but both of you begin to believe that it is.

You have plenty of time alone, to contemplate the voice and what it means. Sometimes it speaks pure poetry. One night Hart finds a book you've left on the dashboard of the car and asks to borrow it. Next morning, it is gone, and every night for a week you leave a note in the same place the book was:

Dear Mr. Hart,
  I hope you enjoy One Hundred Years of Solitude. *When you finish, won't you come by some evening and discuss it? Early evening. Your postmidnight visitations disturb my husband; he needs his sleep.*

The note remains, untouched, until it fades. Two weeks later, the book appears one morning on your welcome mat, wrapped in a rag to keep it dry in the finely sifting snow. No note of thanks, no word at all.

Then, suddenly, the visits stop. Your husband relaxes a little and is less fierce, but his nascent scowl remains. The voice is his pain, and he knows too much about pain to put faith in remissions.

You miss the voice. You hope that Hart is well.

All through February, the days are crisp and brilliant. It only snows at night, and the predawn freeze makes every new snow snap and squeal under your boots. Winds litter the whiteness with the elegant black brushstrokes of fallen twigs, and it is good to be abroad, making your way through the woods with your dog and both of you half-crazy with the excitement of the cold. You follow him, the dog, to the edges of the river and what he shows you there—ice grafted onto nature in sculptured elegance—arrests you utterly.

Ice flowers. Ice grass. Ice twigs. Ice stones. Clear and pure as crystal things, though it is a long time since there was any glassmaker with skill like this. When you have looked your fill and risen, you see the tracks behind you in the snow—one set of human feet and several dogs. You put your own foot in the clearest print to make sure it isn't yours. It is a longer, thinner foot than yours, Hart's foot. If he came once, he may again. You wait. Throwing sticks for the dog is your excuse for waiting, and you stay out until four o'clock nightfall forces you to think of home.

Your house is empty except for its warmth. You are only beginning to thaw when the telephone rings and you pick it up expecting to hear your husband say he won't be home for dinner yet again.

Instead there is a long silence. You speak into it, self-conscious. Who? What? At last, just as you are about to hang up, "Mrs. Doctor Tanner, are you there?"

It is a moment before you know it is *the* voice, it is so shrunken and altered by the apparatus through which it reaches you.

"This is Charles Madison Hart."

You can hear the breaths between his words, always lost before in the night air, and hearing them seems intimate and makes him real.

"I wanted to explain why I can't come to call, and why you shouldn't ask me. I appreciate your kindness very much, you know."

"Then come. Please come at a reasonable hour and come inside and have a cup of tea."

"I can think of nothing more delightful. But I must decline."

"Why?"

"Because of what I've done."

"What have you done?"

His pause is pure flirtation. Then, "I've done quite terrible things. My sister could tell you, except she's too discreet. You know my sister?"

"I scarcely know her."

"Then take my word. And my regrets. I'm quite mad, you know. The doctors couldn't cure me, so they let me go."

"You sound fine now."

"I am. I am. But it's nothing one can count on." You hear him sigh. "As it is, I'm an unpredictable fellow, unfit for any but the life I live. Dangerous, that's what I am. And why I can't accept your kind invitation."

"It stands," you tell him. "If you change your mind."

"My mind changes itself," he replies, before the line goes dead.

In March, you come under siege. His visits become a persistent nightmare and peace an occasional exception. Your husband is wire tightly coiled away from you. The nightly visitations subtract sex from his schedule and you become a lame duck bedmate, a neutered teddy bear, soft, warm, and sexless. Your skin is hungry and your nerves go into mourning, beginning to dream about the dead.

Outside your window, a madman plays King Lear or makes up his own poetry for trees and shingles. Some nights he too dreams sex and shouts his fantasies—perverse, inventive, terrible fantasies—at your barren window. His lust shines in the night. It is a lust of the mind that remembers bodies, distortions nostalgic for reality. Your own dreams twist and turn upon themselves, have you mating with women and trees, never far from the edge of an ice-choked river just melting into spring, and you wake up ashamed.

One night a strange thing happens. The voice is there, the message is lust, and just as the image grows orgasmic, your husband groans in his sleep and instead of falling back deeper into pit and pillows, raises up and rolls on top of you and takes you, not tenderly, but hard and fast, with unaccustomed passion. He says nothing and you answer with a silence of your own, but you are pleased, relieved, encouraged. In the morning, he doesn't remember.

But morning is his time of power, when he solves problems and his energy, renewed by sleep, seems endless. It is morning, then, when he appears unexpectedly and pounds the table with an emphatic fist.

"We've got him," your husband says. "We've finally got him."

"Got who?"

"Got Hart." His grin shows teeth. "I filed a complaint about his mangy dogs, running around loose. They're awful things. Nearly bald, half of them, and going mad from the itch." Your husband's eyes zero in on yours. "He's either got to kill them or cure them." He pulls a paper from his shirt pocket and unfolds it. "I estimate that to cure them, it'll cost in the neighborhood of fifteen hundred dollars. Isolation for a month, and treatment. Plus food. It adds up."

"What if he doesn't want them cured?"

He lays an imaginary shotgun against his cheek, squints down the barrel and pulls the trigger. "Then, pow!"

"Why, Tom?" you ask. "He's harmless."

"He bugs the crap out of me. I haven't had a good night's sleep in weeks. And it's criminal to let animals run around in that condition. It's cruel." His lips lose their fullness and become a grim, straight line set in his jaw.

It does not silence Hart. Instead his visits start earlier, just past midnight, and go on longer, sometimes almost till dawn. They are pleas now, not performances, and have a single theme.

"Don't take my dogs away. You mustn't take my dogs away."

Your husband gets less sleep than ever, but now takes a kind of malicious pleasure in his forced insomnia. He smiles at the ceiling, night after night, awake and listening.

The pleading tears at you. "For God's sake, Tom, go talk to him. Tell him you won't hurt his dogs. Tell him they'll feel better without the mange." So you plead, too, and he refuses to answer either one of you, just stares at the ceiling, arms crossed behind his head. "Please, Tom. Maybe he'll go away if you'll only reassure him."

"If he wants to talk, he can come to my office or call me on the phone. Otherwise, forget it. He doesn't exist."

The man who doesn't exist continues to cry out under your windows, and finally, you can't stand it anymore and sit upright and start to swing your legs around. "Then I will."

"No!" His arm swings out so suddenly and hard that when it

hits, it takes your breath away. You fall back flat on the bed. He offers no solace or apology. You turn away from him and cry.

The voice goes on. "I beg of you, Dr. Tanner. Don't take my dogs away."

They take the dogs by force. The dog catcher's van is accompanied by two state troopers and a public health officer in a sleek police car. When he sees he is outmanned, Hart flees. The dogs scatter, in the woods, along the river, through the golden stalks and stubble in the fields. The men give chase.

Just picture it, the five of them, running fast as they can, encumbered as they are by ropes and nets, by guns and big men's boots. They trample the fields; they sweat and swear; they tear their pants on broken branches. As they close in on one dog on the river bank, about to snare him, one of the troopers steps back incautiously and plunges half his leg into the river's molten ice. He screams. They start at two in the afternoon. By five they have captured all but one, one wily dog, who still outsmarts them. Five dogs taken. Five dogs cower in the catcher's van.

"Maybe we should come back tomorrow for the other one," the public health man, out of breath, suggests, but four pairs of eyes glare back at him, four panting men refuse as one. Hell, no. For this is a religious war.

They stand watch near the entrance to the woods. The sun is at a low slant on the fields and the evening chill makes it seem winter is coming back. All but defeated, they stand. One damn dog, one mangy dog outstanding. Their curses steam. *And* then.

And then, they see a small form dash across the field and take cover behind a golden stand of stalks.

"It might have been a rabbit," the public health man says.

"That was a *dawg*."

"How the hell we gonna catch a dog at this distance? He'll be in woods before we cross the road."

"Like this," the wet-legged trooper says. His sock is slowly freezing around his calf. He plants the butt of his rifle on one beefy shoulder, lines up the stalks, and cocks the gun. They wait in silence till the small form moves.

The trooper fires. Fires again for good measure. Five prisoners, one casualty. They call it a good day's work.

Your husband tells you all about it, with manly glee, and you listen because you have no choice, but after dinner you go to the bathroom and retch up all you've heard and eaten. Going to bed that night, you are equally afraid of your husband and of what the voice will say. It does not come. Your husband sleeps.

Next morning, when he's gone, the telephone rings.

"Your husband is a cruel man."

You can neither agree nor disagree, for different reasons.

"You should leave him."

You tell Hart what you tell yourself. "He's my husband. I married him."

"I want to see my dogs. When can I visit them?"

"You'll have to talk to him. To my husband."

"I wouldn't like to do that. Tell him, please."

"I'll try, but . . ."

"No."

Hart takes a smart revenge. Every night he sits outside your husband's clinic door, saying nothing, quite circumspect in behavior but so strange and awful in his appearance, with his ragged clothes, his boils, his matted hair, that he scares your husband's clients and makes small children cry. The dogs bark incessantly, his own dogs loudest of all. He will not speak to you; your husband will not speak to him. The wholly owned police chief will not make him move away.

The dogs are cured. Your husband, perhaps not feeling his victory is complete, will not release them to Hart, but calls his sister, Mrs. Welton, to come and claim them.

"My, don't they look nice and healthy. Thank you *so* much,

doctor," she says, and writes a check for fifteen hundred and twelve dollars right then and there.

And you wouldn't have known unless, years later, in another incarnation, with another husband at your side, you quite improbably met up with Mrs. Welton at a cocktail party, and she told you: that when you left, her brother Charles went to your husband's house and beat on the door relentlessly until he opened it, then seized Tom by the shirt, shook him hard against the door frame, eyes ablaze, and asked and asked again: *What have you done with her?*

You tell Mrs. Welton to thank her brother for his concern, to tell him you have prospered in another life.

THE GREEN WOMAN
Meghan B. Collins

Born in New Orleans and raised in a cramped apartment in New York City, Meghan Collins amused herself as a child by writing mystery novels. She continued to write for her school papers, but once grown, she says, she tried everything to escape her desire to write. She married young, had three children, and spent many years teaching ballet. When her two older children were in college, she returned to finish her own degree in art history. In 1972 she committed herself to writing a weekly column for a local newspaper and began writing fiction; "The Green Woman" was the result. Sent unsolicited to Ms. magazine, it was discovered, published, and nominated for a National Magazine Award. In 1974, Collins remarried, went to live overseas, and began writing an historical novel about medieval Denmark, a country for which she has a passionate affinity. Maiden Crown was published as a young adult novel in 1979.

Both her novel and this story reflect her use of historical tradition as a scaffolding for her art. In "The Green Woman" a very old genre, the fairy tale, is used to reveal new perceptions when told from the point of view of the traditional "witch." Women's mystical connection to nature is celebrated here as the ancient power to give life; with a humorous nod to female realism, a lusty male is thrown in to ensure the outcome!

APRIL HAD BEEN CHILL AND STORMY this year, so on the first day
that truly felt like spring I was happy to go outdoors in the gentle
sunshine to work in my garden. After a long winter under my
low, dark roof, it lightened me to see young leaves arching in
airy layers overhead. I often paused in my digging to look up
through them to the newborn blue sky beyond.

I was shaking soil from a clump of roots before tossing it into
the barrow when the geese began to scurry about their pen with
a din of honking. Geese are much better watchdogs than my old
shaggy True, who now only raised his head with good-natured
interest to look toward the road. If ever the villagers come to get
me, the geese might warn me in time to run away into the forest.
Still, old True is ferocious against rats and mice, and I would not

dare to keep a cat. You never know what small thing might be brought against you later.

Now I too heard the sound of wheels creaking toward my gate. I stood up to look, shading my eyes with my trowel. Whoever it was could only be coming here, for this was the end of the road.

My house is set in a clearing in the woods. There is enough open space to give sunlight for the garden, but the forest crowds in close, right to the fence that keeps deer from eating my herbs. Thus, trees hid the carriage from view until it was almost beside my front gate.

When I saw it was a closed carriage drawn by two fine roans, my heart gave a horrid lurch within me, for I knew of only one such in all the countryside, and it belonged to the Governor. In that first moment, I thought surely he was sending some men after me. I picked up the front of my skirt and half-turned to run before I noticed the shadowy head of a woman behind the carriage windows.

The equipage tilted to a halt, with one wheel in a rut. A driver in Kendal green livery jumped from the box to open the carriage door. A brightly colored figure within furled herself up like a morning glory to fit through the narrow doorframe.

When she had stepped forth onto the roadside, I recognized her from certain descriptions of Parson Wicker to be the Governor's lady. The coachman opened the gate for her, then leaned upon the gatepost with a frank and impudent interest to watch Milady stroll toward me, herself gazing about curiously.

I tossed my trowel into the barrow and brushed dirt from my fingers as best I could. I wondered what could be bringing me such a visitor. Few from the village dare approach my house by daylight. They don't want anyone to know they come to me, those dropsical old folk who creep up my path in the gloaming to be dosed with foxglove, or the young girls who come seeking a charm to make someone love them.

Now and again, someone will knock on my door in the night to fetch me to the village. The midwife there is skilled, but the one thing beyond her is a breech birth. At such times she sends for me, for I have the art of turning the baby within the womb, which I learned from my mother.

Whatever their distress, though, the sun is well down before any of these good folk slip from behind the trees toward my house. The sawyer would come by day if he wished, for he fears neither God nor the devil, but as it happens, the moonlight shines down on most of his visits. The sawyer—well, the sawyer has a sickly wife. He is a big man, and his eyes are a very clear dark blue, and that is all I care to say about that.

Parson Wicker is sure enough of his soul's safety to visit me by daylight. Many an afternoon he sits by the hour at my table, drinking cider and talking to me as I work. I am sure he tells his parishioners that he seeks to cure my own wretched soul by his visits. Perhaps he thinks so himself. I know better.

As we know, the priests of Rome are not allowed to marry. I have sometimes thought it is because they must stay empty in their own lives to keep space within for all the human woe they carry away from the confessional. But Parson Wicker is no priest, and when the weight of all he knows about the villagers grows too heavy for his heart, he brings it to me because he knows it is perfectly safe to do so.

Yes, he has told me much that he should not, that spry little pink-cheeked man. I keep silent, and often find it useful in my work to know more about the village of Starwater than the busiest gossip in it, though I seldom cross the green myself.

What chagrin would have filled the breast of this fine young lady who now approached me if she knew how much I had heard about her! Her great mansion with its gardens and lake, her extravagance in the purchase of table porcelain, her quarrels with her handsome sulky husband.

She was wearing a long cloak of soft blue wool like a jay's

wing, lined in darker blue. The hood had fallen back from her head. She was so fair that it was hard to see her brows, or where her broad forehead left off and the fine pale hair began.

The path was not very long, yet she seemed to take a long time to reach me, like a boat's sail you see from afar that looms toward you slowly. When she came closer, I could see a strangeness and strength to the beauty of her face. For all she was so soft and fair, you would hesitate to cross her will.

I made her a curtsy and said, "Madam Governor, how do you do."

She inclined her head, accepting without question that I knew who she was. I suppose she was used to being recognized by all. She spoke no greeting in reply, but said at once, "I have business with you, Miss. May we go into your house?"

She did not wait for me to answer, but walked straight past me toward the open doorway. My house is such a little gray weathered box; most peculiar it seemed to watch her elegant figure disappear inside, like a doll-lady on a foreign clock.

I followed her inside and gave her the chair to sit on while I took a bench facing her. She settled down with a little shake of her shoulders, as a bird settles its feathers, and gazed calmly about the room for a few moments before speaking. My notice was caught by the delicate shoes she was wearing, of softest pewter-gray leather, as fine as glove leather, with shoe roses at the instep and scarlet heels. I drew my clogs under the bench and pulled my eyes away.

Sunshine coming in through the open door cast a bright square on the floor planks, and dust motes quivered in the falling rays like a veil of light. Tiny points of light twinkled from the shelves of crocks and jars; otherwise the room was shadowy and cool, with a tang in the air from bunches of dried plants hanging among the rafters.

A long silence fell while the lady scrutinized my face and uncovered head.

"They say," she remarked in a clear, almost joyful tone of accusation, "that witches have red hair."

I sat quietly, looking at her. Then I shrugged. *"They say,"* I answered, repeating her emphasis, "that looking at the new moon in a mirror will drive you mad—but it isn't so."

She considered this for a moment with her lips pursed, and then countered, "Well, but I have heard you can read and write!"

"As my mother taught me before she died, Madam. We must be able to read the herbals, and write labels for our mixtures, you see. And I write down new things that I learn, so as not to forget them myself, and to pass on that knowledge to my own daughter when I have one. Many men know how to read—there is no witchcraft in it just because a woman can."

"Then what do you call yourself if not a witch?" she asked slyly.

"I call myself a green woman, Milady. If anything is wrong with you that plants can cure, I may be able to help you, for that has been my life study." I paused and searched her face, trying to read her thought. "Are you ailing? Tell me about it."

She looked down into her lap and sat twisting the wedding band on her white finger.

"I have heard that if a woman is with child and does not want to be, you are able to—well, you know—make an end to it." She shot me a keen glance from under her fair lashes and looked down again. I frowned, thinking hard.

It is true they come to me sometimes, young girls half crazy with fear, or exhausted young wives with a child in the cradle and one on the floor, and three or four in sizes up from there. How they weep, poor souls, with their heads in my lap. How they have waited and prayed, looking by night and by day for signs that do not come!

They have no fear of me then, no, no. Most gratefully they take the Contessa's powder. But afterward, when their bodies and hearts are light once more, they draw off from me with strange looks. The devil must be in it, they think, that I can in this manner turn aside from them the hand of God.

Has one of these women now, I thought, been tormenting herself in the night with fears of hellfire? Gone to the Governor, perhaps, and complained of me, so that he has sent his lady here to entrap me with questions?

I took a deep breath and ventured, "I am wondering why such rumors would interest you, Madam Governor, a married lady like yourself, with no children of your own, I believe?"

"That is just it," she replied. "Three years now we have been wed, and still no children. I was thinking, you see, that since you know how to make an end, you must know how to make a beginning, too." She turned up her palms in an expressive gesture of appeal.

"Ah, that is another trouble entirely," I said, thinking of a certain almost empty jar on the upper shelf. "I am afraid I cannot help you there."

At these words, her fair softness congealed at once into a substance much harder and colder. Her lips set in a line, and the pupils of her eyes were tiny blank points in circles of gray ice.

"If I were in your place, I should think very carefully before refusing," she said. She leaned forward in her chair and added almost in a whisper, "It has been a long, long time since we have had a witch's trial in these parts."

A hush fell between us now that almost had a thickness to it. It was like the moment when you drop a stone down a well and wait for the sound of its striking.

"To make a life," I mused. "As I told you, that is another thing, much harder than the other. Suppose I do try to help you and nothing comes of it?"

"A long, long time," she repeated. "Since your grandmother's day, if I recall correctly."

I showed my teeth at her in a grin or a snarl, she could take her choice. "You use strong persuasions, Madam. I hope your rewards are equally weighty!"

"Oh yes, I will pay in gold," she assured me, her voice becoming lighter, almost eager, as she felt sure her will had pierced through to me.

"All right," I said slowly. I went on to question her at some length about her health and habits, to get a better idea of what might be amiss. At last I added, "You will have to give me some time to make up the medicine. A week, say. Shall I bring it to you, or will you come back here?"

"I will come back here, I think. It would be as well for my husband not to know of this."

I nodded. A memory came to mind of the one time I had seen the Governor. He was walking into the inn, but paused on the steps to turn around at someone's call. He was a handsome fellow, though just inclining to stoutness. The glistening salt-white of his shirt and his suit of fine black serge well became his pale complexion and glinting dark eyes. (I also recalled Parson Wicker's complaint that the church might install a new pew each year with the money the Governor spent on linen alone.) A certain droop of the Governor's mouth and the lackadaisical manner of his turn spoke of a constitution perhaps not altogether virile.

"Just a moment," I said as Milady rose to leave. "There is something I want you to take with you."

I went to the shelves, took down a jar, and began to spoon some of its contents into a small packet for her.

"Starting from today, try to have your husband take some of this each day. Make it up into a tea for him, a spoonful to the cup."

She laughed shortly. "It would be quite a trick to make my husband drink anything but ale. Yes, one would have to be a magician, I think."

"Put it in a toddy, then, with rum and honey, and give it to him for a bedtime drink. It will work just as well that way."

"Yes, that he would take. What is the stuff?" She looked curiously at the jar I was restoppering.

"Oh, sarsaparilla and other things. It is a tonic."

"And might I take it too?"

I smiled. "No, just your husband. It is in my mind that the press of office might be fatiguing the Governor. This will build up his manly vigor."

A curious half-smile crossed her face and was gone. I could not guess its meaning.

"You do look pale," I observed. "Perhaps your blood is thin. Take some molasses every day to strengthen yourself. I will have your other medicine ready when you come back."

She took the packet without further question and began to saunter toward the door. "I shall return next Wednesday, then. My, what a great stack of firewood you have, and you with no man around the place. Do you have to cut it yourself?"

"No, the sawyer brings it to me from the mill."

"Ah, the sawyer. I have seen him, I think. A big man, with blue eyes?" She stood still, gazing at the wood in a deep reverie, then pulled herself up with a shake of the head, as if gnats were pestering her.

"Good-bye for the present, then," she said.

I bowed to her in the doorway but did not follow her outside. I stood and watched her walk away down the path toward her waiting carriage. Above her head, a jay flew down from the tree-tops to perch on a lower branch. He called at me with his jeering cry.

"Haw!" he seemed to be laughing. "Haw-haw!"

When the last rattle of carriage wheels had died away, when the sheltering woods were once again silent of all but their own sounds, I turned away from the doorsill and sat down in the chair with my grandmother's old handwritten herbal in my lap. It was a long, narrow gray book with "Journal" printed on the cover in dull maroon letters. I myself had pasted new cloth along its spine to strengthen the binding. I did not trouble to open the book at first. I suppose I just wanted to hold it in my hands to feel the healing presence of that little aged creature whose bright face I can barely remember.

My mother and I had searched through the book so many times before, searching for this particular formula, but it was one of the very few Grandmother had not written down. Nor did she, before they came to take her away, show my mother how it was made. Perhaps she herself had bought the mixture from somewhere, as I must buy stoneseed from the Indian trader and Peruvian bark from the apothecary. If that were so, she may not have known how to compound it herself; I don't know.

The times we needed to give out such a medicine, and these came but seldom, Mother and I always just took from the jar the small amount needed. As the level sank down, we grew ever more cautious and thrifty about measuring it. Even so, the last full dose we could eke out had been given three years ago, and since my mother died I have not even admitted to knowing such a cure. What was left in the jar were just flakes that you could hold in your palm—so old that there was probably no power in them anymore, for virtue cannot last forever in plants, no more than in women.

The rest of that day and part of the next I read through all the ledgers that had been handed down to me from those two wise women now gone from my life: Grandmother, whose manner of death I do not dare to think of right now, and Mother, who died quite young of a tumor not all her mandrake extracts could diminish. Partly, as I said, I just wanted to feel their company— to bring back a sense of their real persons, which handwriting seems to call up so strongly. But partly I hoped one formula or another might jump together in a pattern to give me a new idea.

I took down the jar with its few leaves and spread them out on a piece of paper to smell them and taste them. I carried them over to a good light by the window and looked at them under my mother's strong glass, with the gold bumblebee for its handle, that the fine gentleman gave her so long ago.

The mixture contained motherwort, of that I was sure, and wormwood. There appeared to be water nerveroot, and water betony also, and something else that might be black horehound. I remembered that when my mother gave out the cure she did not give the dried mixture itself, but boiled it up in water and strained off an infusion.

Still, I was ringed about with unanswered questions. The time of year when herbs are gathered often makes a difference in their properties. Was I to use the leaves, the roots, the stems? And most important, in what proportion must I mix the different kinds?

One late afternoon, while I sat at table with pen and paper writing out a receipt for possible use, Parson Wicker arrived for a visit, announced by screaming from the geese. I could tell he was troubled, for he did not sit down with his usual eagerness to sip and nibble at the little meal of cider, bread, and cheese that I rose to set out for him. Instead, he walked about the room and stood by the window, thoughtfully tapping his teeth with his forefinger. When he spoke, it was in a manner he had when ill at ease, adding a little humming sound before certain words: "How have you been? I hope you are hmmmwell?"

"I am well enough. But you seem restless today. Are you upset about something?"

"Truth to tell, I am a little. Mrs. Jacob Taylor tells me that the Governor's lady drove past their farm Wednesday in her carriage. So, she must have come here—there is no other house beyond the Taylors'."

"That is true. She was here."

"Oh dear," his ruddy face puckered unhappily. "And I suppose she wanted you to hmmtreat her for some ailment?"

"No, it was just a sociable visit," I replied lightly, but the poor man was altogether too heavy-minded to understand pleasantry. A struggle to imagine the Governor's wife paying a social call to the likes of me began to warp his features into the most comical expression, so I quickly added, "I'm teasing, I'm teasing. But you must understand I cannot tell you why she came to me."

"Oh, I think I can guess that. Not long ago, she was lamenting to me about her childless state, and at the same time she questioned me very closely about your skills. That is why I am so sorely troubled. To think I may have been the cause of her coming here!"

He fiddled with the handle of his mug in silence for a time, and then burst out, "*Why* can you not give this up? You shall only end by being hanged or burned one day. Can you not set aside these magics and medicines and live like ordinary folk?"

I thought of the village green, that pleasant oval, with the little houses set around it. There people smiled when they met in the road, and the women called greetings to each other while they hung out their linens to dry in the sun. Thinking of such friendly neighbors made me pull a wry face at the parson.

"And will I have a kindly welcome, dear sir, when I move into my little cottage on the green? Will the good and trusting folk of Starwater rush to buy the pies I shall bake from my famous secret receipts to earn my living? Will the good wives invite me to tea?"

His eyes rolled up to the rafters to avoid meeting mine.

"Well, but this is not the only village in the world," he demurred. "You could go to another where nobody knows you. You are young still, and hmmpleasing to look at. You might even marry, if you could learn to bridle that sharp tongue of yours."

"We do not marry," I told him haughtily.

"And why not, I should like to know?"

"I don't know. It is a tradition. In a way, I suppose we are like the priests of Rome—we have to keep our own lives empty to be free to cure others."

"Hush, woman! What blasphemy!"

"Well, you asked me," I murmured, smiling to turn his mood. "As for going away, we have been living in this house since time out of mind. Am I now to be run off like a homeless dog because the fine lady might take a whim against me?"

"She is a danger; never doubt it. Did you know that she works her farms and gardens with prisoners' labor? Yes, and has them flogged at her displeasure. A heart of marble, truly."

He hunched his shoulders and looked so wretched that I reached out and patted his hand.

"Please, don't distress yourself so. It is true that I sometimes think with longing of the life you describe, to be safe and sheltered, and part of a friendly, homely world. But it always comes back to this, that what I know cannot be unlearned. Nor would I wish to know less than I do. Whatever the risk, I will not be less than what my life has made me."

I paused to look at him earnestly and added, "It is my own choice, you see. However it turns out, there is no reason you should feel accountable."

He sat looking down at the table for a short while and at last nodded his head several times in acceptance. Without further word or look, he rose and, picking up his tall hat that was covered with road dust, walked slowly out the door.

The next days were long and weary for me. Although many useful plants grow in my home garden—sage, poppy, foxglove, and the like—I also make daily use of wild herbs from the woods and meadows. It may sound like dainty work to wander about with a willow basket, picking flowers and rare greens, but remember, I must go in any weather. Dusty and sun scorched, or windy and raining ice, no matter. Sometimes I must walk many miles to find what I am looking for, and still there is the day's work to do when I get home.

For some of life's needs I can barter. I keep no cow, for instance, since the farm wives of our district pay me in butter and cheese. But there is much I must do for myself, and living alone as I do with no one to help, just the chores of staying alive pare many precious hours from my day.

The only work I truly hate, though, is hunting the bogs for

water plants. There, my flesh crawls with the nearness of snakes I cannot see. I am always in dread of a false step on that quaking ground, which would suck me down slowly, screaming, into the ooze. Sometimes I wake up in the night, drenched in sweat but also shivering cold, having dreamed of that.

So it was good, after a day spent in the bog late that week, to have the sawyer's company in the night. I was drying plants on a screen over the fire when he came in. My hair was sticking to my face in tendrils from the heat, and I felt tired and unkempt, but I was glad to see him. I smiled a greeting and fetched him a mug of ale to sit with while I finished my work.

Later, when all had been tidied away and the hearth swept, I took up the ale jug and carried it to where he was sitting. He threw an arm around my knees.

"Do you know what I like about you?" he muttered, nuzzling his face against my belly. "You make me feel that it pleases you to feed me and love me. I hate that feeling that everything I need wears a body to death."

Surprised and touched, I cradled his dark head in my hands. It was seldom he was so tender. That night he was a gentle breeze lifting me up, not the wild wind or bluff gale I was accustomed to. At some point the thought came to me to worry about all the mixtures I had been tasting, and a fear jumped in my gullet like the sudden leap of a frog. But then, almost as clearly as if she had been there, I could hear my mother's firm voice in my ear: "Dear heart, it is time you had a daughter of your own." At these words, a pure well of peacefulness filled within me, and I feared no more.

Just as she had promised, in the afternoon of the seventh day Milady once more approached my house with her slow, swaying walk like a boat at anchor or a wind-tilted bell. I had already set out for her on the table a stoneware bottle containing the potion I had brewed for her. Seeing it, she picked it up at once and turned it curiously in her hands.

I made her reckon up her monthly dates, which she had

trouble remembering. Then I made some calculations on a piece of paper, while she watched me with uneasy interest, as if I were writing sorcerers' signs.

"Here is what you must do," I told her, when I finished writing. "From the time the moon is in its last quarter you must not have anything to do with your husband. If he presses you, pretend you are ill. In the dark of the moon, begin to take this liquid. Take half a wine goblet both morning and night. From the third day after the new moon, lie with your husband as often as he will for a few days. Can you remember that?"

"Yes."

I stood up so that I could look down on her.

"Now, my pay for this. I want two gold pieces now and three more when you find yourself full."

"When?" she repeated with mocking challenge. "You are so sure, then, of your merit?"

I gathered up all the strength of my being and fixed my eyes on her like a mighty beam of light. Pressing the heels of my hands on the table, I leaned across it toward her and asked in a measured, chiming voice: "Do you now believe I have powers to do it?"

She swallowed and bent her head.

"Then trust what I tell you."

I let the aftertones of my words circle out in the silent room until they died away. Then, resuming my normal voice, I said, "Here, I shall wrap your bottle in a bit of cloth to guard it against breaking. Keep it somewhere cool at home, for heat will rob its power."

She stirred in her chair. Opening a little netted purse, she took out two gold pieces and placed them on the table, meticulously pushing them side by side with her tapered forefinger. As if the act of payment had restored her proper rank, she too now rose and looked about her with an arrogant tilt of her head.

"More firewood!" she exclaimed. "The handsome sawyer treats you well."

"Yes, he is good to me."

"You are so fortunate." She gave a little laugh, sharp as broken glass, and walked away. "Good-bye, then. I hope your potion works as promised. For both our sakes, eh?"

Once she was gone, I should have felt some ease. I should have been able to say to myself, "It is done now. There is nothing more but to wait."

There was something, though, an unnameable shadow in my mind that would not let me settle. During the next days, if I were at sweeping, I would stop and lean on the broom, staring with vacant eyes. Digging in the garden was the same—I would start out of a dream and find that I had been idly drawing lines on the ground with the edge of my trowel.

Thus driven by unrest, I paced and thought. I wished for the wisdom of King Solomon himself, to tell me what else I should do to preserve my life and the one perhaps to come. At length I called to True and set out on the road toward the sawmill.

When we had come near to the bridge, I took a side path through the woods and stood among trees on the edge of the stream, just across from the sawmill. He was working the big saw that is run by the waterwheel, and the noise of it drowned out every other sound in the world. I wondered how he could abide such a din in his ears all day. I waited until I was sure he had seen me, then withdrew into the woods to sit on a stump until he should come. The sound of the saw faded in a dying whine, and before long the flicker of his blue shirt showed through the underbrush.

"Is something wrong?" he asked, for I had never before approached the mill.

"No, I just have a favor to ask, and I wasn't sure when you might come back to my house."

"Ah," he said, squatting down with his back against a tree and reaching out to scratch the dog's head.

"I need some white Solomon's seal to make up a salve, and the nearest place to find it is Vannevar's Lake. It must be eleven miles to walk there. Will you take one of your horses and ride over to get it for me?"

He raised his head and gave me a curious look, without answering for a moment.

"Don't you want to take the horse and go yourself? How can you be sure I would get the right plant?"

"I couldn't do that. Everyone in the countryside knows the sawmill horses by sight. Do you want to scandalize your name?"

That made him twitch. I pressed on: "I can show you a picture of white Solomon's seal in an herbal before you go. It is not hard to recognize. And I will show you how to pack it so it will stay fresh."

"Vannevar's Lake is on the Governor's land. Suppose he has me up for trespass?"

"Go to the mansion and ask permission of the Governor's lady. Ask her pleasantly and I'm sure she will not refuse you. The stuff grows wild in the woods there, after all."

He looked up at me in pure male mischief.

"The Governor's lady, eh? She has a wanton look in her eye, that one. Suppose she will be following me into the woods?"

I smiled. "Well, if the Governor will not do his duty, I'm sure you can make up the lack."

He scowled. "And wouldn't you care?"

"Of course I would care!" I cried out, and then recovered my light tone. "I am just wise like King Solomon, who knew that true love will bear any cost to guard the child."

"You talk riddles," he said impatiently.

"But will you go?"

"All right, then."

"And one thing more. Can you arrange your work to make the trip next Monday? Tuesday at the latest? The time of the moon is very important in these matters, you see."

Again he gave me a peculiar look, but made no objection. And so we parted, after a brief embrace. When he turned his back and started to walk away, though, I felt such a wave of desolation that I followed a few steps after him in spite of myself.

"John!" I called. He turned around, puzzled. "You will come back to me, after?"

A smile creased his cheek, and his blue gaze steadied my heart. "How could I not?" he said simply, and was gone.

So now I have come back to my house all alone. This week I shall turn out all my drawers and cupboards to tidy them. Such a pastime will keep my mind busy. Besides, if they should be coming to get me soon, I do not want the virtuous women of Starwater to be clucking over my housekeeping afterward, saying, "Look, what a sloven she was."

But there is no need for me to worry about that. I have staked all the skill of my mind, and thrown my heart's dear desire in after it. Now there is no more to be done, indeed, but to wait and see what tidings the full moon shall bring.

KRUEVA AND THE PONY
Sally Gearhart

Raised first by her grandmother and then by her mother in the mountains of southwestern Virginia, Sally Gearhart spent much of her youth in university and semiprofessional theater. Looking for a larger role than that of the ingenue, she decided to be a college teacher and in 1956 received her Ph.D. in theater and public address from the University of Illinois. She describes the next fifteen years as a time of painful contradictions: being a lesbian in the restrictive church-related institutions where she taught, and having her own personal drive toward Christianity. Though the leap of faith never came, her conversion to feminism catapulted her out of her job. In 1976 she joined other women to establish a B.A. program in Women's Studies at San Francisco State University, where she has been granted tenure to design and teach courses on women.

Gearhart co-authored/edited Loving Women/Loving Men: Gay Liberation and the Church (1974) with gay minister William Johnson and, with Susan Rennie, A Feminist Tarot (1976).

"Krueva and the Pony" is one of a series of stories about hill women that Gearhart circulated among friends. Once in Seattle she was touched to come upon a dog-eared copy that had been photocopied from a ditto, and she decided then to complete the cycle, which Persephone Press published in 1979 as The Wanderground: Stories of Hill Women.

In "Krueva and the Pony," Gearhart uses a futuristic form, the fantasy, to celebrate woman's ancient powers and culture, and a new language to celebrate her devalued attributes—intuition, nurturance, communion with all living things. The communion between Krueva and the dying pony as she rocks and cradles her out of this round of life is not sentimental but rather marvelous.

"WE'RE BRINGING IJEME HOME," Krueva sent. "She's not in deep fallaway or in retrosense. We don't know what is wrong. She is clearly exhausted. We may have to draw together for a gatherstretch—tomorrow at evening ministrations—and if we do, all the women both there and on rotation must be notified. If you stretch to Evona before we return there, be particularly careful. Some have felt that she must be being watched."

"No. She's not." Ijeme's thought interrupted. Krueva had believed her to be totally unconscious. Ursula picked up the thought, too. Both women turned to the supine figure of Ijeme— Krueva from above where she stood at the edge of the trees, Ursula from her kneeling position as she held Ijeme's head.

Krueva longstretched again. "I'll come again. We should be

there tomorrow afternoon." She checked her monitor sweeps, found allwell, and turned her attention back to Ijeme. Ursula was busy sending soothes through her body.

Krueva shortstretched. "Ijeme. Can you talk?"

"I want to," came back. Ijeme's sending was tense with effort. "Evona is safe. She feared she was being watched, but it was only one of their robos, a lockkeeper at her building, accidentally on her call circuit."

"Accidentally?" from Ursula.

Ijeme seemed to fade away. Then she breathed in hard. "Yes. She complained like an angry tenant and the robo was fixed. She's not had any more interference."

"Sure it wasn't a trap?" from Krueva.

"Sure. I'll have to leave now. I can't sustain. Shall I go light so you can carry me?"

"Not yet." Ursula began physically rubbing Ijeme's cheeks. "We'll stay here a few hours before starting back. We can set a together-shade and all three of us can rest."

Ijeme seemed to relax. Then her eyes fluttered and she tried to sit up. Aloud she said, "The pony!" Ursula soothed her. "We'll hold it. It will be all right."

"She carried me well," said Ijeme.

Ursula saw her body relax and fall into deep rest. She looked at Krueva. "Shall I see to the pony? I think it must die."

"I fear so, too," sent Krueva. "I will see to it." She turned toward the open field where the exhausted and hurt animal had collapsed. She turned just in time to be struck by a strong sense of danger. Something, someone, approached. She warned Ursula with a hand touch and then sent out spanners in all directions doubleforce before drawing them together toward what was clearly the threat. It came from behind them, not from the city. That at least was a comfort. "Wild beasts I can handle," she thought, "even a score of them. But deliver me from one man."

She stepped softly to the side of another tree. "Cat," she thought. "Maybe coming for the pony." She tried to smell, but in vain. She couldn't even make out the blood from the pony's wound. But that was undoubtedly what would draw a bobcat or a lynx. "I'm going to shade with the pony," she shortstretched to Ursula, "and you'd best do so with Ijeme." Ursula was already in shade.

Stealthily but quickly Krueva moved back to the edge of the open field. There lay the pony, its chest heaving with hard breathing. They had laid a rest upon it when they took Ijeme from its back, but now there seemed to be no rest for the throbbing body. Even without a moon Krueva could make out the deep wound on its flank, an ugly opening as long as the pony's own leg. It oozed red blood over the dingy white skin, a thick stream, seemingly endless. Ursula's temporary stanch had broken, and the little animal lay virtually in a pool of its own life force. Krueva touched the wound, and with a gasp discovered that the flesh gave way beneath her hand. It had separated from the bone and the pony's entire flank hung in place only by the skin. Krueva was struck with guilt. "We were so busy with Ijeme," she thought. Then again she felt the oncoming bobcat—almost heard it now with her first ears, so close it seemed. "Hurry," she thought.

Even as she knelt by the pony she was weaving about the two of them a wall of protection. Her breathing was fast and heavy by the time she drew herself up behind the animal. She stretched out on the ground over the low brush until she was on her right side. She settled herself as gently as she could along the animal's backbone so that she could curl her head over the neck. She seemed to fit, to match. The rough mane was knotted and lumpy. She could not get her right arm under the pony's neck for the proper holding. Time was important, so she said, "I will hold you better, pony. I will hold you and rock you. But in a moment. Can you breathe with me?"

There was no response from the heavy body. Krueva determined that it must be in the sleep near death. Without saying more she began to match her breathing with that of the stricken body beside her. In and out. In. And out. Up and hold. Down.

Hold. Up. Hold. Down. Again she drew the curtain of protective shades about them both. Only for a moment did her hand leave the pony's neck to check the placement of her own knife. They were together now and the covering grew stronger. Even in its faintness and deep sleep the pony seemed to respond to Krueva's urgings. Together they built the dome against the cat. Together they bonded for protection against the approaching fear.

Krueva kept her eyes open. "Where is it?" she asked herself. She had withdrawn partially from the cat's coming to concentrate on the shield and on the pony. She was still in light touch with Ursula and Ijeme, but she was having trouble holding her connections to three thought vessels at once. Nowhere could she see the cat. Yet she knew it was near. She strained to see with her eyes the forest's edge only a few yards away. Darkness. More darkness, it seemed, than before. Still pushing in and out with the pony, still lightholding Ursula and Ijeme, Krueva sent spanners toward the cat. No contact. Had it gone? Around again.

There! She was brought up short by a hunger so intense that she physically shook. The cat was ravenous and clearly came in search of the pony's flesh. It was in the open field now, very close. It seemed confused; its presence seemed to dart back and forth; it was trying to understand the dome of protection cast over the pony and the woman. Krueva felt the animal's frustration, its puzzlement.

"This is the tricky part," she said to herself. "Brave pony," she addressed the warm heaving body beside her "Brave pony." No answer. She tried with both arms to stroke the head. Still no response save the heavy pushing in and out. "The cat can for sure hear that," she muttered. "Well, if not the pony, then maybe the cat," she reasoned, and gathering her courage she sent strong spanners out in the direction of the cavernous stomach.

"Bobcat!" she called. There was a connection. But this was bigger than a bobcat. The attention that flowed back into her suggested a mountain lion or at least a small cougar. "It's not time," she thought, "to wound an ego."

"Big cat!" she sent again. "Hear me. Hear me." In a wave of panic she realized that she did not remember the incantation for such an animal. She would have to do with only her strength.

"Big cat!" she sent again. This time the full force of a stalking animal shook her. She was frightened—frightened that the shade would not hold, that the cat would attack, that her sending voice would sound weak, that the cat would not hear her, that the cat would hear her. To her relief she felt Ursula's strength join with her own. "Big cat!" they sent together.

The presence halted. "Who?" it sent. Loud and clear it asked, "Who stops me?"

"We are the forest women, the women from the hills," Ursula was answering. "We have dealt you no harm and have pledged our lives to your protection save when you turn on us. Do you know us?"

"Know you well," sent the cat. No quarter as yet. It was still hungry. Still intent. Perhaps even intent on a meal of women as well as of pony.

Krueva broke in. "We parley with you for the pony."

Silence.

"The animal still lives," Krueva continued. "We ask you to retire without its carcass." Was that laughter from the cat? "Our terms are these," Krueva went on, with more boldness than she felt. "We will talk with the pony and see to its wounds as best we can. If it is deemed good by the pony itself and by us that it return to the mother, then we will help it to go and leave the body so that in the round of life you may gain sustenance from it." There was no answer. Krueva was brazen to add, "It seems a healthy pony and one that no disease has infested. You would eat well of the warm flesh."

The cat understood. "It may not die. Unless I help it."

"If it does not die and we can make it whole, we offer this

promise to you: that the first of any of our flock to choose a return to the mother will be your own. We will make the gift with due ministrations outside our ensconcement."

There was an audible sound from what Krueva felt was a crouching cougar. Then it seemed to understand what it risked losing; it released all its reality. *"Hunger!"* assailed Krueva's body as from the brush almost upon her came a roar. She shaded within the shade, giving all her strength to the sustaining of the barrier between them.

"You cannot come closer, cat, anyway. You know that. Let me speak to the pony. It rides right between life and death. Give me time." Without waiting for an answer, Krueva passed the contact to Ursula. She felt her sister take over the channel to the hungry animal. She was safe enough to relax the shade a bit. Then she turned her strongest self to the wet warm flesh beside her. She did not have to go deep.

"I'm ready to go," sent the pony.

Krueva tried again and in vain to force her arm beneath the heavy head. "Carrier, we will work with your blood. We may be able to help you to life." She tried to think of happier things, of gathering up instead of letting go. Letting go was always so hard. She tightened her arm around the body.

"No. I am ready. I've done all that was important for me to do. And I don't want to wear out my welcome."

"In bringing Ijeme this far you gave us a great gift."

"I have brought others before," sent the pony.

Krueva nodded. She wondered where in the city Ijeme could have come upon such an animal.

"I let her steal me," answered the pony, "outside the city. She was running and I called her to me. We rode well together. Until that fence." The pony moved its head to allow Krueva to place her arm under it. "I cannot move or say more. I ask that you hold me for a while." It stretched its neck, fell back a bit on Krueva's arm, then sent with calmer tones, "I commend my body to my sister, the cat. May she feed well."

Krueva was not surprised to find her own tears mixed with the sweat on the pony's neck. The labored breathing was shorter now and louder. The big heart pounding seemed amplified. This was the hastening of death, the hastening by the dying pony and the hastening by its companion. They lay there, the one clasped by the other, panting in unison to the final rushing of the blood. Krueva clung to the pony, sucked in the breath, and released it in more and more violent bursts. She moved back and forth to the rhythm of the deathholding words. "Easy," she said. "Long."

"Easy. Long.

"I will not be so always.

"Leaning back.

"Leaning back.

"Leaning back upon the sea.

"Easy. Long.

"Easy. Long.

"She will bear you.

"Easy. Long."

The pony inhaled, then stopped at the top of its breath. Krueva held her own lungs full. Then a tremendous stretch. Back the head, down the legs, curving the spine, a long unending mighty stretch until Krueva felt she could not keep the stiffened body from bursting away from her. One last note of the heart and one last sigh of the breath going forth, going out, going down, not to return. The body relaxed. A huge shudder shook the heavy frame, and then silence. Silence and sweat. Silence and smells. Krueva still held the animal in holding stillness, rocking and holding, rocking and holding, saying again and again the words of passing.

She tried to move her arm. It was pinned beneath a thick neck. No use. Dimly she recalled the presence of a real danger beyond. Her shade was still in place, but she had not been present for a long time, it seemed. Tentatively she stretched to Ursula. There was a moment before Ursula answered.

"Allwell. The cat knows and is waiting." There was a long

pause. "Ijeme slept through it all. Though she's crying." Another pause. Krueva joined Ursula's stretch to the cat. It was sitting calmly.

"Give us a long start to carry our friend," Krueva sent. "Then you may have the pony."

There was assent from the cat. Krueva asked Ursula for help in freeing her arm. She was stiff as she rose to her knees, stiff and bloody and vivid with earth and dying smells. She tried to see the cougar. No sign. She looked at the pony, touching its forelock. "May you come again," she said softly.

Lifting the shade entirely, she rose to her own stretch. From her standing posture she could not see but could only feel the body beneath her. In one long stroke of her mind she lastheld it and then started directly for the trees. She felt the cat not far from her path.

They would have to carry Ijeme. And there were important things to do. The whole ensconcement would be waiting for them. She found Ursula and Ijeme holding each other. Ijeme's sending had lost its tightness. "I can walk for a while," she said.

With only one backward look to the pony and the cat, Krueva flanked Ijeme. The three women walked with surprising briskness through the darkened trees.

REQUIEM FOR WILLIE LEE

Frenchy Hodges

Born in 1940 in Dublin, Georgia, Frenchy Hodges spent all her growing years on a farm—milking, feeding, hoeing, fertilizing by hand. When she left at eighteen to go to Fort Valley State College, she never really went back, though her writing returns again and again to those roots. She received an M.A. in Afro-American Studies at Atlanta University, then went north to teach in Detroit's inner-city high schools. She has written three chapbooks of poetry: Black Wisdom, Piece de Way Home, and For My Guy: Love Poetry. In her poetry Hodges uses forgotten folk idioms, and at her frequent poetry readings she accompanies herself on the guitar. She now lives in Atlanta, where she hopes to find time from mothering—she was recently the surprised parent of twins—to write.

"Requiem for Willie Lee" is her first short story. She describes it as a gift that "came upon me full blown at four o'clock in the morning of April 2, 1977. It woke me up in more ways than one and taught me love, compassion, growth. I shall be learning from it for a long time."

Like Richard Wright's Bigger Thomas, Willie Lee is the worst stereotype of the repressed, violent, rage-filled black man who is as much a threat here to the black middle-class schoolteacher as he is to whites. But in a final, loving embrace, the teacher acknowledges that her fate is linked to Willie Lee's, and she makes a requiem "for him for myself and for all the world's people who only know life through death."

I TEACH YOU KNOW and it was summer, one of the few times we get to be like children again. Summers we pack up and go somewhere that only rich folk year-round can afford. And if we can only afford a day and a night, we take what we can get and do not count the loss. For twenty-four hours we groove fine on the dollar we have to spend, and in my purse with the credit cards was exactly eighteen dollars: a ten, a five, and three ones.

El Habre is a rustic resort area halfway between Los An and Sanfran. Not a swanky place, but fronting two miles of the most beautiful oceanic view, the junglic-beach is splattered with endless numbers of summer-camp-type cabins whitewashed and dingy gray measuring about nine by nine and most of them claiming five sleeping places. Crowded with beds, they can only be used for sleeping. Such is El Habre.

But El Habre has one thing more. El Habre has one of the most popular clubhouses in the world and people who have no intention of ever seeing the cabins—some never even knowing they exist—come to enjoy the fun, the food, and the fine show of stars. So, one lazy summer afternoon near the end of my vacation, Gaile (my hostess) and I and her little girl Donaile set out in my trusty old Mercedes for remote El Habre.

Now we, like many people, didn't know of the need for reservations and we experienced a foreboding of the wait to come when we saw the acres and acres of cars in the Temporary Guests' parking lot. We parked and were ushered by red-coated attendants through a multi-turnstile entrance to a waiting room as we cracked private jokes about the three of us and the only occasional dark faces in evidence among the sea of white. The waiting room was a comfortable no-nonsense place with white straight-backed chairs placed everywhere. There were perhaps a hundred people or more. Only three others were black, an older couple looking for all the world like contented grandparents, which in fact they were, as we learned from the restless little boy of about four who was with them. To my right were two hippie couples making jokes and telling stories about places they'd been and things they'd done. Most of the people were encouraging them to keep up this light show by laughing animatedly at every joke and story punch line. I was sorta enjoying them myself, exchanging "ain't-they-sick" glances with Gaile as we kept a wary eye on Donaile across the room playing with the little grand-boy.

Somewhere in the middle of all this, the door burst open and in came Willie Lee, tall, lean, reed slender, country-sun-and-rain black, and out of place. In his right hand was a little girl's. With his left he closed the door. He then thrust this hand to some hidden place in the bosom of his black denim jacket and stood for a moment deliberately surveying the room. Though he had a pleasant mischievous schoolboy face, he seemed to be about twenty-two or three. Right away I knew him. Well, not *him,* but from some wellspring of intuition I knew into him and sensed some sinister intent enter that room in the winsome grin and bold arresting gaze that played around the room.

Silence played musical chairs around the group and the hippies were *it,* ending a story that was just begun. All eyes were on the man and the child at the door.

He swaggered Saturday-night-hip style to a seat across the room from Gaile and me, sat, and the little girl leaned between his knees looking smug and in-the-know about something she knew and we did not. Willie Lee his name was, he said, but somewhere later I heard the child call him Bubba.

Oh, Willie Lee, where did you come from and why are you here where you don't belong with that do-rag on your head, and those well-worn used-to-be-bright-tan riding boots on your feet, and that faded blue sweatshirt and those well-worn familiar-looking faded dungarees? Willie Lee, why did you come here and I know it's a gun or a knife in your jacket where your left hand is and you ain't gonna spoil my last-of-summer holiday!

"What do you think?" *sotto voce,* I said to Gaile.

"Methinks the deprived has arrived," *sotto voce,* her reply.

From the time he entered he took over.

"Don't let me stop nothing, gray boys," he said to the story-tellers. "We just come to have some fun. Yeah! Spread around the goodwill!" He threw back his head and laughed.

That was when I noticed fully the little girl. She was watching him, laughing to him like she knew what was to come and was deliciously waiting, watching him for the sign. She seemed to be about nine. He stuck out his hand and carefully looked at his watch.

"Yeah!" he said, stretching out his legs from some imaginary lounge chair. "Whatcha say, Miss Schoolteacher?" He laughed, looking boldly amused at me.

Years of teaching, and I knew him. Smart, a sharp mind, very intelligent and perceptive but reached by so many forces before

me, yet coming sometimes and wanting something others had not
given, others who didn't know how, some not knowing he
needed, grown in the street and weaned on corners, in alleys, and
knowing only a wild creative energy seeking something all
humans need. I knew him, looked in his eyes and perceived the
soul lost and wandering inside.

"I say forget it, Willie Lee. That's what I say."

A momentary look of recognition crossed his face, and when
he realized what we both knew he laughed a laugh of surprise
that even here some remnant of his failed past jumped out to
remind him of the child he'd been, yet appreciating too, I think,
that here it was he in charge, not I.

Gaile had tensed as I spoke. "Come here a minute, Baby," she
called to Donaile, but the child was already on her way to her
mother, and quickly positioned herself between her legs. She
stood facing this newly arrived pair and stared at them. The little
girl, Willie's sister he said, made a face at the smaller child who
then hid her face in her mother's lap. Still, I looked at Willie
Lee. Then I looked away, regretting having acknowledged his
person only to have that acknowledgment flung laughingly back
in my face, and I resolved to have no more to say to him but to
try and figure out what his plan was and how to escape it un-
harmed.

Again, he must have read my mind.

"Folks," he said, "my sister and I just come to have a little fun.
She's had a little dry run of what to expect, and it's coming her
birthday and I told her, 'Donna,' I say, 'I'ma let you have a little
piece of the action up at El Habre.' She'll be seven next week,
you know, and well, it's good to learn things while you young."
He laughed again.

Then turned to a flushed-looking man sitting on his left.

"Hey, Pops, how's business on Wall Street?" That laugh again.

The poor man looked for help around the room and, finding
none in the carefully averted eyes, finally perceived Willie Lee
waiting soberly for his answer.

"Nnnnn-not in the ssss-stockmarket," he said, to which Willie Lee guffawed.

I found myself looking intently at that laughing face, trying to figure out what to do and how to do it. I reviewed the entrance from the parking lot. We'd come through a turnstile such as large amusement parks have and we'd been ushered to this side room to wait for reservations. Now where were those uniformed ushers who'd directed us here? One had come and called out a party of five about forty minutes ago. I decided to give up my waiting position and be content to read about this fiasco in tomorrow's paper.

So deciding, I stood up resolutely, took Donaile's hand and said to Gaile, "Let's go," and started for the door. The whole room stumbled from its trance to begin the same pilgrimage.

Coldly, "Stop where you are, *everybody!*" he said, arresting us, and we turned to look at him standing and calmly holding a gun.

Defeated, I dropped the child's hand and stood there watching the others return to their original seats.

You will not hurt me, Willie Lee. I stood still, looking at him.

"Slim, you and the sister can go if you want to," he said looking levelly at me. Dreamlike I saw a little lost boy sitting in my class, wanting something—love maybe—but too lost, misguided and misbegotten and too far along on a course impossible to change and too late if we but knew how.

"Thank you," I said, and Gaile and I went out the door, each of us holding one of Donaile's hands.

Something was wrong at the turnstiles, and the sky had turned cloudy and dark. Instead of the neatly dressed ushers we'd seen coming in, there were two do-rags-under-dingy-brim-hatted fellows wearing old blue denims and black denim jackets calmly smoking in the graying day.

When they saw us, I felt the quick tension as cigarettes were halted in midair.

"Where y'all going, Sistuhs?" the short pudgy one said.

"We got tired of waitin' and *he* said we could go," I answered, standing still and looking at them intently.

They looked at each other a moment.

Then, "I think y'all better wait a while longer," the tall droopy-eyed one said.

Some sixth sense told me we'd be safer inside, and then I saw the bulge of the gun at the pudgy one's side sticking from the waist of his pants.

"You're probably right," I said, and with studied casualness, we turned and went back to the room we'd just left.

Things had started to happen inside. Willie Lee was brandishing the little black and sinister gun as he methodically went to each person collecting any valuables people were wearing and money from pockets and bags.

"Get your money out, Slim," he said to me as we came back inside.

Distinctly, I remember returning to my seat, locating my billfold, extracting eight dollars—the five and three ones, thinking I'd not give any more than I *had* to and holding the three ones in my hand and stashing the five in my skirt pocket.

He was snatching watches from wrists and rings from fingers and making people empty their pockets and purses to him and putting these things in a dingy little laundry bag with a drawstring. People seemed dazed in their cooperation while the little girl, Donna, carted booty from all over the room in wild and joyful glee. The room was hot and deathly quiet. Then her hand was in my skirt pocket and she was gone to him and his bag with my three singles and the five.

Gaile was just sitting there and Donaile was leaning quietly between her legs. And I was thinking. Where is everybody? What have they done to them? We'd heard nothing before *he* came. Then I heard something. I heard the sirens and my mouth dropped open. Oh, no! Don't come now. I sat wishing they had not come just then with Willie's job unfinished and the child in the throes of her wild prebirthday glee!

Then he was standing in front of me.

"I'm sorry, Slim, but you see how it is!" he said with amused resolution.

He grabbed the not-on-Wall-Street man, pushed him roughly toward the door.

"Okay, everybody out," he said.

Things got confusing then. Outside we vaguely heard shouts and what I guess was gunfire, and not the holiday fireworks it sounded like. We all went rushing to the door. The door got jammed, then was not. More shots were heard and screams and cries. Outside, amid rushing legs, a turnstile smoker lay groaning and bleeding on the ground. The child Donna ran screaming to where he groaned and lay. Holding tight to Donaile's hand, Gaile and I ran toward the turnstile amid wild and crowded confusion. Then someone was holding me.

"Let me go!"

"Bitch, come with me!" a mean voice said. "You too, Bitch, and bring the kid!" This to Gaile.

We were shoved and pushed into the rear seat of a Scaporelli's Flower Delivery station wagon. Crowded next to us were the two hippie girls clinging to each other and crying. The back doors were slammed, and Willie Lee hustled the pleading Wall Street man in the front seat, jumping in behind him. And Droopy-Eye of the turnstile jumped in the driver's seat and started the car. Donaile was crying and clinging to Gaile. The course we took was bizarre and rash because people were running everywhere. And still more people were running from the gilded entrance of the El Habre Clubhouse to scatter confusedly along the course we sped. Too many people scattered along this fenced-in service drive where running people and a racing car should never be. He tried to dodge them at first, blowing his horn, but they would not hear and heed, so soon he was knocking them down, murdering his way toward a desperate freedom. The blond hippie girl began to heave and throw up on her friend. I closed my eyes begging the nightmare end. And then I smelled the flowers. Looking back, I saw them silently sitting there.

I looked at the back of Willie Lee's head, where he, hunched forward, gun in hand, tensely peered ahead.

"Willie Lee, it just won't work." I kept my eyes on the back of his head.

"Shut up, Bitch," Droopy-Eye said.

Willie Lee looked back to me.

"Man, that's Miss Schoolteacher. She knows *everything*," he exaggerated. "Slim, it'll work 'cause *you* part of our exit ticket now, since Ol' Sam here brought y'all in."

"Willie Lee, give it up," I said.

"Man, let's dump the dizzy bitch! I was just grabbing any-body," he excused himself. Then as an afterthought, "I never did like schoolteachers no way."

Then up ahead they saw the gate.

"Hey, Sam, crash that gate. No time to stop," Willie said, peering behind.

"Man, ain't no cops gonna run down no people. You got time to open that gate!" This from a man who'd run people down.

Willie Lee peered again through the flowers at the road behind.

"Willie Lee, the road will end when you reach the gate. It's a dirt road then where you have to go slow, unless," I added, "you're ready to die and meet your maker."

"Damn, this bitch think she know everything!" Droopy-Eye said while Willie Lee just looked at me.

Donaile was crying still. Gaile was too. Wall Street was now quietly sitting there, just sitting and staring straight ahead. The hippie girls were crying.

I turned around and looked behind. The running people had receded in the distance, framed in stagelike perspective by the big El Habre Clubhouse where we'd been going to enjoy an

afternoon show. And tomorrow my vacation would end, if my life
didn't end today.

Droopy-Eye stopped the car and Willie Lee got out and
opened the gate. Now began dust and sand as the station wagon
plowed too fast down the gravelly, dusty road. Down before us,
we could see the ocean's white-capped waves. And between us
and the ocean was the circular courtyard flanked by four or five
small buildings and one other building larger than the rest.

"The road will end at those buildings," I said. "What you
gonna do then, Willie Lee?"

"I'ma chunk yo' ass in the ocean, Bitch, if you don't shut up."

I kept looking levelly at Willie Lee. He kept hunched forward
looking down the slowly ending road. We reached the courtyard
entrance, a latticed, ivy-covered archway, and Droopy drove the
station wagon through.

"Oh, shit, the road *do* end!" Droopy moaned as he stopped the
car.

When the motor was cut, we heard the ocean's waves, and
back in the distance, the people running and screaming behind.
Why are they coming this way, I wondered, remembering the
time we kids ran home to our burning house. They must be
cabin dwellers, I thought.

"What now, Willie Lee?" I said.

Willie and Droopy jumped out of the car.

"Okay, everybody out!" Willie directed.

When Wall Street, the last, had finally climbed out, Willie
shouted, "Okay, Slim, y'all take off. Sam, you take Wall Street,
and the two girls come with me." And they began to hustle the
three toward the bigger building with the cafeteria sign.

When I awakened, it was to see Gaile running with Donaile
toward the woods where the cabins were and where beyond was
the busy sea. As I ran behind them, I looked back to see Sam
and Willie crashing in the cafeteria door, dragging and pushing
the man and the girls inside, just as a Wonder Bread truck began

to enter the courtyard from behind. It was filled with guns-ready police. I screamed to Gaile to wait for me.

When we'd reached the bottom of the hill, we heard shouting and gunfire. We ran on cutting right to a service path that led through the green woods lush with undergrowth. About every fifty feet on either side of the path were the cabins, whitewashed, dank and gray. *Thank you, Willie Lee, for letting me free.* Running and running, stopping some to breathe and rest and to try and soothe the terrified child. *You shouldn't have come here, Willie Lee, bringing your sister to see you fail.* Soon we heard others coming, loud and excited in the tragedy of this day.

Why couldn't you stop, Willie Lee, when it started going wrong and kept on going that way? You're not a fool, because I know you from each year you've been in my classes, and when I've tried to teach you, reach you, touch you, love you, you've snarled "Take your hands off me" and I've kept myself to myself and tried my best to forget every one of you and this afternoon at El Habre was part of my plan to get as far away from you as I can and here you are set on tearing up my turf. Will I never get away from you?

Once while I stopped, resting, some people passed.

"They killed the one with the droopy-eyes," they said, "but the other was only wounded and got away."

"He's coming this way, they say."

Then another: "I got my gun in the cabin. When I git it, I'ma help hunt'im and I hope I get to blow'im away."

"They say he's looking for his girl friend, a teacher or somebody that got away."

Willie Lee, why are you looking for me? Why don't you give yourself up and die? Will I never get away from you?

"Gaile, I've got to go find him," I said. "You take Donaile and try to get away."

I didn't stay for her protest but started walking resolutely back over the path we'd come. The day was dark and the woods were dark and the clouds were dark in the sky. I met and passed people who looked curiously at me. He is looking for me, I thought, and maybe they wondered, thought they knew. I had visions of him knocking people down, shooting anyone trying to stop him, keep him from having his way. Still, why *was* he looking for me? And then I knew. For the same reason I was now looking for him. He was my student who'd failed and I was the teacher who'd failed him. Not for hostage, not for harm, but to die! To die near me who knew him. Well, not *him*, but knew into him just the same. He, who's going to die. Is dying. And now he knows. And I'm the only person who knows him and can love the little boy hurting inside.

His jacket was gone and so was his do-rag and blood was caked in his straightened unkempt hair. His eyes unseeing, he peered ahead and stumbled dying past me.

"Willie Lee," I called his name.

He stopped and in slow motion, semicrouched, gun half-raised, he turned, peering at me through time. In the green-gray light, I opened wide my arms and silently bade him come. He dropped his gun and came paining into my arms.

It was another world then. People continued to run by bumping us as they did. Glancing about, I saw a cabin nearby.

"Let's go in here," I said.

"Yeah, this what I want," he said. "Someplace to stop."

I looked inside and saw the cabin was bare except for the beds. I climbed through the door and helped him in, leading him to the one double bed. Two singles above and one single below on the side.

"What is this place?" he asked in wonder as our eyes grew accustomed to the darker inside. Drab even in this darkened day.

"This is one of the resort cabins," I said. "Part of El Habre too."

"What do they *do* here?" he asked.

"Sun and swim and sleep," I said. "Hear the ocean on the beach below?"

"And for this," he gestured around the room in unbelieving wonder, "shit, people *pay?*"

"Yes," I said, "for this." I looked to him and was held by his waiting eyes. "*Shit,*" I turned away, "people pay. For the sun and the earth and the good growing things and the moon, and the dawn and the dew, people take their hard-earned bread and come here and stay and pay. *They pay!*"

Until then, I had been calm. *Steady, Teach, or you'll lose again.* I softer added, "*We* pay. We all pay."

He was quiet then and dropped his head. He looked at his hands and then at his feet. Then he looked at me.

Soberly, "Well, I spoiled it for them today, didn't I? I spoiled it today real bad," he chuckled, "didn't I?" Then he threw back his head and laughed and laughed.

And I threw back my head and just laughed and laughed hugging him.

"Yes, you did!" I said. "Yes, you really did!"

Perhaps our laughter called the people. And there they were outside the cabin windows peering and laughing in. I went to the windows then and gently pulled the shades and as best I could I comforted the dying man, making a requiem for him for myself and for all the world's people who only know life through death.

THE RIGHT THING

Fanny Howe

Fanny Howe spent much of her youth around theaters and with poets and artists in the Cambridge, Massachusetts, area, since her mother, Irish novelist and playwright Mary Manning, co-founded the Poets Theater there and her father taught law at Harvard University. In 1961 she dropped out of Stanford University and began writing seriously, supporting herself by working as a clerk and accountant. She started teaching poetry and fiction in 1968, got married and had three children—Ann Lucien, Danzy, and Maceo. In 1969, Houghton Mifflin published her collection of short stories, Forty Whacks, *and in 1970 a collection of poems,* Eggs. *Her three novels—*First Marriage, Bronte Wilde *(both 1975), and* The White Slave *(1978)—were published by Avon. She has received a National Endowment for the Arts award and the Radcliffe Institute and MacDowell Colony fellowships. Currently, Howe teaches at the Writing Program at MIT and lives with her children, her sister and family in a house on the edge of Boston.*

With corrosive sarcasm, Howe dissects the hypocrisy of white liberalism in the intentions and conditional politics of the Boston couple who adopt a black child as a "social obligation" and as a present to their daughter. More repulsive than the mother's decision to return the child is her self-congratulatory belief that she has done the "right thing." An allegory for our times, the story forces us to examine our own honesty in "adopting" social causes.

THE WHITE COUPLE who adopted the black child were not happy with what they got. Carol, the wife, had wanted a "mixed" female; John, the husband, had not really wanted another child at all. But aside from being a social obligation, it was also a present for their daughter Jessica, who got a dog the year before. They named the baby Malcolm, a name they never would have used on a white boy, and took him home.

To social workers, Carol and John were the ideal adoptive couple. They owned their own house on the fringes of Boston. John was employed by the state college as an assistant professor of music; Carol did part-time work as a research assistant for a Harvard man. They were comfortable, clean, and socially aware.

"I just can't go through another pregnancy," Carol had said, "but I don't want my daughter to be an only child either, the way I was."

Carol had pale blond hair that was cut straight below her ears. She wore horn-rimmed glasses. A wide, mobile mouth. With her bespectacled and balding husband, she shared a preoccupation with material order. Neither could tolerate chaos of any kind, not in their house or in their community. Each aspired after social justice because it made good common sense. And to each the slogan "peace and freedom" made great sense, as it did to most comfortable people.

They drove the baby home in the heat of a June day. He was already six months old, and the foster parents who had raised him so far had described him as "easy." Malcolm lay on Carol's lap, not a big baby, his eyes fixed on her face. He wore a little blue suit and held his hands together. His eyes were round and alert for a baby, his nose flat, his lips dry and pink. Carol ran her hand across his soft curls.

"I hope we're doing the right thing," she said.

John's glasses flared in her direction. Sweat glistened along his pale-red hairline. Heaps of cars fumed in traffic around them.

"We'll see," he said, as he always did, though his eyesight was very weak.

When they got home, Jessica was seated on the front porch, waiting. A high-browed girl with long legs and red-gold curls, she jumped up and down, thrilled with the baby. The dog, a sheep dog named Mozart, leaped about Carol's legs impatiently.

"Down, down!" Carol cried, lifting the baby high as they all trooped up into the house.

Their rooms were furnished in a modern, almost austere fashion—Danish stick furniture, glass-topped tables, bare floors polished with bowling alley wax, and bright-colored throw rugs. All books were locked away, upstairs, in John's study.

They marched upstairs in single file to the small room set aside for the baby. The walls and crib were white; the rug was a green shag. Already the diaper service had delivered the first batch, and cream for diaper rash sat in a jar beside the pins.

Carol laid the baby on his back on the changing table, while Jessica and John flanked her, gaping.

"God, I hope I can remember how to do it," she was saying. "It'd better all come back to me, or else!"

She paused reverentially, for she never did anything in a hurry, and gazing out the window, said, "This is the way to do it. No pregnancy, no labor."

He began to thrash his legs up and down, and Carol directed her attention to his pants. He had made a mess.

"Oh, God," she whispered, holding her nose. "I can't take it." John took over, as Carol moved away.

"What's wrong, Mom?"

"Nothing. It just takes getting used to."

Jessica stepped in to help her father. She went to the bathroom for a wet washcloth to clean the baby off, and after that she rubbed cream on his bottom.

"I'm sorry," sighed Carol. "I'll get over it, I'm sure."

But she never did. It was the first in a series of things she couldn't take about Malcolm. The second was his sex. Raised by her mother alone, she was not used to the other sex. Even her husband was a stranger, not fully welcome, as her mother and daughter were, into the heart of her affections. John and Carol were held together by a similar mental outlook upon society, and by Jessica. They kept out of each other's hair, delicately. While John tinkered, Carol organized women's groups, parent-teacher confrontations, summer programs for urban children, and pro-busing rallies.

Soon Carol gave John the main responsibility for raising Malcolm. John's only professional obligations included two or three courses in music theory; the rest of the time he worked on building a harpsichord. Carol felt that John, economically more privileged than she, should compensate for her losses as a child, when she was poor. While he was gliding, she was struggling. Luckily, his temperament was an obliging one. "Peace at any cost" was his motto.

So John assumed basic responsibility for Malcolm, while Carol continued to pour her spare energies into Jessica. She drove her to ballet lessons, swimming and piano lessons; she took her to puppet shows and children's theater. She adored her daughter, but so did John, and he had to question why Carol had insisted on adopting another child.

"For Jessica," she would insist.

And it was true that Jessica was enthralled with Malcolm. She carried him up and down stairs, from room to room, showed him how to work his toys, lay on the rug with him cooing, fed him and changed him. He was at first "easy," as they were told he would be. But he grew robust very fast and by Christmas he was walking, climbing stairs, knocking things off tables, and throwing stuff around. In Carol's eyes, he was worse than their rambunctious sheep dog.

She hired babysitters for Malcolm, when John was gone and Jessica at school, and sometimes on weekends when they went on family outings.

"Give me a break," she would say. "I just want a little time alone with you guys."

Jessica and John conceded, always, to Carol, but felt bad about leaving Malcolm behind. By this time, Malcolm had names for each member of the family—Jecca, Dada, and Momma. He had been taught these names by Jessica, and they stuck.

There were certain occasions when Carol would take Malcolm with her. These were invariably marches or meetings involving the issue of race. Boston was, at this time, obsessed with race. Blacks and whites could think of little else with such confusion and intensity. The national conflict over where to live—in the city, the country, or the suburbs—was magnified tenfold in this city where the sun never seems to shine.

For Carol the decision to stay in Boston, made years before, was founded on her political ideology, as was her adoption of Malcolm. With Malcolm, she could be conspicuously counted as a friend of the militants, even as a Third World woman. So she took him with her to "racialized" affairs, though never to the Stop & Shop in white Chestnut Hill. She was not oblivious to the hypocritical side of these actions, and, for the first time in her life, discovered she was not altogether good and righteous. She did not enjoy the discovery and went to a therapist to purge herself.

"I feel so guilty," she told the man. "Either I hate Malcolm, or I pity him. There's no in between. I even hate his name! It reminds me of cucumbers."

"But you gave him that name, didn't you," asked the man.

"Yes. For political reasons."

"Then that's something to feel guilty about. The rest is— well, something to deal with. I mean, it's very hard to control the feelings, but it can be done."

"I don't want to spend the rest of my life controlling my feelings."

"Well, what's the alternative?"

"I don't know, but I'll think of something."

She spent the rest of the afternoon at the public library, perusing books about child-rearing and problems with adoption. They offered no solutions, and she went out to the dreary February twilight, her mood much like the weather. She gazed around her at the city, with a sudden surge of disgust.

"Maybe if we move to Florida, or California, the problem will disappear," she figured. "Maybe it has something to do with this city, its racism."

Driving home, she envisioned the family in a new environment, but her spirits did not lift.

"Or maybe," she went on, "I should just split, with Jessica. John can have Malcolm."

There are certain thoughts which arise—conscious calculations of great force—and stun the thinker. Carol was shocked at herself for being so scheming. But if it was a hard task controlling the emotions, it was a harder one controlling the thoughts. Anything could happen in the head.

She had reached that moment in life where either one's mask becomes, irrevocably, one's own face; or where the mask is thrown away as useless and one stands, frankly flawed, before the crowd. She could, she knew, continue as she was, pretending to love the little boy in her house, and thereby, over time, prove herself a martyr to the cause of racial integration. On the other hand, she could actually do the opposite: liberate herself of her husband and her home and, taking her daughter with her, make a fresh start as a completely selfish person. At least, for a little while she imagined she could.

Freed by her knowledge of her own imperfection, she began to experiment with the flaws. She would not let John touch her in bed on those rare occasions when he made a sensual suggestion, saying that he was not necessary to her survival, she could live without sex and not miss it, and that she would prefer sleeping in a room of her own. He did not protest.

But the main heat of her effort went into the mental torture of Malcolm. For a few weeks, she played mental games with him, designed to undermine his curiosity and to let him know how greatly he disgusted her. The very sight of him released a rush of anger, and he became cowering and overly humble in her presence, smiling too frequently at her, up from under, his eyes fearful. This response from him only increased her anger.

"Don't pretend you like me," she would snap.

"I hate your smile," she would hiss.

"Just go away."

She only did this when they were alone together. She was

sure no one knew the depths of her irritation. And, at last, over breakfast, she said to John:

"I think we ought to have a trial separation."

"What? Why?"

"I can't take another day of it."

"And what about the kids?"

She smiled, "I'll take Jessica, don't worry. You'll only have Malcolm to worry about."

"Oh, no, wait a minute," he said, raising his hand like a traffic cop. "Uh-uh, no, that's the limit."

Carol nibbled bacon, looking down.

"Then what do you suggest?"

He smiled. "I'll take Jessica, and you take Malcolm."

"You've got to be kidding. Jessica would never stand for it. She'd want to be with me."

"Are you sure about that?"

He stood up at the sound of Malcolm calling loudly from his crib upstairs. It would turn to a cry in a minute, and John couldn't stand the sound of a crying child. Carol listened to him go, a soft patient pad up the stairs, and realized she was not sure about that. Jessica might want to be with her father, after all. It was a possibility she had neglected.

"Oh, God," she moaned. "Maybe I'm stuck."

When John returned, carrying Malcolm, who could walk, she looked at them and said, "Jessica wouldn't want to be parted from Malcolm. We'd better try to stick it out."

John said nothing. Like a young branch, he was a model of passive resistance. All he needed to be content was time and peace to pursue his mild activities. Carol realized he was not so much weak as pliable, one of the lucky ones who have no interest in power or mental games.

Spring came, and rocks were tossed against buses traveling around Boston. The newspapers and streets threw off images of small black faces pressed against glass, of cops and white teen-agers and their mothers. The streets, warming up, were littered with debris and broken by potholes from snowplows. Whites didn't dare drive through black areas and blacks didn't dare drive through white areas. While great pink magnolias spread their wings along Commonwealth Avenue, yellow school buses folded and steamed only a few blocks away.

A couple of times Carol had to drive into perilous territory for a meeting, and for these occasions she took Malcolm. Her black child would ward off danger, she believed. But at one meeting a young black woman approached her, while Carol smilingly squeezed Malcolm on her lap. The woman approached with a critical eye and running her hands over Malcolm's ashy skin said: "You don't know how to take care of him. His skin needs oil, it's dry."

Carol, humiliated, lied that she had just run out of oil, and asked if the woman could recommend a special kind.

"Johnson's is just fine," said the woman.

Malcolm fussed through the hot meeting, so Carol took him home early. She did not oil his limbs more than twice, and did not bring him to a meeting again. His skin, in the summer heat, grew ashier still, and developed scaly patches which he picked at. He was not a whiny child but had outbursts of weeping for no apparent cause. Jessica was the only one who could handle these moods, and like any elder sister cajoled him with false promises—candy, a trip, a game. The attention she gave him, inherent in even the falsest of promises, cheered him back into high spirits.

By the time he was three, the scabs on Malcolm's skin were an embarrassment to Carol, and she took him to the neighborhood clinic. The doctor said it was a form of eczema and recommended a special cream. Carol got John or Jessica to apply the cream to Malcolm's dry spots, but they didn't clear.

With the arrival of another summer, the prospect of sweltering in the city was intolerable. So the family splurged on a beach house for two weeks, and were, for the first time in years, free from the obsessions of urban living. A private beach, an acre of land on Cape Cod, and they were happy. It seemed to Carol, then, that they were suffering unduly from their life in the city.

"Maybe we should think of moving," she said to John from the screen porch; they could hear, through darkness, the sea lapping over rocks.

"I've been thinking the same thing," he said.

"But your job . . ."

"I'm never going to get tenure, so why stick around? I could probably earn as much money as a carpenter."

"But where should we go?"

"California?"

"I'd be near my mother again," she said with great joy.

Their return to the city's heat only increased their determination to leave. They had the capital to move on, without difficulty, and John sent in a letter of resignation to the college the first of August. Carol put the house on the market for a sale sometime in the fall. They hoped to leave around Christmas.

As soon as he was toilet trained, Malcolm was sent to a child-care center, for full days. Carol chose one of the more under-staffed and ill-equipped centers, because of the predominance of black children there. She felt, she said, he needed as much contact with his own race as he could get. She also felt, but did not say, that he was society's responsibility, because he was not quite her own. Besides, she had to devote herself to the problems of moving and had to drive Jessica from lesson to lesson and friend to friend, and that was exhausting.

At the child-care center, Malcolm was either ingratiating or sobbing. He gazed up the length of grown-ups with the eyes of a beggar. Often he sat off by himself picking at his scabs, and once when the head teacher asked him to stop, he said he was "just picking the paint off."

"What paint?" she asked.

"That. Black paint." He pointed at his skin.

The head teacher promptly reported this remark to Carol, who cried, "He said *that?*"

And after weeks of avoiding it, she thought about Malcolm again. This time she placed his image in the future against a flat blue California sky, palm trees, and oranges. The Pacific Coast, as she knew it, meant the life of the body, all golden, all tow-headed. Malcolm, stocky, black, and covered with sores, did not exactly fit.

"Will there be other blacks in La Jolla?" John asked her one day.

"I know a couple with an adopted daughter, she's mixed, but I think they're still there."

"Maybe we should go to L.A. or San Diego."

"That's not the point of our moving!"

"True," he agreed.

Another day, when dropping Malcolm off at the center, she saw a handsome black couple dropping two daughters at the door, and she said to Malcolm, "Wouldn't you like to have parents like that? They look just like you."

He smiled and nodded, uneasily.

Sometimes a child is born into a family where it never feels comfortable. It is almost as if she or he has been sent as a messenger on an errand and is held prisoner by these strangers for many years. Yet it never occurs to anyone involved that there may have been some mistake made, at the level of supernatural cause, which produced this situation. And so the child suffers, as do the parents.

For the messenger child, who is being held prisoner, a sister or brother often becomes the object around which she or he grows. For Malcolm, who sensed that his presence in the family was openly insecure, Jessica was the source of development and happiness. From her he learned what was acceptable, what was laughable, what was wrong. His fear, at finding himself in an overcrowded child-care center, was not that he was far from home but that Jessica was not with him, guiding and protecting him. He was surrounded by boisterous aliens.

What was he doing there? Where would they put him next? Who would unzip his pants if he had to pee? When was he going to leave? Where would he go then? His mind was awash with unanswered questions. He only knew that if he smiled at a grown-up he was left alone, and he could play with some toy in peace. Playing, then, he would hum one of the songs Jessica had taught him, and feel her presence hovering over his head.

The house was filling up with cardboard boxes. The days were growing chill, the leaves falling. Malcolm got a bad chest cold and had to stay home for a few days. With Jessica in school, he tried to stay out of Carol's way, upstairs in his bedroom, playing and coughing.

She wanted to be pleased with his behavior, but instead his humility annoyed her, his meek smile came to her like a spray of poison. His eyes expected the worst from her and brought it out. She teased him mercilessly. She had never, since childhood, indulged herself in cruelty for its own sake. With a limpid curiosity, she knew what she was doing, and did it more.

"You hate me, don't you," she said. "After all I've done for you, you hate me. I can't believe it. Don't pretend you like me, with that smile. You don't have to smile, you can just come out and say it, you hate me. I'm not even your real mother, so why pretend."

Malcolm stared at the bologna sandwich in his hand. He laid it down and concentrated on picking at a scab on his wrist.

"Don't do that!" she cried, slapping his hand. "You're making it worse! Eat."

"I'm not hungry," he murmured.

"I asked you if you wanted a sandwich and you said yes. Now eat it."

She hung over him, from behind, feeling herself capable of

physical violence. He started to pick up the sandwich, but she grabbed it from him and crushed it in her hand, throwing it across the kitchen into the sink.

"Go upstairs," she said.

He did so, immediately. Sitting in his chair, Carol felt a gush of compassion and guilt. But she stayed still, as if it were enough to feel it, for, sure enough, all feelings pass.

However: "This can't go on," she said.

Now she thought of the people she knew, in the city, the neighborhood, how they had been watching her for symptoms of failure, since the day she brought Malcolm home. She had, she thought, successfully concealed all signs of trouble from the public eye. But Malcolm's eczema, the quality of his skin, was giving her away.

Then she recalled some changes in Jessica's behavior. Her daughter was conscious of her mother's attitudes, and was becoming overtly protective, at home, of Malcolm. She would defend her little brother for the smallest infraction of the rules, and say to her mother, "Don't be mean to him," or "I did it, not him."

And this was more than Carol could bear. The loss of her daughter's adoration was bound to happen some day, when she was a teen-ager maybe, but not now. And, given the fact that they were all moving west together, there would be no escape from the problem. She refused to go on feeling she was a prisoner in her own house, the victim of this child.

"Why, I wonder, do I feel this way about him?" she asked herself. And this was the one question she never asked anyone else, then or later, when it became unnecessary.

Snow came, a level film of white, a hint of the deeper end of winter. Wonderful, then, to imagine golden bulbs of fruit, and not electric lighting, as the gift of a season. Boxes were already heading west; the furniture would leave the morning of the day they left in their car. Two weeks before their departure, as the snow fell, Jessica said to her mother from her pillow and bed:

"Will Malcolm and I share a room in California?"

"I don't know," said Carol.

She sank on the edge of her daughter's bed, could see from there the white drops on a black windowpane.

"Why?" she asked Jessica.

"I just wondered."

"I honestly don't know," she said, "if he's coming with us or not."

"What?"

"I mean, I don't know."

"Come on, Mom." The girl sat up. "What happened? Did his real mother find him? Does she want him back?"

Carol closed her eyes behind her glasses. "Yes," she said, "exactly. How did you guess? But don't tell him!"

"I won't, I promise. But did you see her? What does she look like?"

"I didn't see her, they won't let me. You know. But I think he'd be happier with her, don't you?"

Jessica said she guessed so, and her mother stood up, drifting to the door. "Now go to sleep," she called. She didn't turn back, for she had confidence in her daughter, how she would sleep on command, almost, at least be quiet until she fell asleep.

Carol went downstairs and sat in the living room with a pile of sewing. John was playing some Bach pieces on the harpsichord. Malcolm had been asleep since seven. Carol, biting a loose button off a pair of Malcolm's pajamas, wore the expression of one watching an intense battle scene on television. It was being played out on John's thin back, hunched over the keys.

"It's the best time to do it," she would soon tell John. "Now. While we're leaving."

"So your friends won't know?"

"Well, that's part of it, of course. But for Jessica, too. If we return him to the state now, it will just be part of the whole separation from the East Coast."

"She'll still feel it. Deeply."

"Not if she thinks he's going to his real mother. That will seem like justice. You know how children like justice."

John squirmed. "But what about him?"

"He'll be better off. They'll find a nice black family for him. He'll be miserable in California, where we're going. He'll feel like a freak. And you know it hasn't been working out—look at his skin—it just hasn't worked."

"I didn't think it was that bad," said John.

"Well, you're in a dream world."

He gazed off into space with a rueful air. For she was not altogether wrong in this judgment. While he considered himself a good and honorable man, most of his life was acted out in his head, which made certain portions of it readily disposable. Wherever he went, he would feel the same things, behave the same way. This abstract manner of surviving made him easy to live with. Like Carol's, his one visceral passion was his daughter. He loved Malcolm no more or less than the sheep dog Mozart. He did not exactly imagine that Malcolm had the same emotions that he did, although if someone suggested he dehumanized Malcolm he would eagerly protest.

"I honestly don't think it's right," he said to Carol. "We made a commitment to Malcolm when we adopted him."

"I wanted a mixed female," said Carol. "Besides, I had no conception of the problems it involved."

"You meant well."

"Right."

"Hmmm," he sighed.

He looked at his wife with faint disapproval.

"It's the best thing," she said.

Moral righteousness, being an essential mental tool for survival, entered Carol's heart. For now she felt morally justified to the state, and to Malcolm.

However, the social worker did not see it this way. She was mad.

"You realize he'll be passed from foster home to foster home from now on," she lectured. "He's too old to be adopted, except by some miracle, and he'll probably end up in the streets. People do return babies, it's true. It's not unusual for a white couple to return a black or mixed child. But always within the first few months. You've had this child for more than three years! How could you wait so long?"

"I was trying my hardest," said Carol, "to make it work."

"And you failed."

Carol's eyes burned. The question of failure had not arisen in her mind before. Not of her failure anyway.

"It's not that simple," she said.

"You are making it that simple, just by this act—by returning him to the state like a pair of shoes that don't fit."

"I'm sorry—"

"Forget it," snapped the white woman. "Bring him in on Monday morning."

"But the movers are coming then."

The woman gave Carol a look of such intense disapproval that Carol blushed and jumped up.

"Okay," she swore. "I'll bring him in."

The icy air, outdoors, made her teeth cold; she was grinding them unconsciously, feeling sore inside and out. "Things do work out for the best; you must have faith," said a priest once to her. "It may not be the best for you, but for someone else."

"What a horrible thought." She didn't like it.

Still, she was consoled at home by Jessica's romantic faith that Malcolm was going to be reunited with his mother. Carol almost came to believe it herself, as she listened to Jessica imagine the first meeting between mother and son.

"Can't I tell him?" she begged Carol.

"No, dear. The social worker said to let it be a surprise."

"But why?"

"I don't know."

"I wish I could see what she looks like! Do you think she'll look like Malcolm? It'll be *weird*. Can't I come too, when you take him?"

"No, dear."

Jessica had a hard time keeping the news from Malcolm. It was almost more than she could bear, and the repression of her instinct worked havoc with her stomach. She couldn't eat, and developed a bellyache. She lay flat, face down, on Malcolm's bed, while he played with trucks. His suitcase was already half-packed, clothes meticulously folded—the way Carol always worked. Jessica eyed its open mouth, her innards tightened, she wanted to cry.

Malcolm asked, "Tummyache?"

"Yes," she moaned.

"Want to throw up?"

"Yes. But I can't. Nothing will come up."

"Oh."

He lowered his chin and growled for his truck's engine, sliding it across the bare floor; the shag rug was already rolled and ready to go. Jessica watched him, noting that his manipulation of the truck was more sophisticated than it was a week before, his growl more true to life.

"Make it crash," she instructed him.

He whirled it toward the wall, roaring and wailing as it knocked gently against his suitcase.

"Pretty good," she said. "You're getting good at trucks."

"I am?"

"Yup. Come on, let's have a race."

She slid off the bed and joined him on the floor, for a short time forgetting the mysterious forces at work on the two of them.

But, inevitably, the next morning Malcolm left. John and Jessica cried when he was gone, as rain fell in mushy, half-frozen lumps against the window. Carol took it upon herself to take him downtown. Gray snow was piled in dense heaps along the edges of the streets. Traffic ground slowly forward, windshield wipers bopping.

Carol appraised Malcolm's wide-eyed stare. He knew he was not going to "California," but somewhere else. That was all he knew. Carol thought of all the boring papers she would have to sign—it would probably take all morning—and the hostility of the social workers was almost more than she could bear.

"How do you feel?" she asked Malcolm.

He shrugged from inside his blue snowsuit.

"Well, everything will be all right. Don't worry."

He was quiet, then murmured, "Mommy?"

"What," curtly.

"Are you going to pick me up?"

"Uh, you have to spend the night there."

She reached out and turned on the radio. The morning news surfaced with the usual tales of urban disaster—fires, robbery, mugging, murder, rape—to which she listened without emotion because she would be free of it all soon.

When they finally parked, she looked at the gray building and felt some dread. They got out and Malcolm slipped on the ice, so she had to hold both his hand and his bag. The pressure of his hand raised a vague emotional quarrel, but she was a reasonable person, and her reasons came to mind, fast, all of them racial. They crossed the street, gingerly.

On the other side, they went into the building, side by side; and some time later she came out, alone.

THE THORN
Mary Gordon

As a young writer, Mary Gordon was haunted by the specters of male writers who advised her to write like Conrad about large, important issues, and if she wrote about social relationships, then to give them significance by distancing them, like Henry James. In fact, she first wrote Final Payments in the third person so that she wouldn't appear trivial. When a woman writer suggested she change the voice of the protagonist to the first person, it became the story she meant to write. For what Gordon loved in writing was not distance but radical closeness, not the cosmic but the quotidian. "I don't know what the nature of the universe is," she writes, "but I have a good ear." It's ironic that with the publication of her first novel Gordon was acclaimed as a writer with a large moral vision. Final Payments is about the nature of sacrifice, of morality, of self-fulfillment—final things.

Gordon, who was born in Rockaway, New York, in 1949, has written two novels: Final Payments (1978), which was nominated for the National Book Critics Circle Award, and The Company of Women (1981). Her short stories have been published in such popular and literary magazines as Ladies' Home Journal, Redbook, Southern Review, Virginia Quarterly Review. She studied creative writing at Barnard and Syracuse University and now lives and teaches in Poughkeepsie, New York.

Like the child's father in this story, her own father died when she was eight. He was a scholar and taught her to be one. "He was besotted with me, his only child." "The Thorn" is a poignant rendering of a child's attempt to understand the unknown in terms of her limited knowledge of the known. It is also about the profound burden of love.

IF I LOSE THIS, she thought, I will be so far away I will never come back.

When the kind doctor came to tell her that her father was dead, he took her crayons and drew a picture of a heart. It was not like a valentine, he said. It was solid and made of flesh, and it was not entirely red. It had veins and arteries and valves and one of them had broken, and so her daddy was now in heaven, he had said.

She was very interested in the picture of the heart and she put it under her pillow to sleep with, since no one she knew ever came to put her to bed anymore. Her mother came and got her in the morning, but she wasn't in her own house, she was in the bed next to her cousin Patty. Patty said to her one night, "My mommy says your daddy suffered a lot, but now he's released from suffering. That means he's dead." Lucy said yes, he was, but she didn't tell anyone that the reason she wasn't crying was that he'd either come back or take her with him.

Her aunt Iris, who owned a beauty parlor, took her to B. Altman's and bought her a dark blue dress with a white collar. That's nice, Lucy thought. I'll have a new dress for when I go away with my father. She looked in the long mirror and thought it was the nicest dress she'd ever had.

Her uncle Ted took her to the funeral parlor and he told her that her father would be lying in a big box with a lot of flowers. That's what I'll do, she said. I'll get in the box with him. We used to play in a big box; we called it the tent and we got in and read stories. I will get into the big box. There is my father; that is his silver ring.

She began to climb into the box, but her uncle pulled her away. She didn't argue; her father would think of some way to get her. He would wait for her in her room when it was dark. She would not be afraid to turn the lights out anymore. Maybe he would only visit her in her room; all right, then, she would never go on vacation; she would never go away with her mother to the country, no matter how much her mother cried and begged her. It was February and she asked her mother not to make any summer plans. Her aunt Lena, who lived with them, told Lucy's mother that if she had kids she wouldn't let them push her around, not at age seven. No matter how smart they thought they were. But Lucy didn't care; her father would come and talk to her, she and her mother would move back to the apartment where they lived before her father got sick, and she would only have to be polite to Aunt Lena; she would not have to love her, she would not have to feel sorry for her.

On the last day of school she got the best report card in her class. Father Burns said her mother would be proud to have such a smart little girl, but she wondered if he said this to make fun of her. But Sister Trinitas kissed her when all the other children had left and let her mind the statue for the summer: the one with the bottom that screwed off so you could put the big rosaries inside it. Nobody ever got to keep it for more than one night. This was a good thing. Since her father was gone she didn't know if people were being nice or if they seemed nice and really wanted to make her feel bad later. But she was pretty sure this was good. Sister Trinitas kissed her, but she smelled fishy when you got close up; it was the paste she used to make the Holy Childhood poster. This was good.

"You can take it to camp with you this summer, but be very careful of it."

"I'm not going to camp, Sister. I have to stay at home this summer."

"I thought your mother said you were going to camp."

"No, I have to stay home." She could not tell anybody, even Sister Trinitas, whom she loved, that she had to stay in her room because her father was certainly coming. She couldn't tell anyone about the thorn in her heart. She had a heart, just like her father's, brown in places, blue in places, a muscle the size of a fist. But hers had a thorn in it. The thorn was her father's voice. When the thorn pinched, she could hear her father saying something. "I love you more than anyone will ever love you. I love you more than God loves you." *Thint* went the thorn; he was telling her a story "about a mean old lady named Emmy and a nice old man named Charlie who always had candy in his pockets, and their pretty daughter, Ruth, who worked in the city." But it was harder and harder. Sometimes she tried to make the thorn go *thint* and she only felt the thick wall of her heart; she couldn't remember the sound of it or the kind of things he said. Then she was terribly far away; she didn't know how to do things, and if her aunt Lena asked her to do something like dust the ledge, suddenly there were a hundred ledges in the room and she didn't know which one and when she said to her aunt which one did she mean when she said ledge: the one by the floor, the one by the stairs, the one under the television, her aunt Lena said she must have really pulled the wool over their eyes at school because at home she was an idiot. And then Lucy would knock something over and Aunt Lena would tell her to get out, she was so clumsy she wrecked everything. Then she needed to feel the thorn, but all she could feel was her heart getting thicker and heavier, until she went up to her room and waited. Then she could hear it. "You are the prettiest girl in a hundred counties and when I see your face it is like a parade that someone made special for your daddy."

She wanted to tell her mother about the thorn, but her father had said that he loved her more than anything, even God. And she knew he said he loved God very much. So he must love her more than he loved her mother. So if she couldn't hear him her mother couldn't, and if he wasn't waiting for her in her new room then he was nowhere.

When she came home she showed everyone the statue that Sister Trinitas had given her. Her mother said that was a very great honor: that meant that Sister Trinitas must like her very much, and Aunt Lena said she wouldn't lay any bets about it not being broken or lost by the end of the summer, and she better not think of taking it to camp.

Lucy's heart got hot and wide and her mouth opened in tears. "I'm not going to camp; I have to stay here."

"You're going to camp, so you stop brooding and moping around. You're turning into a regular little bookworm. You're beginning to stink of books. Get out in the sun and play with other children. That's what you need, so you learn not to trip over your own two feet."

"I'm not going to camp. I have to stay here. Tell her, Mommy, you promised we wouldn't go away."

Her mother took out her handkerchief. It smelled of perfume and it had a lipstick print on it in the shape of her mother's mouth. Lucy's mother wiped her wet face with the pink handkerchief that Lucy loved.

"Well, we talked it over and we decided it would be best. It's not a real camp. It's Uncle Ted's camp, and Aunt Bitsie will be there, and all your cousins and that nice dog Tramp that you like."

"I won't go. I have to stay here."

"Don't be ridiculous," Aunt Lena said. "There's nothing for you to do here but read and make up stories."

"But it's for *boys* up there and I'll have nothing to do there. All they want to do is shoot guns and yell and run around. I hate that. And I have to stay here."

"That's what you need. Some good, healthy boys to toughen you up. You're too goddamn sensitive."

Sensitive. Everyone said that. It meant she cried for nothing. That was bad. Even Sister Trinitas got mad at her once and told her to stop her crocodile tears. They must be right. She would like not to cry when people said things that she didn't under-stand. That would be good. They had to be right. But the thorn. She went up to her room. She heard her father's voice on the telephone. *Thint,* it went. It was her birthday, and he was away in Washington. He sang "happy birthday" to her. Then he sang the song that made her laugh and laugh: "Hey, Lucy Turner, are there any more at home like you?" because of course there weren't. And she mustn't lose that voice, the thorn. She would think about it all the time, and maybe then she would keep it. Because if she lost it, she would always be clumsy and mistaken; she would always be wrong and falling.

Aunt Lena drove her up to the camp. *Scenery.* That was another word she didn't understand. "Look at that gorgeous scenery," Aunt Lena said, and Lucy didn't know what she meant. "Look at that bird," Aunt Lena said, and Lucy couldn't see it, so she just said, "It's nice." And Aunt Lena said, "Don't lie. You can't even *see* it, you're looking in the wrong direction. Don't say you can see something when you can't see it. And don't spend the whole summer crying. Uncle Ted and Aunt Bitsie are giving you a wonderful summer for free. So don't spend the whole time crying. Nobody can stand to have a kid around that all she ever does is cry."

Lucy's mother had said that Aunt Lena was very kind and very lonely because she had no little boys and girls of her own and she was doing what she thought was best for Lucy. But when Lucy had told her father that she thought Aunt Lena was not very nice, her father had said, "She's ignorant." *Ignorant.* That was a good word for the woman beside her with the dyed black hair and the big vaccination scar on her fat arm.

"Did you scratch your vaccination when you got it, Aunt Lena?"

"Of course not. What a stupid question. Don't be so goddamn rude. I'm not your mother, ya know. Ya can't push me around."

Thint, went the thorn. "You are ignorant," her father's voice said to Aunt Lena. "You are very, very ignorant."

Lucy looked out the window.

When Aunt Lena's black Chevrolet went down the road, Uncle Ted and Aunt Bitsie showed her her room. She would stay in Aunt Bitsie's room, except when Aunt Bitsie's husband came up on the weekends. Then Lucy would have to sleep on the couch.

The people in the camp were all boys, and they didn't want to talk to her. Aunt Bitsie said she would have to eat with the counselors and the K.P.'s. Aunt Bitsie said there was a nice girl named Betty who was fourteen who did the dishes. Her brothers were campers.

Betty came out and said hello. She was wearing a sailor hat that had a picture of a boy smoking a cigarette. It said "Property of Bobby." She had braces on her teeth. Her two side teeth hung over her lips so that her mouth never quite closed.

"My name's Betty," she said. "But everybody calls me Fang. That's on account of my fangs." She opened and closed her mouth like a dog. "In our crowd, if you're popular, you get a nickname. I guess I'm pretty popular."

Aunt Bitsie walked in and told Betty to set the table. She snapped her gum as she took out the silver. "Yup, Mrs. O'Connor, one thing about me is I have a lot of interests. There's swimming and boys, and tennis, and boys, and reading, and boys, and boys, and boys, and boys, and boys."

Betty and Aunt Bitsie laughed. Lucy didn't get it.

"What do you like to read?" Lucy asked.

"What?" said Betty.

"Well, you said one of your interests was reading. I was wondering what you like to read."

Betty gave her a fishy look. "I like to read romantic comics. About romances," she said. "I hear you're a real bookworm. We'll knock that outa ya."

The food came in: ham with brown gravy that tasted like ink. Margarine. Tomatoes that a fly settled on. But Lucy could not eat. Her throat was full of water. Her heart was glassy and too small. And now they would see her cry.

She was told to go up to her room.

That summer Lucy learned many things. She made a birchbark canoe to take home to her mother. Aunt Bitsie made a birchbark sign for her that said "Keep Smiling." Uncle Ted taught her to swim by letting her hold onto the waist of his bathing trunks. She swam onto the float like the boys. Uncle Ted said that that was so good she would get double dessert just like the boys did the first time they swam out to the float. But then Aunt Bitsie forgot and said it was just as well anyway because certain little girls should learn to watch their figures. One night her cousins Larry and Artie carried the dog Tramp in and pretended it had been shot. But then they put it down and it ran around and licked her and they said they had done it to make her cry.

She didn't cry so much now, but she always felt very far away and people's voices sounded the way they did when she was on the sand at the beach and she could hear the people's voices down by the water. A lot of times she didn't hear people when they talked to her. Her heart was very thick now: it was like one of Uncle Ted's boxing gloves. The thorn never touched the thin, inside walls of it anymore. She had lost it. There was no one whose voice was beautiful now, and little that she remembered.

BETTY

Margaret Atwood

Margaret Atwood, born in Ottawa in 1939, is the author of eight volumes of poetry, most notably Power Politics (1971) and Two-Headed Poems (1981), and four internationally acclaimed novels: The Edible Woman (1970); Surfacing (1972), her most explicitly feminist novel, which has recently been made into a film; Lady Oracle (1976), a spoof on the harlequin romance, and Life Before Man (1979), as well as a critical study of Canadian literature, Survival. One of the few women political cartoonists, her strip "Kanadian Kulture Komics" appears in the weekly, This. Atwood has been active in fighting for authors' rights in Canada and has worked to keep the integrity of Canadian publishing intact and separate from that in the United States. She lives on a farm near Alliston, Ontario, with novelist Graeme Gibson and their three-year-old daughter.

Atwood has written that her work's central theme is "the creation, exploration and eventual destruction of, or by, certain mythologies, especially those involving victor/victim patterns with their endless variations of . . . complicity and subversion of the human." In Surfacing, her most successful exploration of certain "mythologies of self," the narrator strips down and dives into human history and her own psychic roots. Upon surfacing she promises: "This above all, to refuse to be a victim. Unless I can do that I can do nothing. I have to give up the old belief that I am powerless and because of it nothing I can do will ever hurt anyone." Returning again to this theme in "Betty," Atwood tries to get beyond a single-sided view of the victim. Here, neither glorified nor dismissed as one-dimensional, Betty remains a mystery to the young narrator, who must grapple in her own life with "the dark side of Betty's terrible niceness."

When I was seven we moved again, to a tiny wooden cottage on the Saint Mary's River, upstream from Sault Sainte Marie. We were only renting the cottage for the summer, but for the time being it was our house, since we had no other. It was dim and mousy smelling and very cramped, stuffed with all the things from the place before that were not in storage. My sister and I preferred to spend most of our time outside it.

There was a short beach, behind which the cottages, with their contrasting trim—green against white, maroon against robin's-egg blue, brown against yellow—were lined up like little shoe boxes, each with its matching outhouse at an unsanitary distance behind. But we were forbidden to swim in the water, because of the strong current. There were stories of children who had been swept away, down toward the rapids and the locks and the Algoma Steel fires of the Soo which we could sometimes see from our bedroom window on overcast nights, glowing dull red against the clouds. We were allowed to wade, though, no further than the knee, and we would stand in the water, strands of loose weed tangling against our ankles, and wave at the lake freighters as they slid past, so close we could see not only the flags and sea gulls at their sterns but the hands of the sailors and the ovals of their faces as they waved back to us. Then the waves would come, washing over our thighs up to the waists of our bloomered and skirted seersucker bathing suits, and we would scream with delight.

Our mother, who was usually on the shore, reading or talking to someone but not quite watching us, would sometimes mistake the screams for drowning. Or she would say later, "You've been in over your knees," but my sister would explain that it was only the boat waves. My mother would look at me to see if this was the truth. Unlike my sister, I was a clumsy liar.

The freighters were huge, cumbersome, with rust staining the holes for their anchor chains and enormous chimneys from which the smoke spurted in gray burps. When they blew their horns, as they always did when approaching the locks, the windows in our cottage rattled. For us they were magical. Sometimes things would drop or be thrown from them, and we would watch these floating objects eagerly, running along the beach to be there when they landed, wading out to fish them in. Usually these treasures turned out to be only empty cardboard boxes or punctured oil cans, oozing dark brown grease and good for nothing. Several times we got orange crates, which we used as cupboards or stools in our hideouts.

We liked the cottage partly because we had places to make these hideouts. There had never been room before, since we had always lived in cities. Just before this it was Ottawa, the ground floor of an old three-tiered red-brick apartment building. On the floor above us lived a newly married couple, the wife

English and Protestant, the husband French and Catholic. He was in the air force and was away a lot, but when he came back on leave he used to beat up his wife. It was always about eleven o'clock at night. She would flee downstairs to my mother for protection, and they would sit in the kitchen with cups of tea. The wife would cry, though quietly, so as not to wake us—my mother insisted on that, being a believer in twelve hours of sleep for children—display her bruised eye or cheek, and whisper about his drinking. After an hour or so there would be a discreet knock on the door, and the airman, in full uniform, would ask my mother politely if he could have his wife back upstairs where she belonged. It was a religious dispute, he would say. Besides, he'd given her fifteen dollars to spend on food and she had served him fried Kam. After being away a month, a man expected a good roast, pork or beef, didn't my mother agree? "I kept my mouth shut and my eyes open," my mother would say. He never seemed that drunk to her, but with the polite kind you couldn't tell what they would do.

I wasn't supposed to know about any of this. I was considered either too young or too good; but my sister, who was four years older, was given hints, which she passed along to me with whatever she thought fit to add. I saw the wife a number of times, going up or down the stairs outside our door, and once she did have a black eye. I never saw the man, but by the time we left Ottawa I was convinced he was a murderer.

This might have explained my father's warning when my mother told him she had met the young couple who lived in the right-hand cottage. "Don't get too involved," he said. "I don't want her running over here at all hours of the night." He had little patience with my mother's talents as a sympathetic listener, even when she teased him by saying, "But I listen to *you*, dear." She attracted people he called sponges.

He didn't seem to have anything to worry about. This couple was very different from the other one. Fred and Betty insisted on being called Fred and Betty, right away. My sister and I, who had been drilled to call people Mr. and Mrs., had to call them Fred and Betty also, and we could go over to their house whenever we wanted to. "I don't want you to take that at face value," our mother said. Times were hard, but our mother had been properly brought up, and we were going to be, too. Nevertheless, at first we went to Fred and Betty's as often as we could.

Their cottage was exactly the same size as ours, but since there was less furniture in it, it seemed bigger. Ours had Ten-Test walls between the rooms, painted lime green, with lighter squares on the paint where other people had once hung pictures. Betty had replaced her walls with real plywood and painted the inside bright yellow, and she'd made yellow-and-white curtains for the kitchen, a print of chickens coming out of eggshells. She'd sewed herself a matching apron from the leftover material. They owned their cottage rather than renting it; as my mother said, you didn't mind doing the work then. Betty called the tiny kitchen a kitchenette. There was a round ironwork table tucked into one corner, with two scrolled ironwork chairs painted white, one for Betty and one for Fred. Betty called this corner the breakfast nook.

There was more to do at Fred and Betty's than at our house. They had a bird made of hollow colored glass that perched on the edge of a tumbler of water, teetering back and forth until it would finally dip its head into the water and take a drink. They had a front-door knocker in the shape of a woodpecker: you pulled a string and the woodpecker pecked at the door. They also had a whistle in the shape of a bird that you could fill with water and blow into and it would warble, "like a canary," Betty said. And they took the Sunday colored funnies. Our parents didn't. They didn't like us reading trash, as they called it. But Fred and Betty were so friendly and kind to us, what, as my mother said, could they do?

Beyond all these attractions there was Fred. We both fell in love with Fred. My sister would climb into his lap and announce that he was her boyfriend and she was going to marry him when she grew up. She would then make him read the funnies to her and tease him by trying to take the pipe out of his mouth or by tying his shoelaces together. I felt the same way, but I knew it was no good saying so. My sister had staked her claim: when she said she was going to do a thing she usually did it. And she hated my being what she called a copycat. So I would sit in the breakfast nook on one of the scrolled ironwork chairs while Betty made coffee, watching my sister and Fred on the living-room couch.

There was something about Fred that attracted people. My mother, who was not a flirtatious woman—she went in for wisdom, instead—was livelier when he was around. Even my father liked him and would sometimes have a beer with him when he got back from the city. They would sit on the porch of Fred's cottage in Betty's yellow wicker chairs, swatting at the sand flies and discussing baseball scores. They seldom mentioned their jobs. I'm not sure what Fred did, but it was in an office. My father was "in wallpaper," my mother said, but I was never very clear about what that meant. It was more exciting when they talked about the war. My father's bad back had kept him out of it, much to his disgust, but Fred had been in the navy. He never said too much about it, though my father was always prompting him; but we knew from Betty that they were engaged just before Fred left and married right after he came back. Betty had written letters to him every single night and mailed them once a week. She did not say how often Fred had written to her. My father didn't like many people, but he said that Fred wasn't a fool.

Fred didn't seem to make any efforts to be nice to people. I don't think he was even especially handsome. The difficulty is that though I can remember Betty down to the last hair and freckle, I can't remember what Fred looked like. He had dark hair and a pipe, and he used to sing to us if we pestered him enough. "Sioux City Sue," he would sing, "your hair is red, your eyes are blue, I'd swap my horse and dog for you. . . ." Or he would sing "Beautiful Brown Eyes" to my sister, whose eyes were brown, as compared with my own watery blue. This hurt my feelings, as the song contained the line "I'll never love blue eyes again." It seemed so final, a whole lifetime of being unloved by Fred. Once I cried, which was made worse by the fact that I couldn't explain to anyone what was wrong; and I had to undergo the humiliation of Fred's jocular concern and my sister's scorn, and the worse humiliation of being comforted by Betty in the kitchenette. It was a humiliation because it was obvious even to me that Betty didn't grasp things very well. "Don't pay any attention to *him*," she said, having guessed that my tears had something to do with Fred. But that was the one piece of advice I couldn't take.

Fred, like a cat, wouldn't go two steps out of his way for you really, as my mother said later. So it was unfair that everyone was in love with Fred, but no one, despite her kindness, was in love with Betty. It was Betty who always greeted us at the door, asked us in, and talked to us while Fred slouched on the couch reading the paper. She fed us cookies and milk shakes and let us lick out the bowls when she was baking. Betty was such a nice person; everyone said so, but no one would have called Fred exactly that. Fred, for instance, did not laugh much, and he only smiled when he was making rude remarks, mostly to my sister. "Stuffing your face, again?" he would say. "Hey, baggy-pants." Whereas Betty never said things like that, and she was always either smiling or laughing.

She laughed a lot when Fred called her Betty Grable, which he did at least once a day. I couldn't see why she laughed. It was supposed to be a compliment, I thought. Betty Grable was a famous movie star; there was a picture of her thumbtacked to the wall in Fred and Betty's outhouse. Both my sister and I preferred Fred and Betty's outhouse to our own. Theirs had curtains on the window, unlike ours, and it had a little wooden box and a matching wooden scoop for the lye. We only had a cardboard box and an old trowel.

Betty didn't really look like Betty Grable, who was blond and

not as plump as our Betty. Still, they were both beautiful, I
thought. I didn't realize until much later that the remark was
cruel, for Betty Grable was renowned for her legs, whereas our
Betty had legs that started at her waist and continued downward
without a curve or a pause until they reached her feet. At the
time they seemed like ordinary legs. Sitting in the kitchenette,
I saw a lot of Betty's legs, for she wore halter tops and shorts,
with her yellow apron over them. Somehow Betty could never
get her legs to tan, despite the hours she spent crocheting in her
wicker chair, the top part of her in the shade of the porch but
her legs sticking out into the sun.

My father said that Betty had no sense of humor. I couldn't
understand this at all. If you told her a joke she would always
laugh, even if you got it mixed up.

My father also said that Betty had no sex appeal. This didn't
seem to bother my mother in the least. "She's a very nice girl,"
she would answer complacently, or, "She has very nice coloring."
My mother and Betty were soon collaborating on a scheme for
making the preserving easier. Most people still had Victory Gardens, though the war was over, and the months of July and
August were supposed to be spent putting up as many jars of
fruit and vegetables as you could. My mother's garden was half-
hearted, like most of her housekeeping efforts. It was a small
patch beside the outhouse where squash vines rambled over a
thicket of overgrown tomato plants and a few uneven lines of
dwarfed carrots and beets. My mother's talent, we had heard her
say, was for people. Betty and Fred didn't have a garden at all.
Fred wouldn't have worked in it, and when I think of Betty now
I realize that a garden would have been too uncontained for her.
But she had Fred buy dozens of six-quart baskets of strawberries,
peaches, beans, tomatoes, and Concord grapes on his trips into
the city, and she persuaded my mother to give up on her own
garden and join her in her mammoth canning sessions.

My mother's wood stove was unbearably hot for such an opera-
tion, and Betty's little electric range was too small, so Betty got

"the boys," as she called Fred and my father, to set up the derelict wood stove that until then had been rusting behind Betty's outhouse. They put it in our backyard, and my mother and Betty would sit at our kitchen table, which had been carried outside, peeling, slicing, and talking, Betty with her round pincushion cheeks flushed redder than usual by the heat and my mother with an old bandanna wrapped around her head, making her look like a gypsy. Behind them the canning kettles bubbled and steamed, and on one side of the table the growing ranks of Crown jars, inverted on layers of newspaper, cooled and sometimes leaked or cracked. My sister and I hung around the edges, not wanting to be obvious enough to be put to work, but coveting the empty six-quart baskets. We could use them in our hideout, we felt; we were never sure what for, but they fitted neatly into the orange crates.

I learned a lot about Fred during Betty's canning sessions: how he liked his eggs, what size socks he took (Betty was a knitter), how well he was doing at the office, what he refused to eat for dinner. Fred was a picky eater, Betty said joyfully. Betty had almost nothing else to talk about, and even my mother, veteran of many confidences, began to talk less and smoke more than usual when Betty was around. It was easier to listen to disasters than to Betty's inexhaustible and trivial cheer. I began to think that I might not want to be married to Fred after all. He unrolled from Betty's mouth like a long ribbon of soggy newspaper printed from end to end with nothing but the weather. Neither my sister nor I was interested in sock sizes, and Betty's random, unexciting details diminished Fred in our eyes. We began to spend less of our playtime at Fred and Betty's and more in our hideout, which was in a patch of scrubby oak on a vacant lot along the shore. There we played complicated games of Mandrake the Magician and his faithful servant Lothar, with our dolls as easily hypnotized villains. My sister was always Mandrake. When we tired of this, we would put on our bathing suits and go wading along the shore, watching for freighters and throwing acorns into the river to see how quickly they would be carried away by the current.

It was on one of these wading expeditions that we met Nan. She lived ten lots down, in a white cottage with red trim. Unlike many of the other cottages, Nan's had a real dock, built out into the river and anchored around the posts with piles of rocks. She was sitting on this dock when we first saw her, chewing gum and flipping through a stack of airplane cards from Wings cigarettes. Everyone knew that only boys collected these. Her hair and her face were light brown, and she had a sleek plump sheen, like caramel pudding.

"What're you doing with *those?*" were my sister's first words. Nan only smiled.

That same afternoon Nan was allowed into our hideout, and after a cursory game of Mandrake, during which I was demoted to the lowly position of Narda, the two of them sat on our orange crates and exchanged what seemed to me to be languid and pointless comments.

"You ever go to the store?" Nan asked. We never did. Nan smiled some more. She was twelve; my sister was only eleven and three quarters.

"There's cute boys at the store," Nan said. She was wearing a peasant blouse with a frill and an elastic top that she could slide down over her shoulders if she wanted to. She stuck her airplane cards into her shorts pocket and we went to ask my mother if we could walk to the store. After that, my sister and Nan went there almost every afternoon.

The store was a mile and a half from our cottage, a hot walk along the shore past the fronts of other cottages where fat mothers basked in the sun and other, possibly hostile, children paddled in the water; past rowboats hauled up on the sand, along cement breakwaters, through patches of beach grass that cut your ankles if you ran through it and beach peas that were hard and bitter tasting. In some places we could smell the outhouses. Just before the store, there was an open space with poison ivy, which we had to wade around.

The store had no name. It was just "the store," the only store for the cottagers, since it was the only one they could walk to. I was allowed to go with my sister and Nan, or rather my mother insisted that I go. Although I hadn't said anything to her about it, she could sense my misery. It wasn't so much my sister's desertion that hurt, but her blithe unconsciousness of it. She was quite willing to play with me when Nan wasn't around.

Sometimes, when the sight of my sister and Nan conspiring twenty paces ahead of me made me too unhappy, I would double back and go to Fred and Betty's. There I would sit facing backward on one of Betty's kitchen chairs, my two hands rigid in the air, holding a skein of sky-blue wool while Betty wound it into balls. Or, under Betty's direction, I crocheted sweaty, uneven little pink and yellow dolls' dresses for the dolls my sister was, suddenly, too old to play with.

On better days I would make it as far as the store. It was not beautiful or even clean, but we were so used to wartime drabness and grime that we didn't notice. It was a two-story building of unpainted wood which had weathered gray. Parts of it were patched with tar paper, and it had colored metal signs nailed around the front screen door and windows: Coca-Cola, 7-Up, Salada Tea. Inside, it had the sugary, mournful smell of old general stores, a mixture of the cones for the ice-cream cones, the packages of Oreo cookies, the open boxes of jawbreakers and licorice whips that lined the counter, and that other smell, musky and sharp, part dry rot and part sweat. The bottles of pop were kept in a metal cooler with a heavy lid, filled with cold water and chunks of ice melted to the smoothness of the sand-scoured pieces of glass we sometimes found on the beach.

The owner of the store and his wife lived on the second floor, but we almost never saw them. The store was run by their two daughters, who took turns behind the counter. They were both dark and they both wore shorts and polka-dot halter tops, but one was friendly and the other one, the thinner, younger one, was not. She would take our pennies and ring them into the cash register without saying a word, staring over our heads out the front window with its dangling raisin-covered flypapers as if she were completely detached from the activity her hands were performing. She didn't dislike us; she just didn't see us. She wore her hair long and done in a sort of roll at the front, and her lipstick was purplish.

The first time we went to the store we found out why Nan collected airplane cards. There were two boys there, sitting on the gray, splintery front steps, their arms crossed over their knees. I had been told by my sister that the right thing to do with boys was to ignore them; otherwise they would pester you. But these boys knew Nan, and they spoke to her, not with the usual taunts but with respect.

"You got anything new?" one of them said.

Nan smiled, brushed back her hair, and wiggled her shoulders a little inside her peasant blouse. Then she slid her airplane cards slowly out of her shorts pocket and began riffling through them.

"You got any?" the other boy said to my sister. For once she was humbled. After that, she got my mother to switch brands and built up her own pack. I saw her in front of the mirror about a week later, practicing that tantalizing slide, the cards coming out of her pocket like a magician's snake.

When I went to the store I always had to bring back a loaf of wax-papered bread for my mother, and sometimes a package of Jiffy Pie Crust, if they had any. My sister never had to: she had already discovered the advantages of being unreliable. As payment, and, I'm sure, as compensation for my unhappiness, my mother gave me a penny a trip, and when I had saved five of these pennies I bought my first Popsicle. Our mother had always refused to buy them for us, although she permitted ice-cream cones. She said there was something in Popsicles that was bad for you, and as I sat on the front steps of the store, licking down to the wooden stick, I kept looking for this thing. I visualized it as a sort of core, like the white fingernail-shaped part in a kernel of corn, but I couldn't find anything.

My sister and Nan were sitting beside me on the front steps. There were no boys at the store that day, so they had nothing else to do. It was even hotter than usual, and airless; there was a shimmer over the river, and the freighters wavered as they passed through it. My Popsicle was melting almost before I could eat it. I had given my sister half of it, which she had taken without the gratitude I had hoped for. She was sharing it with Nan.

Fred came around the corner of the building and headed toward the front door. This was no surprise, as we had seen him at the store several times before.

"Hi, beautiful," he said to my sister. We moved our rumps along the step to let him in the door.

After quite a long time he came out, carrying a loaf of bread. He asked us if we wanted a lift with him in his car: he was just coming back from the city, he said. Of course we said yes. There was nothing unusual about any of this, except that the daughter, the thinner, purple one, stepped outside the door and stood on the steps as we were driving off. She folded her arms across her chest in that slump-shouldered pose of women idling in doorways. She wasn't smiling. I thought she had come out to watch the Canada Steamship Lines freighter that was going past, but then I saw that she was staring at Fred. She looked as if she wanted to kill him.

Fred didn't seem to notice. He sang all the way home. "Katie, oh, beautiful Katie," he sang, winking at my sister, whom he sometimes called Katie since her name was Catherine. He had the windows open, and dust from the rutted gravel road poured over us, whitening our eyebrows and turning Fred's hair gray. At every jolt my sister and Nan screamed gleefully, and after a while I forgot my feelings of exclusion and screamed too.

It seemed as if we had lived in the cottage for a long time, though it was only one summer. By August I could hardly remember the apartment in Ottawa and the man who used to beat up his wife. That had happened in a remote life; and, despite the sunshine, the water, the open space, a happier one. Before, our frequent moves and the insecurities of new schools had forced my sister to value me: I was four years younger, but I was loyal and always there. Now those years were a canyon between us, an empty stretch like a beach along which I could see her disappearing ahead of me. I longed to be just like her, but I could no longer tell what she was like.

In the third week of August the leaves started to turn, not all at once, just a single red one here and there, like a warning. That meant it would soon be time for school and another move. We didn't even know where we would be moving to this time, and when Nan asked us what school we went to, we were evasive.

"I've been to eight different schools," my sister said proudly. Because I was so much younger, I had only been to two. Nan, who had been to the same one all her life, slipped the edge of her peasant blouse over her shoulders and down to her elbows to show us that her breasts were growing. The rings around her nipples had softened and started to puff out; otherwise she was as flat as my sister.

"So what," said my sister, rolling up her jersey. This was a competition I couldn't be part of. It was about change, and, increasingly, change frightened me. I walked back along the beach to Betty's house, where my latest piece of grubby crocheting was waiting for me and where everything was always the same.

I knocked on the screen door and opened it. I meant to say, "Can I come in?" the way we always did, but I didn't say it. Betty was sitting by herself at the iron table of the breakfast nook. She had on her shorts and a striped sailor top, navy blue and white with a little anchor pin, and the apron with the yellow chickens coming out of their eggs. For once she wasn't doing anything, and there was no cup of coffee in front of her. Her face was white and uncomprehending, as if someone had just hit her for no reason.

She saw me, but she didn't smile or ask me in. "What am I going to do?" she said.

I looked around the kitchen. Everything was in its place: the percolator gleamed from the stove, the glass bird was teetering slowly down, there were no broken dishes, no water on the floor. What had happened?

"Are you sick?" I said.

"There's nothing I can do," Betty said.

She looked so strange that I was frightened. I ran out of the kitchen and across the hillocky grass to get to my mother, who always knew what should be done.

"There's something wrong with Betty," I said.

My mother was mixing something in a bowl. She rubbed her hands together to get the dough off, then wiped them on her apron. She didn't look surprised or ask me what it was. "You stay here," she said. She picked up her package of cigarettes and went out the door.

That evening we had to go to bed early because my mother wanted to talk to my father. We listened, of course; it was easy through the Ten-Test walls.

"I saw it coming," my mother said. "A mile away."

"Who is it?" my father said.

"She doesn't know," said my mother. "Some girl from town."

"Betty's a fool," my father said. "She always was." Later, when husbands and wives leaving each other became more common, he often said this, but no matter which one had left it was always the woman he called the fool. His highest compliment to my mother was that she was no fool.

"That may be," said my mother. "But you'd never want to meet a nicer girl. He was her whole life."

My sister and I whispered together. My sister's theory was that Fred had run away from Betty with another woman. I couldn't believe this: I had never heard of such a thing happening. I was so upset I couldn't sleep, and for a long time after that I was anxious whenever my father was away overnight, as he frequently was. What if he never came back?

We didn't see Betty after that. We knew she was in her cottage, because every day my mother carried over samples of her tough and lumpy baking, almost as if someone had died. But we were given strict orders to stay away, and not to go peering in the windows as our mother must have known we longed to do. "She's having a nervous breakdown," our mother said, which for me called up an image of Betty lying disjointed on the floor like a car at the garage.

We didn't even see her on the day we got into my father's secondhand Studebaker, the back seat packed to the window tops with only a little oblong space for me to crouch in, and drove out to the main highway to begin the six-hundred-mile journey south to Toronto. My father had changed jobs again; he was now in building materials, and he was sure, since the country was having a boom, that this was finally the right change. We spent September and part of October in a motel while my father looked for a house. I had my eighth birthday and my sister turned twelve. I almost forgot about Betty.

But a month after I had turned twelve myself, Betty was suddenly there one night for dinner. We had people for dinner a lot more than we used to, and sometimes the dinners were so important that my sister and I ate first. My sister didn't care, as she had boyfriends by that time. I was still in public school and had to wear lisle stockings instead of the seamed nylons my sister was permitted. Also, I had braces. My sister had had braces at that age too, but she had somehow managed to make them seem rakish and daring, so that I longed for a mouthful of flashing silver teeth like hers. But she no longer had them, and my own mouth in its shackles felt clumsy and muffled.

"You remember Betty," my mother said.

"Elizabeth," Betty said.

"Oh, yes, of course," said my mother.

Betty had changed a lot. Before, she had been a little plump; now she was buxom. Her cheeks were as round and florid as two tomatoes, and I thought she was using too much rouge until I saw that the red was caused by masses of tiny veins under her skin. She was wearing a long black pleated skirt, a white short-sleeved angora sweater with a string of black beads, and open-toed black velvet pumps with high heels. She smelled strongly of lily of the valley. She had a job, my mother told my father later, a very good job. She was an executive secretary and now called herself Miss instead of Mrs.

"She's doing very well," my mother said, "considering what happened. She's pulled herself together."

"I hope you don't start inviting her to dinner all the time," said my father, who still found Betty irritating in spite of her new look. She laughed more than ever now and crossed her legs frequently.

"I feel I'm the only real friend she has," said my mother. She didn't say Betty was the only real friend she had, though when my father said "your friend" everyone knew who he meant. My mother had a lot of friends, and her talent for wise listening was now a business asset for my father.

"She says she'll never marry again," said my mother.

"She's a fool," my father said.

"If I ever saw anyone cut out for marriage, it was her," said my mother. This remark increased my anxiety about my own future. If all Betty's accomplishments had not been enough for Fred, what hope was there for me? I did not have my sister's natural flair, but I had thought there would be some tricks I could learn, dutifully, painstakingly. We were taking home economics at school and the teacher kept saying that the way to a man's heart was through his stomach. I knew this wasn't true—my mother was still a slapdash cook, and when she gave the best dinners she had a woman in to help—but I labored over my blanc-mange and Harvard beets as if I believed it.

My mother started inviting Betty to dinner with men who were not married. Betty smiled and laughed and several men seemed interested, but nothing came of it.

"After the way she was hurt, I'm not surprised," my mother said. I was now old enough to be told things, and besides, my sister was never around. "I heard it was a secretary at his company he ran off with. They even got married, after the divorce." There was something else about Betty, she told me, although I must never mention it, as Betty found it very distressing. Fred's brother, who was a dentist, had killed his wife because he got involved— my mother said "involved" richly, as if it were a kind of dessert— with his dental technician. He had put his wife into the car and run a tube in from the exhaust pipe, and then tried to pretend it was suicide. The police had found out, though, and he was in jail.

This made Betty much more interesting in my eyes. It was in Fred's blood, then, this tendency toward involvement. In fact, it could just as easily have been Betty herself who had been murdered. I now came to see Betty's laugh as the mask of a stricken and martyred woman. She was not just a wife who had been deserted. Even I could see that this was not a tragic position, it was a ridiculous and humiliating one. She was much more than that: she was a woman who had narrowly escaped death. That Betty herself saw it this way I soon had no doubt. There was something smug and even pious about the way she kept mother's single men at a polite distance, something faintly nunlike. A lurid aura of sacrificial blood surrounded her. Betty had been there, she had passed through it, she had come out alive, and now she was dedicating herself to, well, to something else.

But it was hard for me to sustain this version of Betty for long. My mother soon ran out of single men, and Betty, when she came to dinner, came alone. She talked as incessantly about the details surrounding the other women at her office as she had about Fred. We soon knew how they all took their coffee, which ones lived with their mothers, where they had their hair done, and what their apartments looked like. Betty herself had a darling apartment on Avenue Road, and she had redone it all herself and even made the slipcovers. Betty was as devoted to her boss as she had once been to Fred. She did all his Christmas shopping, and each year we heard what he had given to his employees, what to his wife and children, and what each item had cost. Betty seemed, in a way, quite happy.

We saw a lot of Betty around Christmas; my mother said she felt sorry for her because she had no family. Betty was in the habit of giving us Christmas presents that made it obvious she thought we were younger than we were. She favored Parcheesi sets and angora mittens a size too small. I lost interest in her. Even her unending cheerfulness came to seem like a perversion, or a defect almost like idiocy. I was fifteen now and in the throes of adolescent depression. My sister was away at Queen's; sometimes she gave me clothes she no longer wanted. She was not exactly beautiful—both her eyes and her mouth were too large— but everyone called her vivacious. They called me nice. My braces had come off, but it didn't seem to make any difference. What right had Betty to be cheerful? When she came to dinner, I excused myself early and went to my room.

One afternoon, in the spring of grade eleven, I came home from school to find my mother sitting at the dining-room table. She was crying, which was so rare that my immediate fear was that something had happened to my father. I didn't think he had left her; that particular anxiety was past. But perhaps he had been killed in a car crash.

"Mum, what is it?" I said.

"Bring me a glass of water," she said. She drank some of it and pushed back her hair. "I'm all right now," she said. "I just had a call from Betty. It was very upsetting; she said horrible things to me."

"Why?" I said. "What did you do?"

"She accused me of . . . horrible things." My mother swabbed at her eyes. "She was screaming. I've never heard Betty scream in my life before. After all that time I spent with her. She said she never wanted to speak to me again. Where would she get such an idea?"

"What idea?" I said. I was just as mystified as my mother was. My mother was a bad cook, but she was a good woman. I could not imagine her doing anything that would make anyone want to scream at her.

My mother held back slightly. "Things about Fred," she said. "She must be crazy. I hadn't seen her for a couple of months, and then suddenly, just like that."

"There must be something wrong with her," my father said at dinner that night. Of course he was right. Betty had an undetected brain tumor, which was discovered when her strange behavior was noticed at the office. She died in the hospital two months later, but my mother didn't hear about it till afterward. She was contrite; she felt she should have visited her friend in the hospital, despite the abusive phone call.

"I ought to have known it was something like that," she said. "Personality change, that's one of the clues." In the course of her listening, my mother had picked up a great deal of information about terminal illnesses.

But for me, this explanation wasn't good enough. For years after that, Betty followed me around, waiting for me to finish her off in some way more satisfactory to both of us. When I first heard about her death I felt doomed. This, then, was the punishment for being devoted and obliging, this was what happened to girls such as (I felt) myself. When I opened the high school yearbook and my own face, in page-boy haircut and tentative, appeasing smile, stared back at me, it was Betty's eyes I superimposed on mine. She had been kind to me when I was a child, and with the callousness of children toward those who are kind but not enchanting I had preferred Fred. In my future I saw myself being abandoned by a succession of Freds who were running down the beach after a crowd of vivacious girls, all of whom looked remarkably like my sister. As for Betty's final screams of hatred and rage, they were screams of protest against the unfairness of life. That anger, I knew, was my own, the dark side of that terrible and deforming niceness that had marked Betty like the aftermath of some crippling disease.

People change, though, especially after they are dead. As I passed beyond the age of melodrama I came to see that if I did not want to be Betty, I would have to be someone else. Furthermore, I was already quite different from Betty. In a way, she had absolved me from making the demanded choices by having made them so thoroughly herself. People stopped calling me a nice girl and started calling me a clever one, and after a while I enjoyed this. Betty herself, baking oatmeal cookies in the ephemeral sunlight of fifteen years before, slid back into three dimensions. She was an ordinary woman who died too young of an incurable disease. Was that it, was that all?

From time to time I would like to have Betty back, if only for an hour's conversation. I would like her to forgive me for my rejection of her angora mittens, for my secret betrayals of her, for my adolescent contempt. I would like to show her this story I have told about her and ask her if any of it is true. But I can think of nothing I want to ask her that I could phrase in a way that she would care to understand. She would only laugh in her accepting, uncomprehending way and offer me something, a chocolate brownie, a ball of wool.

Fred, on the other hand, no longer intrigues me. The Freds of this world make themselves explicit by what they do and choose. It is the Bettys that are mysterious.

THE QUIET WOMAN

Mary Heaton Vorse

The following has been adapted from an appraisal by E. M. Broner.

Mary Heaton Vorse was born in 1874 to affluent parents who took her on their extensive travels. She became fluent in several languages—indeed, felt foreign nowhere in her life—and stayed in Paris to study art. She was widowed twice and had to provide for herself and her three children from 1915 to 1966. She was acutely aware of being a working woman.

She allowed herself to investigate, to be curious, and to feel deeply about what she saw, and she always saw and reported on the condition of women. In 1912 she covered the Lawrence, Massachusetts, textile strike. Vorse gave ample space in her reportage to the women's auxiliaries of the labor movement, the Women's Emergency Brigade in the 1937 sit-down strike at GM's Flint plant. She followed them into the kitchen and interviewed them.

Vorse wrote her accounts of domestic struggle, of the coming of international war, for a variety of presses from Masses to the New York Times, *the Washington* Post, *the New Yorker, and the New Republic. She wrote of migrant workers and union organizers in Florida and saved the testimony of the murders committed against the organizers by the Klan in Lakeland in 1937. She wrote for Harper's of racketeering on the New York waterfront. She wrote of migrant workers in California, the textile worker in New England, the lumbermen of the Northwest, the cannery workers in Florida. She was as gifted as Lincoln Steffens or Upton Sinclair. She wrote 16 books and 400 articles, yet she has been almost totally forgotten—her papers only recently unearthed.*

"The Quiet Woman," first published in the Atlantic Monthly in 1907, reflects one task of the feminist critic: to recover lost writers of fiction. Amazingly contemporary, Vorse was sensitive to the unspoken between women, to what women did not tell one another.

THE DUSK WAS WIPING OUT THE COLORS of the world, spreading over the tender greens and pale pinks an indefinite nameless color more beautiful than any we know. The apple trees loomed up, great masses of bloom, and their sweetness drifted to Katherine mingled with the smell of young leaves and spring— it was as if all the souls of the myriad growing things had breathed themselves forth into the night.

The dusk deepened and then grew blonder; the moon was coming up. One could see again that the trees were green, one could see the small flowers in the lawn. The white trees cast deep shadows on the young grass. Everything was very still; Katherine thought that the beating of her own heart was too loud for the miracle of the night. Everything—the trees and sky and hills—

gave her the sense that something wonderful was about to happen; surely they were only the setting for some greater miracle. Then there came over her an appalling sense of desolation. It was terrible that on this most lovely night she must be so alone, that there should be no kind hand anywhere to meet hers. Katherine's need of companionship grew more poignant; the beauty of the night weighed on her as too great a burden to be borne alone; but she listened in vain for the sound of a human voice mingled with the voices of the night. The neighboring houses turned blank, unlighted faces to her; Katherine was as solitary as if she had been adrift on some unknown sea.

Then, in the garden on the slope of the hill below a white shadow moved; it flitted about, unsubstantial, unreal, now stopping as if to look at the night, now moving on slowly, then lost to sight among the flower-laden shrubs. At last it stood out in a little open space, attentive, even reverent, in its attitude. Without realizing what she did, Katherine trailed through the wet grass toward the motionless figure, her shawl hanging loose around her; it was as if one white spirit went forth to meet another like itself. She made her way through the loosely planted shrubbery which divided one garden from the other, and was near the other woman before she turned her head toward Katherine. She greeted Katherine quietly as if she had been waiting for her. They stood a moment in silence, then the woman said:

"I could not have stayed out here alone—" she stopped shyly and turned toward Katherine to see if she were understood, and Katherine wondered if here was someone as terribly alone as herself, as in need as she of sympathy. They looked at the night together, as silent as old friends who do not need to talk to one another; they did not know each other's names, and yet already they had ceased to be strangers; the fellowship of spring had brought them together.

A voice called from somewhere beyond a screen of white apple trees, a man's voice, gay, mocking, jovial:

"Mother! mother! Where are you? Mother, you'll be *moon-struck*."

The woman turned gravely to Katherine.

"My son is calling me," she told her. "Good night, I am glad you came." Then she added wistfully, "This is the first time in many years that I have had a friend by me as I looked at the night."

With the sound of the man's voice and his gay, chaffing, "Mother, you'll be *moonstruck*," the mirage of the night had vanished; the frail, subtle tie that a moment before seemed to bind the two women into friendship had snapped. They hurried their several ways a little ashamed of themselves—for what, they didn't know exactly.

Next morning, when Katherine came out, there was a woman working in the garden below. Katherine made no doubt that it was her friend of the moonlight and made her way toward her.

"I am your new neighbor, Katherine Paine," she said.

The older woman smiled at her, greeting her in silence; but it was a silence with a more enfolding welcome than any words Katherine had ever heard, and she knew that they had gone on with their friendship begun so oddly the night before, for all they ignored their first meeting as something too apart from the or-dinary events of life to be discussed in broad daylight.

They walked several paces through the lovely garden before the older woman said, "I don't know whether you know my name or not—it's Eunice Gaunt." Her voice had none of the New England aggressiveness; it was indeed singularly sweet; it had a shy little note of hesitation very charming to listen to; and she chatted away about her garden as if to an old friend.

From the house there came the same jovial voice of the night before: "Mother, mother! Oh, there you are!" and a man swung down the path. He stared at Katherine in a way that was just short of disconcerting. It was almost as if he had said, "Yes, on the whole, I think you're a very pretty girl." He looked bold, stub-born, domineering; but one forgave him all that—there was a

large gaiety about him that went to one's heart. As he put his
hand on his mother's shoulder with an air of assured ownership,
it flashed over Katherine that all the same this dark bold man
was an odd sort of son for the delicate, sweet little lady to have
mothered.

She was saying, "This is our new neighbor, Miss Paine—"

"Mr. Gaunt?" Katherine murmured in acknowledgment of his
formal greeting.

"His name is Wetherill," Eunice Gaunt corrected tranquilly.

"Why in the world did you think my name was Gaunt?" he
demanded. The stand-and-deliver tone of his question and the
little lurking amusement in his voice embarrassed Katherine;
before she could answer, his mother explained:

"I told her my name was Eunice Gaunt—and so of course—"

He burst out into loud, gay laughter. "Couldn't you," he asked,
"for respectability's sake, add a 'Wetherill'?"

Mrs. Wetherill smiled gently at him. She seemed to have ab-
stracted herself from the scene; it was as if she had actually
walked away from them and left them together alone, as she
replied, "I think of myself, I suppose, as 'Eunice Gaunt.'"

"She's only had forty years to get used to 'Wetherill,' Miss
Paine." He turned a humorous eye on his mother, who kneeled
down to examine a plant; she had ceased to have any connection
with them.

"Well," said Wetherill, "I must go. I'm delighted to have met
you, Miss Paine; it's nice you're our near neighbor—I'm especially glad that you and my mother have made friends so soon.
Good-bye. Good-bye, 'Eunice Gaunt.' Please don't work too hard."
He bent over her and drew her toward him. "*Promise* me you
won't work too hard. —She does a man's work in this garden
every day, Miss Paine. —You'll go in and lie down like a good
girl. —Yes? and you'll call Ezra if you've anything heavy to
lift. —Yes?" He kissed his mother, and, with a pleasant nod to
Katherine, was off.

"Come," Mrs. Wetherill said. "I want you to see my daffodil

border under the hedge." She took up the conversation where her son had broken it, quite as if he had not been there at all. "Do you mind my asking you," she continued, "what wind blew you here?"

"I always took care of my mother," Katherine answered; "she had been ailing for years. She died not long ago, and I wanted a quiet place to rest."

Katherine had told the whole story of her uneventful life. It had left her at twenty-six with the eyes of a young girl.

For a moment Mrs. Wetherill looked at Katherine kindly, sweetly, as a sister might. Then, as if brooding over what she read in the girl's face, "How we eat up one another's lives!" she said.

Katherine had gone out that morning with an empty heart, and she came back with it filled. "Eunice Gaunt" had some way taken her in, opened the door of her heart to her; and Katherine wondered how she had passed by all the boundaries of reserve. She wondered again, as she had the night before, if her friend was perhaps as lonely as she; if, like herself, she needed so greatly the touch of a friendly hand; then she put that from her as absurd; there was a spiritual quality about the older woman, a sweet content that made the idea of her needing anything impossible, and companionship least of all.

Katherine had rented the house for the summer from an old friend of her mother's; so during the first few weeks of her stay a procession of ladies came to call, as they had evidently been asked to do by the owner of the house.

Mrs. Carling was the first to put the inevitable question, "How do you like Thornton?"

"Very much," Katherine answered, and added that she found her neighbor charming.

"Your neighbor?" Mrs. Carling wondered.

"Mrs. Wetherill," Katherine explained.

"Why, has *she* been up here?" asked the other.

"She 'runs in,' " said Katherine. "I think I 'ran in' first"; and Mrs. Carling gave forth an astonished, "Well, well!" To Katherine's look of inquiry, she explained, "She's a very quiet woman and rarely goes anywhere, and when she does, never a word out of her! Not a bit like her son. Henry's sociable enough."

She went away, leaving Katherine with the impression that Mrs. Wetherill's "running in" on her, which she had so taken as a matter of course, was for Mrs. Wetherill something very much out of the common. The other ladies of the village, as they called one after another, made this certain. The news of Mrs. Wetherill's neighborliness had gone forth, had been discussed, it was evident; and Katherine became very well acquainted with two people whom she amused herself by calling Mrs. Wetherill and Eunice Gaunt. One she knew only by hearsay. She was a silent woman, but so kindly that in the hard little New England village she was well beloved. Though she was no recluse and attended club meeting, doing her share of work in the village, she seldom opened her lips; and as for strangers—why, Mrs. Wetherill never went to see *them*. Of Mrs. Wetherill, Katherine was sure that she had never had so much as a glimpse; she couldn't in the least identify her with Eunice Gaunt. Eunice Gaunt for all her shy, hesitating manner had plenty to say—to Katherine anyway; companionship with her had a significance far beyond any companionship Katherine ever had. There was a certain freshness to all her words, as if her very silence had kept her mind young. Her thoughts came out clear and shining, minted quite fresh. How different the two, the Mrs. Wetherill of Thornton and her friend Eunice Gaunt were, Katherine could gauge by the curiosity their friendship excited. How alone Eunice Gaunt had been she saw only too plainly by the subdued, almost tremulous eagerness with which she gave Katherine her friendship.

She couldn't help wondering why her friend was shut so closely in the house of herself, Eunice Gaunt couldn't indeed have been more separated from the world around her had there been question of locks and keys.

"The house of herself," was Eunice Gaunt's own word.

"We all of us keep the real 'me' locked up in the house of ourself," she had said once to Katherine. "Sometimes it is self-consciousness that turns the key, and sometimes shyness, and more often circumstances." Then she added wistfully, "Some happy people come in and out at will." They walked side by side toward the little wood. Then Eunice Gaunt put her hand on the younger woman's with an indescribable gesture of tenderness. "You open the door for me, my dear," she said.

They stood face to face, silent in the contentment of perfect understanding, and Katherine went home, to wonder again why this loving, lovable woman should live so aloof from her fellows. How aloof this was she found out the first time they went out together; it was a party at Mrs. Carling's, and not only, as Mrs. Carling said, was there "not a word out of Mrs. Wetherill," but no promise of words or anything else. A diffident, smiling little old lady was all she seemed, who, as Mrs. Carling had put it, "wouldn't say 'Boo' to a goose"; one would as soon have expected treasures of companionship and understanding from the tufted chair on which she was sitting. As they left the house Henry Wetherill joined them.

"Well, mother," he chaffed, "did you tell them how to raise strawberries as good as yours?"—and without waiting for an answer, "Mother, you know," he explained, "is forever telling people how to raise things like hers; but *I* always have thought she was like the housekeepers who leave out the important thing when they give away their receipts."

There was a little edge of patronizing sarcasm in his tone, a mere suggestion only, so imperceptible that Katherine thought she must be mistaken. Mrs. Wetherill hadn't noticed it. She smiled absently at her son, and absently she left on Katherine the burden of keeping up a conversation, which she did not unwillingly. She liked Henry Wetherill, even if his abrupt way of asking questions disconcerted her to dumbness.

Mrs. Wetherill turned in at her own gate, saying good-bye to

Katherine with the same gentle formality she had shown in taking leave of the other ladies.

"I'll walk over with Miss Paine," Henry announced; and Mrs. Wetherill replied with a smiling, aloof, "Very well, dear," and "Good-bye, Katherine."

Once at Katherine's gate, "I think I'll come up and sit on your piazza," he said, "if you'll let me, I mean." He might have been asking permission smilingly of a child of twelve. He arranged himself comfortably in a big piazza chair, and from his attitude a passerby would have gathered that he was a daily visitor, so much at home he seemed.

He stared at Katherine in his embarrassing way, and when she felt herself flushing and caught a twinkle of a smile in his eyes, she had an unreasoning impulse to run away and lock the door in the face of this man, who stared one into self-consciousness and then smiled tolerantly over one's confusion.

There was, however, no hint of the smile in his voice as he said, "You don't know how glad I am that you and mother are such friends. I'm like my father, I hate a gadding, gossiping woman; but I think mother goes too far the other way."

Katherine warmed to him over his concern for his mother, and for a while they chatted together. To Katherine's shy invitation to come again, "As often as you like," he answered warmly.

When he left, Katherine felt that her house was empty, his large radiant personality had so filled it. This was not to be the last she saw of him that day. Later, as she made her way through the shrubbery in search of his mother, she heard Wetherill's voice saying, "Why don't you put them where Mrs. Wetherill told you to?"

His voice was not raised beyond his usual tone, but it cut like a knife. One couldn't call it bullying; it was a finer and more wounding way of getting what one wanted. "Why," he continued in exactly the same pitch, "don't you answer me?"

Katherine knew he could continue indefinitely on the same

insulting key. Through the bushes she could see the old gardener grubbing away at a flowerbed, Wetherill standing over him. While the old man did not answer or pause in his work, every outline of his old, bent figure expressed indignant protest. Mrs. Wetherill stood a few paces distant, trowel in hand; she was gazing off at the distant horizon, calm-browed, apparently unconscious of everything around her.

"*Why* didn't you put them where you were told? You think you know everything about a garden, but you're here, aren't you, to do what Mrs. Wetherill says?"

Katherine had gained the open lawn and was only a few steps away from her friends.

"Why—" Henry began again.

The old man jumped to his feet, his brown face red under the tan.

"I *be* doin' what she told me," he cried angrily. Then, appealing to Mrs. Wetherill, "Ain't I settin' them plants where you said?"

It seemed to Katherine that Mrs. Wetherill brought herself back as from a distance, and that it was an effort for her to realize what was going on.

"Why of course you are, Ezra," she answered, "why not?" She looked with surprise at the angry faces of the two men; then she saw Katherine. "Why, my dear child," she cried joyously, and stopped herself abruptly.

"Do you mind telling me," Henry asked his mother politely, "why in the world you let me sail into Ezra as I've been doing on your behalf, when after all he was doing what you said?"

She looked at him mildly. "I didn't hear what you were saying, Henry," she replied. Henry threw out his hands despairingly.

"Did you ever see such a pair, Miss Paine? I was perfectly sure Ezra was planting those roses where I heard mother tell him not to. I go for him loud enough to be heard across the street, and there she stands and, perfectly unruffled, lets me maul him. Actually she hasn't heard a word!"

He turned to his mother. "Where were you anyway? I never saw such an absent-minded woman! I talk and talk to her and I might as well be at the other side of a plate-glass window. Ezra, you old fool, why didn't you tell me sooner?"

Henry was entirely restored to good humor now, and his question to Ezra was almost an apology; but the old man did not answer or take any notice of him beyond hunching an offish shoulder.

"Look at them, Miss Paine," Henry exclaimed. "They never speak! Sometimes I think I'll buy a parrot for company!" He had put a large arm around his mother's neck and lifted her face up toward him like a child's. "Why don't you listen when I talk to you?" he demanded with savage affection.

"You're so like your father, dear," she replied irrelevantly.

Henry Wetherill hastened to fulfill his promise of coming often to see Katherine. Indeed, he formed a pleasant habit of "dropping in" for a few moments' chat, and while he was there he would not takes his eyes from her. She resented this at first; in the end she liked it, in much the fearsome way she liked Henry Wetherill. She was filled with a sense of excitement when she was with him. Conversation with him was an adventure. She could never tell when he would swoop down on her and extinguish her. What he did to give her this impression she could not for the life of her have told; but with him she felt she had to fight for her life or cease to be; the irritating part of it was that he was largely and serenely unaware of the effect he produced, and it is a humiliating thing to be fighting for life with a force which doesn't even realize that there is a fight.

So, between her companionship with the mother and her friendship with the son—for that, in spite of everything, was what it was coming to be—Katherine found her life very full.

She turned her face resolutely from that blank time when she would have to go away—after her tenancy had finished there was really no good excuse to keep her in a snowbound New England village—and when one day Henry Wetherill abruptly asked her what her plans for the winter were, she told him promptly, "Oh, I'll go south, I suppose."

At that moment Mrs. Carling came in, and when, in a few minutes, Henry Wetherill left, Mrs. Carling hardly waited for his broad shoulders to be turned before she raised significant eyebrows at Katherine, and followed it up with a surprised, "Well, you *have* done it—to be sure!"

"Done it!" Katherine wondered.

"Mother and son both! Well I declare," her visitor pursued with relish.

Evenly, but with inward annoyance, Katherine turned the subject. Mrs. Carling, however, had given her a clue to something that had mystified her. For the past few weeks Henry's mother, in some indescribable fashion, had seemed to slip away from her. There had been nothing one could put one's finger on; one could only say in the good old phrase that "things were different." There had been a mute appeal in her friend's eyes that Katherine now thought she understood.

"I must stop his coming here so much," Katherine decided; but in the bottom of her heart she knew how powerless she was to stop Henry Wetherill in anything that he wanted to do.

As he came up the path next day Katherine noticed that his brows were drawn in a sombre line. But as he saw her on the piazza waiting for him, he smiled at her brilliantly, and Katherine felt as if the sun had come out in the midst of a thunderstorm.

"Do you know," he began without preamble, his eyes looking directly into hers, "what I was thinking about when I came up the walk? I was wondering what would become of us all when you went. You don't know, I suppose, what you mean to me— I'm as lonely in a way as mother. Until you came I didn't know there was any other way to be—" He faltered a moment; and there was something very appealing in his hesitation: after all, he needed companionship and affection as do the weaker people of the world, and this touched Katherine to the quick. They stood facing each other, troubled and embarrassed, Katherine's heart beating fast. Now she knew: yesterday's absurdity had become the reality of today.

"You see how it is—you can't go away; you mustn't. I've *got* to have you." Then, as Katherine would have spoken—for it seemed to her that for all his tone of eager pleading she was being swept down the swift-flowing stream of his desire, and she wanted very much to tell him the truth, which was that she didn't love him in the very least—he stopped her.

"I know what you want to say. You want to tell me you don't care for me. I know that. But you don't hate me—you like me even, and after we're married I'd be a poor sort of a fellow if I couldn't make you care."

He cared; that was the principal thing after all, his manner seemed to say.

"It's all so right, don't you see," he pleaded eagerly. "You so belong to us."

The "it's all so right" was what won her. What if she didn't love him? It *was* all so right. The "us" touched her too. His constant thought for his mother was one of the things that drew her most to him.

"How would your mother feel about it?" Katherine asked shyly.

His mother's attitude in the matter had evidently never occurred to him. He looked at her blankly. "Why shouldn't she like it?" he demanded with a touch of anger. It was as if he had said, "Let her not like it and she'll see what she'll get"; and the little vague terror that he had given her from the first came over her; but it vanished as he laughed his loud boyish laugh.

"What an idea!" he shouted; "why, I can't remember mother's

not liking anything I've done since I was grown up. She likes *everything* I do," he repeated with serene assurance. "What made you think she wouldn't like it—my marrying you?" he persisted.

"Why, it's seemed to me that the more I saw of you the less I saw of her; the better I got to know you the more she withdrew herself," Katherine faltered.

He looked at her, a tender glow in his eyes. "Don't worry about that," he assured her lightly. "Mother's only part there most of the time; she's the most absent-minded woman in the world—always in the clouds."

And Katherine forbore telling him how much "Eunice Gaunt" was "there" when her son wasn't. He evidently was not aware of her curious smiling aloofness. Katherine longed to ask him if he never got behind it, never saw the other side; but she only insisted, "I don't think she'll like it."

"What a funny girl you are," he said, smiling. "We'll find mother and ask her, and then—"

"And then," Katherine interrupted, "if she doesn't like it—I love her so dearly I couldn't for the world—"

"You'll see," Henry Wetherill repeated. There was not a shadow of doubt in him; if there was anything he was sure of, it was his mother.

They found Mrs. Wetherill in the garden. "Mother," he called to her joyously, "this foolish girl thinks you wouldn't like me to marry her." His tone was gay, happy, assured. There was a certain finality in it also, as if she already belonged to him, as he added, "Tell her you think she'll be a good wife to me."

For a fraction of a second, Mrs. Wetherill stared at them wide eyed. Then, "She would make the best wife in the world for anyone," she cried warmly, and kissed Katherine.

"You see," Henry triumphed, and Katherine wondered if he actually had not noticed that his mother had turned white at his words; if he could not see how her hands trembled as she smiled her little vague smile at him.

"I'll leave you to talk things over," he told them. Mrs. Wetherill stood watching him until he disappeared beyond the tawny lilies into the house.

"Now tell me the truth," Katherine said gently, taking both her friend's hands in her own.

Mrs. Wetherill raised her troubled, sombre face to hers; her mouth quivered pitifully; slow tears gathered in her eyes.

"You don't need to say anything," Katherine went on still more tenderly. "I can understand. He's your only son—"

But as Henry Wetherill's mother whispered under her breath, "Oh, I can't live it all over again," Katherine understood that here was more than a mother who finds it hard to give up her dear son.

"You're so near me," Mrs. Wetherill went on, so low that it was as if she were afraid to hear her own words, "that I can't let you suffer what you would have to. You're so near me that you seem to me like my own child—"

In this moment they passed beyond the door of friendship. They stood for the moment closer than it is often possible for one human being to come to another. They were at the very threshold of Eunice Gaunt's hidden life. For Katherine's sake she had opened a door that such women keep closed even against themselves.

"I hoped," she went on, "that you would see for yourself— you see so many things other people don't—"

"You don't think I'd be happy with Henry," Katherine suggested gently. She was beginning to read the riddle of her friend's life, her curious relation with her son; her attitude toward the world began to have a new meaning.

"Men like Henry don't know how they hurt women like us," Henry's mother said gently. It was an apology, not an accusation. "Henry's like his father," she went on in the same gentle tone. "All the Wetherill men are alike. They crush the weaker people around them out of existence; they don't mean to—they don't even know they do it." While she told what her son was, she had to cry out in the same breath, "It's not his fault." With a gesture of unfathomable motherliness, as if Katherine was really her daughter, she put her hand on the girl's head and gazed long into her eyes.

"My dear," she asked, "do you *love* Henry? Your face is the face of a little girl, as it was when I first saw you—"

"He said," Katherine faltered, "that it didn't matter, that he would make me like him."

"Poor Henry," said his mother; "if you had loved him, there wouldn't have been anything to say. I should have lived over through you all that has been hard in my life. It would have been like having my own at war with my own. I should have had to know that no day of yours went by without its humiliation, without its bruise. I should have known that it was my son's fault. He couldn't help doing it—and you couldn't help him. You would try and try, and then you would see that neither patience nor submission nor love could change him."

All the things Katherine had failed to understand fitted in together like parts of a puzzle. Now she knew why her friend was as she was. Henry's father and Henry had shut her into the "house of herself" with their noisy wounding anger, with their wounding laughter. She had a sharp vision of Henry's bullying tenderness, of his mocking laugh, of the glimpse she had had of his insatiable irritation; and a fear of him came over her, the fear of the weaker animal for the stronger. She meditated over what she saw, and Eunice brooded over her own past; at last she cried out—it was her only moment of bitterness—

"They are the men with no woman in them. They are the ones who first created our meannesses and weaknesses and then laughed and scolded and sneered at us for being as they made us." Her voice softened. "They can't help themselves for their unconscious abuse of power," she said.

This was her final judgment of the two men who had made up her life—her husband and her son. It was her only revolt, her only outward sign of discontent. Now she stood upright, as immovable as a figure of justice, and in her Katherine saw more than a woman telling the long tragedy of her life. It was as if through the voice of her friend she heard the immemorial cry of all the weaker creatures who have suffered through the strong. Without passion or anger she put in words woman's world-old quarrel with man. Bits of it would come to Katherine long afterwards.

"They are the sort of men who make cowards and liars of women," was one.

"I understood the meannesses of women when I had been married a few years."

"Often I have seen on a woman's face a look of anger or fear or cunning, and I knew that here was another of me. There are more of us than you think, and we use in self-defense guile, or flattery, or affection, or submission, according to our natures."

"There are few women who haven't been sneered at and reproached for being women."

She told her story, a few sentences at a time; and unconsciously she showed Katherine her final victory, her acceptance of life as it was, the conquest of her own inward peace. She told how she had borne their unconscious brutality, first with tears, then with smiling aloofness; her road to escape had been a withdrawal from them and from everyone, for she had left no point where they could hurt her.

"How did you bear it all?" Katherine asked at last.

Her friend looked at her in gentle surprise. "I loved both of them dearly always," she said. "And I knew they loved me even more dearly. Love goes deeper than understanding. We've lived our lives, Henry and Henry's father and I, talking different languages; but I have always been upheld by their love for me and, curiously enough, by their dependence on me. If you—had cared—" she did not finish, but smiled at Katherine, all tenderness in her eyes. Then Katherine knew that the secret of her inner content was more than self-mastery; she had always had them, whatever else had been lacking; mysteriously they had made up to her for all the pain they had all unconsciously given her.

She had no time to answer, for Henry was bearing down on them, gay and confident. At the two women's serious aspect, "Well?" he asked, raising his eyebrows in question.

"I have been telling Katherine not to marry you," his mother said steadily.

He stared aghast. "You have been telling her *what?*" he repeated; his tone was low, there was in every word the concentration of anger. "What does she mean?" he demanded of Katherine. "Answer me."

"There's no use asking her," Mrs. Wetherill told him simply. "I'm sorry, Henry, I had to do it. You could never have made Katherine happy."

She had told him everything he could understand.

"Let her speak for herself," Wetherill commanded sternly. "Katherine, will you marry me?" The entreaty in his voice, his anger, his very lack of understanding went to Katherine's heart. She was nearer loving him that moment than she had ever been. Had they been alone she realized that she must have promised whatever he wished—and then run away. With her friend's protecting arm around her she managed to falter forth, "No, oh no!"

He turned on his mother.

"You've made mischief between us!" Anger vibrated in his low voice. "You've dared, *you, you*, to judge whether I could make her happy! *You* know whether this means anything to me! *You* know whether I've ever cared for anyone else. The first woman I care for— Oh!" He was white with the rage and despair of it. The creature on earth he loved most had turned on him, treacherously. His world had gone to pieces under his feet, and he raged at it. It was the man's side of it, old as time; and like the first man betrayed by his faithful servant, he raged against the faithlessness of women.

There was nothing mean in his anger; it didn't occur to him to try and control it because of Katherine; such as he was he showed himself. He resorted to no trick of gentleness to win her. Like his kind he had got everything through the brute force of his will, as his ancestors had got everything by might of arm. If all the protest of women from all time against the unconscious abuse of power had been his mother's story, all man's rancor against woman was in his denunciation. As his anger spent itself, he stood before the two women in very despair at his impotence. He didn't understand them; he didn't understand anything. There was not one of the many questions he put himself that he could answer. His own had turned on him. Why? He couldn't tell. The woman he loved had all but given herself to him, and then turned from him. Why? He didn't know. All he knew was the common knowledge of the men of his kind, that women were the enemies of men, creatures one couldn't understand, moved by irrational impulse, untrustworthy and fickle. And as his mother watched him she understood, she trembled for him in a very anguish of pity. He stood before them, a tragic, lonely figure, suffering as a child suffers without knowing why; then he turned from them abruptly and left them. Katherine threw her arms around her friend.

"You shan't stand it," she cried. "Come away with me. You mustn't live with him any longer."

But Eunice Gaunt did not hear her. She watched Henry out of sight while slow tears gathered in her eyes. She breathed so low that Katherine barely heard her.

"Oh, my poor son!" and again, "My poor son!" and then, "Oh, how could I hurt you so much?"

THE BARKING

Ingeborg Bachmann
Translated by Ingeborg Day

Ingeborg Bachmann, born in Klagenfurt, Austria, in 1926, was a poet, short story writer, critic, dramatist, and novelist until her tragic death from burning in 1973. She studied law and philosophy, receiving her Ph.D. from the University of Vienna in 1950, where the subject of her dissertation on Martin Heidegger's existential philosophy forecast her later concerns as a writer. She experimented with many forms: radio plays dealing with escapism and people's ultimate responsibility for each other; two collections of short stories, one of which, The Thirtieth Year, *has been translated by Michael Bullock; two volumes of poetry (the first,* Die Gestundete Zeit [Borrowed Time], *published in 1953, won the prestigious "Gruppe 47" award); and two opera librettos. Her selected poetry,* Gedichte, *which appeared in 1964, won the Georg Buchner prize. Her only completed novel,* Malina *(1971), was described by one critic as "the process of subjective exploration pushed to its limits."*

Bachmann shared with other German postwar writers the pessimistic conviction that the disintegration of values prophesied by Nietzsche is almost complete. In all her work, as in "The Barking" (translated for the first time into English in Ms. magazine), there is an implicit awareness of German guilt and escapism. "The Barking" is a tour de force in the gradual revelation of the true character of a man through the lies that two women tell each other to protect both him and themselves. The reader alone experiences the women's failure to relate except through the famous man.

OLD MRS. JORDAN had been called "old Mrs. Jordan" for the last three decades, because after her there had been first one young Mrs. Jordan and now another young Mrs. Jordan. She lived in Hietzing, but in a run-down house, in a one-room apartment with a tiny kitchen and a bathroom without a tub. Every month she received one thousand schillings from her famous son Leo, the professor. She was able to live on that, even though those thousand schillings had greatly diminished in value over the last twenty years and now she was barely able to pay an elderly woman, a Mrs. Agnes, to "look in" on her twice a week and clean up a bit. From that money she saved for birthday and Christmas presents for her son and her grandchild from the professor's first marriage. Punctually each Christmas, the first young Mrs. Jordan sent the boy to old Mrs. Jordan to collect his gift. Leo was too busy to think about his mother, and since he had become well known and his local reputation had blossomed into international fame he was even busier.

A change came about only when the latest young Mrs. Jordan began to visit the old woman as often as possible. The old woman soon admitted to herself that the second young Mrs. Jordan was really a nice, sweet girl, and she said each time: But, Franziska, this isn't right. You shouldn't come so often, and what a waste of money! You probably have enough expenses, but Leo, of course, is such a good son!

Each time Franziska came, she brought something with her: delicacies, and sherry, and a few little things from a bakery. She had guessed that the old woman liked to drink a little, and now and then a bit more than just a sip. Old Mrs. Jordan also found it important to have food in the house "for company," since Leo might stop by and mustn't notice that she didn't have much of anything and that she worried all day over how to budget her money and how much had to be left over for presents.

Her apartment was extremely neat, but there was a slight smell of old woman in it—something she wasn't aware of but which quickly drove Leo Jordan away. Besides, he had little time to waste and absolutely no idea what to talk about with his eighty-five-year-old mother. He had told Franziska how amused he had been in the past, whenever he had had affairs with married women, because old Mrs. Jordan had slept poorly then and made odd, complicated allusions: that she was afraid for his life and that his women's husbands were dangerous and jealous and bloodthirsty. She had relaxed when he married Franziska, who had no jealous husbands lurking in bushes but was happy and young, an orphan, not from an educated family though she had an educated brother. (Educated families and individuals were very important to Mrs. Jordan, even though she never met any such people, only heard stories about them.)

The old woman and Franziska talked almost exclusively about Leo, who was the only productive topic for the two of them, and Franziska had to look through the photo album many times: Leo in a carriage, Leo at the beach, then Leo through the years—on trips, gluing stamps into his stamp book, and so on—until he went into the army. The Leo she came to know through the old woman was totally different from the one she was married to. When the two women sat drinking their sherry, the old woman would say, He was a complicated child, an unusual boy—actually you might have predicted how he's turned out.

Franziska listened happily to old Mrs. Jordan's assertions for a while—how Leo had always been so very good to his mother, always helping her in all possible ways—until she noticed that something was off somewhere, and then she realized to her dismay what it was: the old woman was afraid of her son.

The old woman (who thought of this as a clever trick which Franziska would never see through, since she admired her husband blindly) would sometimes say, quickly and under her breath, But please, not a word to Leo—you know how solicitous he is, he might get upset—don't tell him there is something wrong with my knee; it's such a little thing, but he might get upset.

Franziska knew that Leo never got upset, certainly not about his mother, and that he always listened to his wife's stories about her visits rather absentmindedly, but she suppressed her first understanding of the situation. She had, unfortunately, already told him about the knee, but now she swore to the old woman she wouldn't say a word about it; Leo had first been angry and then had said, pacifying her, that he really couldn't drive out to Hietzing for such a trifle. Tell her—and he rattled off some medical terms—she should buy this and that, and do and walk as little as possible. Franziska had bought the medications without comment, and said in Hietzing that she had secretly, without mentioning any names, talked to her husband's assistant, who had given her this advice. But she couldn't imagine how she alone, without the help of a practical nurse, would manage to keep the old woman in bed. And she didn't dare ask Leo about it, because a nurse cost money. She found herself between two fronts: old Mrs. Jordan didn't want to listen to her; Leo Jordan, for quite different reasons, didn't want to listen either.

During the time of the inflamed knee, Franziska lied to her husband a few times, quickly drove to Hietzing (supposedly on her way to the hairdresser), cleaned up the little apartment, and brought along assorted things—a radio, for instance. Afterward, she felt uneasy—Leo was bound to notice such an expenditure. She quickly switched a few sums around in her checking account and transferred money from her savings account. (They had agreed that the savings account would be her iron reserve, and used only for some kind of catastrophe which, they hoped, would never happen. It would have to be a very minor catastrophe in any case, since it was a rather meager amount, from the time when she and her brother had divided what little remained after the death of their parents. All that was left was a run-down shed of a house in southern Carynthia, slowly falling apart.)

She finally called a general practitioner in the neighborhood and had him treat the old woman. She paid him, again from her iron reserve. More important than the money was the fact that she couldn't let the doctor know who she was, or who the old woman was, because it would have been bad for Leo's reputation, and Leo's reputation was important to Franziska, too. The old woman had, at times, used a crutch in the past, but after the knee episode she needed it all the time, and so Franziska sometimes drove her into town.

Shopping with her was a laborious procedure. Once she only needed a comb, but combs like those "in her time" were not to be had. And while the old woman was polite, and stood in the store with dignity, she angered the salesgirl by looking suspiciously at the price tags, and couldn't keep from whispering loudly to Franziska that these were robber prices and that they should go somewhere else. The salesgirl, who couldn't understand why a comb was such a big problem for the old woman, said insolently that they wouldn't get a cheaper comb anywhere. Self-consciously, Franziska picked up the comb the old woman had liked and paid for it quickly, saying, It's a Christmas present from us, a little early; prices really have gone up horribly. The old woman felt her defeat and said nothing; but even at robber prices, if you used to be able to get such a comb for two schillings and now it cost sixty, well, she could no longer understand much in this world.

After some time they had exhausted the topic "good son." Now, more and more often, Franziska brought the conversation around to the old woman herself. All Franziska knew about her was that Leo's father had died early, of a heart attack, very suddenly, on a staircase. That must have been a long time ago, because if you bothered to figure it out and actually counted the years, this woman had been a widow for nearly fifty years: first busy rearing her only child, and then an old woman, alone. She never spoke about her marriage, only in connection with Leo, who'd had a difficult life without a father. Never, obsessed as she was with Leo, did she compare his life to that of Franziska, who had lost both parents early; only Leo had had a difficult life.

Then it turned out that his life hadn't been pure hardship after all. All his schooling had been paid for by a distant cousin: Johannes, whom Franziska had heard about in a few critical sentences—some relative, swimming in money, an eternal loafer, middle-aged now, with ridiculous interests, dabbling in art, collecting Chinese lacquer things—in a word, a parasite such as exists in all families. Franziska also knew that Johannes was homosexual and had been amazed that Leo, who should at least professionally have been able to view homosexuality and other phenomena neutrally and scientifically, bad-mouthed this cousin, as if Johannes had caught objets d'art, homosexuality, and an inheritance—all at once and all through his own fault.

But at that time Franziska still admired her husband to a degree that only allowed her to be irritated, and hurt. To her relief, whenever they talked of those hard times, she also heard from the old woman that Leo was immeasurably grateful and had helped Johannes very much. Johannes had been in numerous difficulties, the kind one had best not talk about. The old woman hesitated and, taking courage—she was, after all, sitting next to a woman married to a psychiatrist—said: You must understand that Johannes is sexual.

Franziska controlled herself and did not burst out laughing. She was sure this was the boldest the old woman had been in years. She was becoming more and more open with Franziska and described how Leo had often given Johannes advice (of course without charging Johannes for it), but things were hopeless with Johannes. When someone had no intention of changing for the better, it was understandable that Leo felt rebuffed.

Franziska carefully translated this naïve tale and understood even less why Leo should speak so critically and spitefully about his cousin. At the time she was still unable to see the obvious reason: Leo disliked being reminded of an obligation. He disliked being reminded of Johannes or his mother or his earlier women, all of whom were to him a conspiracy of creditors. He escaped from these reminders by disparaging them, both to himself and to others. He talked the same way about his first wife: she had been a paragon of devilry, baseness, and lack of empathy—all of which had become obvious during the divorce, when her noble father had hired a lawyer to secure part of the money for the child, money she had given Leo during his second difficult period, as a young doctor. It was a frighteningly high sum to Franziska, but, she was told, one could expect nothing less from "the baroness," as Leo called his first wife. Her family had always treated him as an upstart; they'd never had the slightest idea of who they'd had in their midst. Leo found it amusing that the baroness had never remarried; after him, no fool had come along, as young and dumb and poor as he had been back then, who would marry such a precious woman. Of his work she had understood nothing, nothing; and as for the arrangement with his son, she did act fairly in this matter, but only to show all the world how noble she was, for no other reason.

That thorny, arduous climb to the status of genius doctor had become religion to Franziska by then, and she told herself again and again of how he had made his way to the top under indescribable difficulties and despite the obstacle of that awful marriage. The burden that his mother was to him, financially and emotionally, wasn't easy for him either, and Franziska was able to take this one burden from his shoulders. Even though it would not have occurred to her, under different circumstances, to spend her free hours with an old woman, those hours became, when she thought of Leo, something special: a gesture, a proof of love for him, allowing him to keep his attention totally focused on his work.

And Leo was good to Franziska. He said she overdid her care for his mother—a call now and then would be enough. For the last few years, the old woman had had a telephone, which she dreaded more than appreciated. She disliked using it, and when she did, she always shouted loudly into the receiver, and then couldn't hear very well what the other person said. Besides, the telephone cost entirely too much, but Franziska mustn't tell Leo that.

The old woman, excited by Franziska, her second glass of sherry in front of her, began to talk about old times, her very early years. It turned out that she wasn't from an educated family, that her father had been a mitten-and-sock knitter in a small factory in lower Austria; that she had been the oldest of eight children but had had a wonderful time nonetheless on her first job. She had worked for a Greek family, immensely rich. They'd had a little boy, the most beautiful child she had ever seen, and she became his governess. And being a governess was a very good position, nothing demeaning about it. The young wife of the Greek had servants enough—oh, yes, she'd been extraordinarily lucky, it was difficult at that time to get such a good job.

The name of the child had been Kiki. When the old woman began to speak more and more often about him—recalling in detail what Kiki had said, how sweet and funny and affectionate he had been, the walks they had taken together—a glow came into her eyes that was never there when she spoke of her own child. Kiki had been a little angel, without bad manners—she emphasized that: without bad manners. The separation must have been dreadful. They didn't tell Kiki that his governess was leaving, and she had cried all night. Years later she had tried to find out what had happened to the family. Once she had heard they were traveling, then again that they were in Greece, and now she didn't know what had become of Kiki, who must be over sixty—yes, over sixty, she said, deep in thought. She'd had to leave because the Greeks were going on their first long trip at the time and couldn't take her along and she received a beautiful parting gift from Kiki's mother.

The old woman got up, rummaged around in a small box, and showed Franziska a pin, genuine diamonds. She still asked herself if she hadn't been let go because the young woman had realized that Kiki liked her better than his own mother. She was able to understand that, but it had been a terrible blow, and she had never gotten over it.

Franziska thoughtfully examined the pin, which might indeed have been valuable, though she didn't know anything about jewelry. She felt that this Kiki had meant more to the old woman than Leo.

The old woman hesitated to talk about Leo's childhood. When she did begin, she would break off, alarmed, saying quickly, Those were trifles. Boys are so hard to raise, and he never did it intentionally. He had such a hard life then, and it was difficult for me, too, but you get everything back a thousandfold when a child grows up and then finds his way and becomes famous, so famous—he was really much more like his father than me, you know.

Franziska carefully replaced the pin, and the old woman became alarmed again. Please, Franziska, not a word about it to Leo—about the pin—he doesn't know about it, but I have my plans; if I get sick I could sell it, and I wouldn't be even more of a burden to him. Franziska hugged the old woman tightly, and felt afraid. You must never do that, promise me that, selling this pin. You are no burden to us at all.

On her way home she drove aimlessly through town, there was such turbulence in her. The old woman would sell her pin while she and Leo were spending large amounts of money, traveling and entertaining. She couldn't stop thinking about what she should say to Leo, yet something unsettling, a sense of alarm, had begun to take hold of her. Somehow—even if the old woman was confused and did exaggerate—she was right. Franziska ended up saying nothing about it at home, mentioning gaily, in passing, that Mother was doing well.

Before their trip to the London Congress, Franziska secretly entered into a contract with a garage that rented taxis and limousines. She paid a deposit and later told the old woman, We've had an idea. You shouldn't be out on your own, so now you just call a taxi each time; it costs very little. It's a token of appreciation from an old patient, but don't talk about it and especially not to Leo. You know him, he doesn't like anyone thanking him. You go into town whenever you need something and have the car wait, and only let Mr. Pineider drive you, the young one. He doesn't know, by the way, that his father has been a patient of Leo's; that comes under professional secrecy, you know. Promise me, for Leo's sake, that you'll take a car; it will make us feel better.

In the beginning, the old woman hardly made use of the taxi, and Franziska was cross with her when they returned from England. The old woman's leg was worse again, because she had done all her shopping on foot and had once even taken the streetcar into the inner city. Energetically, as to an obstinate child, Franziska said: This simply must not happen again.

About then, the topics of conversation involving Kiki and the life of a young nursemaid in Vienna, before World War I and before her marriage, had been exhausted. Now Franziska told stories, especially when she returned from trips with Leo: about a fabulous speech he had delivered at the congress, for instance. He had given a special copy of the speech to Franziska to bring to his mother. The old woman read the title laboriously: "The Significance of Endogen and Exogen Factors in Connection with the Occurrence of Paranoid and Depressive Psychoses of Former Concentration Camp Inmates and Escapees." Franziska explained that this was only a short preamble to a much larger work Leo was writing, that she was allowed to work with him and that it would probably be the most important book in its field, a definitive work of incalculable importance.

The old woman was strangely silent. She surely didn't understand the importance of this work, maybe nothing at all of what her son was doing. Then she said, surprisingly, I hope he won't make too many enemies with that, here in Vienna, and such a topic. . . .

Franziska became excited. But that would really be very good; it is a provocation, after all, and Leo isn't afraid of anyone. This is the only type of work for him. It goes far beyond scientific importance.

Yes, of course, said the old woman quickly, and he knows how to defend himself, and you're bound to have enemies if you're famous. I'm only thinking of Johannes, but that was so long ago. Did you know that he was in a concentration camp toward the end of the war, for a year and a half? Franziska was surprised; she had not known that, but now she didn't understand the connection either.

The old woman said she no longer wanted to talk about the subject, but then talked about it after all. It had all been quite dangerous for Leo—having a relative who, well, you understand. Yes, of course, said Franziska. She was still disturbed, though, even after this explanation, because the old woman had such a cumbersome way of expressing things and then not expressing them after all. Franziska didn't know just where she stood, even though she was suddenly filled with pride, that someone in Leo's family had been through something so awful and that Leo in his tactful, unassuming way had never spoken about it, not even about the danger this had meant to him as a young doctor.

The old woman no longer wanted to talk, but said, out of context, Do you hear that, too?

What?

The dogs, she said. Years ago, there weren't that many dogs in Hietzing, but I've heard some bark again and at night they bark, too. Mrs. Schönthal next door has a poodle, but he rarely barks, a very sweet dog. I see her almost every day when I go shopping, but we only say hello to each other; her husband isn't educated.

Franziska had to drive back into town quickly. This time she wanted to ask Leo what it meant that his mother had suddenly started to talk about dogs, whether it was a symptom that might have something to do with her age. Franziska had also noticed that the old woman had become very excited over ten schillings that had been lying on the table and were gone after Mrs. Agnes had left. Such excitement over ten missing schillings—something she surely imagined—also seemed to be a sign of an ongoing process of some kind; the cleaning woman could not possibly have taken them. She was what one called in better circles a "decent" woman, who came more out of pity than for the money, which she didn't need. It was a favor, nothing less. Old Mrs. Jordan's haphazard gifts—a worn-out, ancient handbag or some other useless object—would hardly have kept Mrs.

Agnes coming; she had long understood that she had nothing to expect from the old woman or from her son. Franziska had talked calmly with the old woman, as with a child, since she didn't want to lose those valuable household services over some stubbornness born of age and groundless suspicion.

More and more often she found the old woman at the window when she arrived, and they no longer sat next to each other when Franziska came to drink sherry and eat small bakery cakes. The business with the dogs continued, at the same time her loss of hearing became more severe, and Franziska wasn't sure what to do next. Something had to be done, and one of these days Leo, from whom she kept everything, would no longer be able to avoid dealing with his mother.

Only it happened that just then things began to get complicated between her and Leo, and she discovered that she was intimidated by him—afraid of him, really. Just once, in a fit of her old courage, in an effort to get over a fear she didn't understand, she suggested during dinner: Why don't we have your mother live with us here? We have enough room, and then our Rosi would be with her all the time, and you wouldn't have to ever worry about her. Besides, she's so quiet and never asks for anything, she'd never disturb you and certainly not me.

Leo, who was in a good mood that evening and seemed to be secretly enjoying something—she had no idea what, yet she used this opportunity—laughed and said: What an idea. You have absolutely no feeling for the situation! My dear, old people shouldn't be uprooted. It would only depress her and she needs her freedom. She's a strong woman who has lived alone for decades. You hardly know her the way I do. She would die of fear here! Think of all the people who come to our house. She'd worry for hours over using the bathroom, afraid one of us wanted to use it. Now, little Franziska, don't make such a face. I find your obsession sweet and admirable, but you'd kill her with that wonderful idea of yours. Believe me, I simply know more about such things.

But what about the dogs . . . ? Franziska stuttered because she hadn't wanted to talk about that at all and immediately wished she could take back every word.

What, said her husband, totally changed. Does she still want a mongrel?

I don't understand, said Franziska. Why should she . . . you don't really mean she wants a dog?

Well, of course, and I'm certainly glad that this childish interlude passed so quickly. She simply couldn't take care of a dog, too, not at her age. She's supposed to take care of herself. That's more important to me. She doesn't have any idea in her progressive senility what a pest a dog is.

She never said that, Franziska answered shyly. I don't believe she wants a dog. I meant to say something completely different, but it doesn't matter, I'm sorry. Will you have some cognac? Are you going to work some more? Can I type something for you?

During her next visit, Franziska didn't know how to go about asking the wary old woman something she needed to know. She started in a roundabout way. By the way, I saw Mrs. Schönthal's poodle, really a pretty dog. I like poodles very much, all animals. I grew up in the country. We always had dogs. . . . I mean, my grandparents and other people in the village . . . and cats, of course, too. Wouldn't it be good for you to have a dog or a cat, now that you can't read so easily . . . though that'll improve again, of course. . . . I, for instance, would love a dog; it's just, you know, in the city a dog is a burden and it's not ideal for the dog, either, but here in Hietzing it would run around in the yard and you could take it for walks. . . .

The old woman said excitedly, A dog, no, no, I don't want a dog. Franziska realized she had made a mistake, but at the same time she felt she hadn't hurt the old woman's feelings as she might have by suggesting a myna bird or a canary. She must be upset about something quite different.

After a while, the old woman said very quietly, Nuri was a

very beautiful dog. I got along very well with him. That was, let me think, that must have been five years ago, but then I gave him away, to an asylum or someplace where they sell dogs to other people. Leo doesn't like dogs. What had excited her so had indeed been something else.

No, what am I saying here—it was all completely different—there was something in that dog I didn't understand. He hated Leo. Every time Leo came, he rushed at him and barked like mad, and then he almost bit him. Leo was so indignant—that's natural, of course, a dog that's so dangerous—but Nuri never was like that at any other time, not even with strangers, and then I gave him away, of course. I couldn't have him bark at and bite Leo. No, that was too much—Leo should feel comfortable when he comes to visit and not have to get upset over a spoiled dog.

Franziska thought that Leo, even without a dog that jumped at him and disliked him, came very rarely, even less often now that Franziska visited his mother for him. When had he been here last? Once, they had gone on a little ride, the three of them, along the Weinstrasse and into the Helenenthal, and then they had taken the old woman to lunch at some inn; but except for that one time, only Franziska visited.

Please don't mention anything to Leo, that incident with Nuri really upset him; he's very easily hurt, you know, and I can't forgive myself to this day for being selfish enough to want to have Nuri. Old people are selfish, dear Franziska, you don't understand that now because you're still so young and generous, but when you get to be very old, those selfish desires come along, and one simply must not give in to them. If Leo didn't take care of me, where would I be? What would have happened to me? His father died so suddenly and was never able to plan ahead, and there wasn't any money, either. My husband was a little frivolous, not a spendthrift, you understand, but he had his troubles and no head for money; in that respect Leo isn't like him at all. Way back then I was able to work, because I had to, for the boy, and I was still young, but what would I do today? My one fear has always been having to go to some old people's home, and Leo would never allow that, and if I didn't have this apartment, I'd have to go to a home and no dog is worth that.

Franziska listened stiffly and thought, So that's how it is, then, that's how it stands, she gave the dog away for him. What kind of people are we, she said to herself—unable to think: what kind of human being is my husband? How cruel everyone is, and she thinks she is selfish while we have everything.

So as not to show her tears she quickly unpacked a small parcel from Meinl, little things, and pretended not to understand. Oh, by the way—I don't know where my head is these days—I only brought you some tea and coffee, and a little lox and Russian salad; it really doesn't go together very well, but I couldn't concentrate while I did my shopping. Leo is going on a trip and his manuscript isn't ready, but he's going to call you tonight and in a week he'll be back again.

He should take a rest, said the old woman. Why don't you take care of that; you two haven't had any time off this year. Franziska said excitedly, That's a great idea. I'll talk him into it somehow, one has to be a little crafty with him, but he does constantly overwork and I'll have to put brakes on him.

Franziska didn't know that this was her last visit with the old woman and that she no longer needed to be crafty, because other events occurred, and with such tornadolike fury that she almost forgot the old woman and a lot of other things.

The old woman called her son to ask why Franziska hadn't been to see her. She worried, she said; but her son sounded gay and unworried, and once he came for a visit and stayed twenty minutes. He didn't touch the cookies she offered him, didn't drink her sherry, and didn't talk about Franziska, but he did talk quite a bit about himself and that made her happy, since he hadn't done that for a long time. He was going on a trip;

he had to take some time off. When she heard "Mexico," she did become alarmed—wasn't that the place where they had scorpions and revolutions, savages and earthquakes? But he laughed at her, kissed her, and promised to write.

He did send a few postcards, which she read devoutly. Franziska's greetings were not on the cards. But Franziska called her from Carynthia—how young people throw their money away—asking whether everything was going well. She spoke about Leo, and the old woman shouted every few minutes, This is getting too expensive, child! But Franziska talked on, yes, she had succeeded, he was taking some time off now, finally, and she had to see her brother, some things to do, that's why she hadn't been able to go with Leo. Family things in Carynthia. Because of the house.

Then the old woman received a curious letter from Franziska, just a few lines, conveying nothing except affection and that she wanted the old woman to have this photograph, taken by her, of Leo, apparently on the Semmering, laughing, surrounded by a snowy landscape. The old woman decided not to say anything to Leo, and he never asked. She hid the picture in her box under the pin.

She was unable to read books now, and bored by the radio; she only wanted newspapers, and Mrs. Agnes brought her those. In the newspapers, over which she pored for hours, she read the obituaries: it gave her a certain satisfaction when someone younger than herself had died. Well, now, even Professor Haderer, he couldn't have been more than seventy. Mrs. Schönthal's mother died, too, of cancer, not even sixty-five. The old woman stiffly extended her condolences in the grocery store without looking at the poodle, and then went home again and stood by the window. She slept better than old people supposedly do, but she woke up often, and then she immediately heard the dogs.

She was frightened every time the cleaning woman came. Since Franziska's visits had ended, anyone's coming and going disturbed her. And it seemed to her that she was changing: she was now seriously afraid of suddenly falling in the street, or of not being in control of herself. Whenever she needed something in town, she dutifully called young Mr. Pineider, who drove her around. She got used to this small comfort.

She completely lost her sense of time, and when Leo came to see her, deeply tanned, just for a minute, she didn't know whether he'd just come back from Mexico or when he'd been there. But she was too clever to ask, and then she surmised from one sentence that he had just returned from a trip to Italy. Absentmindedly she said, Good, good, that was good for you. And while he was telling her about something, the dogs began to bark, and she felt herself encircled by a soft, soft fear, and then she realized that she no longer feared her son. The fear of a whole lifetime had suddenly left her.

When he said on his way out, Next time I'll bring Elfi with me, you do have to meet her—she had no idea what he was talking about. Was he no longer married to Franziska, and since when, and how many wives had he had—she couldn't remember how long he had lived with Franziska—and she said, Do bring her along. Good. If she's only good for you. For a moment she was sure Nuri was with her again and would fly at Leo, bark at him, so near was the barking now. Out of habit she thanked him, just in case, and he asked, amazed, But for what? Ah, now I've forgotten to bring you my book after all. A phenomenal success. I'll have it sent.

She allowed him to hug her and found herself alone again, given over to the barking. It came from all the gardens and apartments of Hietzing. An invasion of beasts had begun: they came closer, barking at her incessantly. And she stood there, upright as ever, no longer dreaming of her time with Kiki and the Greeks, no longer thinking of the day her last ten schillings had disappeared and Leo had lied about it to her. She only continued, strenuously, to try to understand things better. She wanted to throw away her mementos, especially the pin and the photo, so that nothing of Leo would be found after her death, but she couldn't think of a good hiding place, only the trash can. But she trusted Mrs. Agnes less and less, and she suspected that the woman would rummage through the garbage and find the pin. Once she said, a little too harshly, Why don't you at least give the bones and scraps to the dogs?

The cleaning woman looked at her, amazed, and asked, What dogs?

The dogs, of course, insisted the old woman imperiously, I want the dogs to have them. A person one couldn't trust, a thief, would probably take the bones home. The dogs, I say. Don't you understand? Are you hard of hearing? Really no wonder at your age.

Then the dogs barked less loudly and she thought someone had taken them away, or given them away, because now it was no longer the strong and insistent and solid barking it had been before. The less they barked, the less she let it get her down, she was waiting for the recurrence of the stronger barking, one must be able to wait, and she surely was. Then it was suddenly no longer a barking—though it definitely came from the dogs in the neighborhood—nor a snarling either, but off and on the great, wild, triumphant howling of a single dog, a whimpering afterward, and in the background the barking of the others, slowly receding.

One day, almost two years after the death of his sister Franziska, Dr. Martin Renner received a bill from a firm Pineider for cab fares, all carefully dated, which had been authorized by Mrs. Franziska Jordan and toward which she had paid an advance. But since only a few trips had been made while she was alive, and most of them after her death, he called the firm to get an explanation for this mysterious bill.

The explanation didn't tell him much either, but since he didn't wish to call his former brother-in-law, nor to see him again, he paid, in installments, for the taxi fares of a woman whom he had not known and with whom he had nothing to do whatsoever.

He came to the conclusion that old Mrs. Jordan, who had been driven around by Pineider, must have died some time ago, and that the firm—possibly out of piety—had let several months go by before asking for their due.

A SUCCESS STORY

Margaret Drabble

Margaret Drabble describes her early childhood in Yorkshire, England, where she was born in 1939: "I was brought up on the edge of countryside very similar to the country around Haworth. My family was of the same size and constitution as the Bronte family; my siblings and I [her sister is novelist A. S. Byatt] were interested in writing, and in our childhood composed magazine stories together."

Educated at Cambridge, Drabble has written a novel every other year since 1963: A Summer Bird Cage (1964), The Garrick Year (1965), The Millstone (1965), Jerusalem The Golden (1967), The Waterfall (1969), The Needle's Eye (1972), The Realm of Gold (1975), The Ice Age (1977), and, most recently, The Middle Ground (1980), the story of a professional feminist's boredom with the cause, as well as a biography of Arnold Bennett and a critical study of Wordsworth. Writing out of the tradition of social realism, Drabble gives a rich, almost documentary sense of English life. Her female characters (especially the early ones), straining toward some heightened sensibility and raised expectations, are often brought up short by their "female nature."

In "A Success Story," Margaret Drabble depicts with wry amusement a woman's reversion to "type." A thoroughly liberated woman in all other ways, a success in her career, Kathie Jones would rather be admired for her legs than her mind. "It's an awful thing to say," writes Drabble as if to shock the feminists who are her most ardent supporters, "but that's how some women are."

THIS IS A STORY about a woman. It couldn't have been told a few years ago: perhaps even five years ago it couldn't have been told. Perhaps it can't really be told now. Perhaps I shouldn't write it, perhaps it's a bad move to write it. But it's worth risking. Just to see.

This woman was a playwright. She was one of the few success-ful women playwrights, and she had had a hard time on the way up, for she came from a poor background, from a part of the country hostile to the arts, from a family which had never been to the theater in its life. She wasn't really working class: more lower middle class, which made her success all the more remark-able, as her plays didn't have shock value, they were quite com-plicated and delicate. But they worked: they were something new. She made her way up: first of all she was assistant stage-hand at her local repertory, then she worked in the office at a larger provincial theater, as she didn't really have much interest in life behind the scenes—and all the while she was writing her plays. The first one was put on by the rep she was working in, and it was very much noticed. Kathie (that was her name—Kathie Jones) used to say modestly that it was noticed because she was a woman, and women playwrights were a rarity, and there was something in what she said. But her modesty couldn't explain why she went on writing, professionally, had her plays transferred to the West End, had them filmed, and did really very nicely. She was good at the job, and that was why she suc-ceeded. She was also good, somewhat to her own surprise, at all the things that went along with the job, and which had kept women out of the job for so long: she was good at explaining herself, at arguing with megalomaniac directors, at coolly stick-ing to her own ideas, at adapting when things really couldn't be made to work. She had good judgment, she was calm and professional, she could stand up for herself.

She was not, of course, world famous; let us not give the impression that she was an international name. No, she was a success in her own country, in her own medium. Some of the gossip columns thought her worth mentioning, some of them didn't. Not that there was much to mention: she was a quiet, hard-working girl, with her own friends, her own circle of close friends—some of them writers, one or two friends from the early days at grammar school in the Midlands, one or two journalists. She was considered rather exclusive by some, and she was. She didn't much care for a gay social life, partly be-cause she hadn't time, partly because she hadn't been brought up to it and didn't quite know how to cope. She lived with a man who was a journalist and who traveled a great deal: he was always going off to Brazil and Vietnam and up Everest. He was an exceptionally good-natured man, and they got on well together. Sometimes she was sorry when he went away, but she was always so busy that she didn't miss him much, and anyway it was so interesting when he came back. He, for his part, loved her, and had confidence in her.

So really, one could say that her life had worked out very nicely. She had a job she liked, a reputation, a good relationship, some good friends, a respectable though fluctuating income. At the time of this story, she was in her early thirties and had written five successful plays and several film scripts. She had a play running at a lucrative little theater in the West End and was amusing herself by working on a television adaptation of a play by Strindberg. Her man was away: he was in Hungary, but he would be back soon, he would be back at the end of the week. At the moment at which we close in upon her, she was just putting the phone down after speaking to him: they had exchanged news, she had told him what was in his post, which she always opened for him, he had said that he loved her and was looking forward to coming back and kissing her all over but particularly between her stockings and her suspenders, if she would please wear such antiquated garments on his return to greet him. Then he told her to enjoy her evening; she was just about to go out to a rather grand party. So she was smiling as she put down the telephone.

She was quite a nice-looking woman. This we have not mentioned till this point, because it ought not to be of any importance. Or ought it? Well, we shall see. Anyway, she wasn't bad looking, though she was nothing special. She had rather a long, large-featured face, with a large nose: she had big hands and large bones. Some people thought her beautiful, but others thought she was really plain. You know the type. As a child, she had been plain, as her mother had never tired of saying, and consequently she had no confidence in her appearance at all. Nowadays she didn't care much, she was happy anyway, and as long as her lover continued to take an interest in the serious things of life, like her legs, then she wasn't much interested in looking in the mirror. In fact, she hardly ever did, except to brush her hair, and she wore the same clothes most of the time until they wore out. But tonight was different. She would have to have a look at herself, at least. So when she'd put the phone down she went into the bathroom to have a look.

Tonight was rather a special, grand sort of party, not the usual kind of thing, so she'd put on her best dress, a long green-blue dress that she'd once thought suited her rather old-fashioned looks. She wasn't so sure, now, she wasn't at all sure what she looked like these days; the older she got, the more variable she seemed to be. Not that it mattered much, one way or the other. But one might as well wear one's best dress once in a while. She'd bought it for one of her own first nights, years ago, and hadn't worn it much since. She didn't go to her own first nights anymore, or anyone else's for that matter. It had cost a lot of money for those days. (Not that she spent much money on clothes now—in fact, she spent less.) Staring at herself, hitching it a bit at the shoulder, she wondered whether she'd put it on because she was still, whatever she told herself, slightly nervous about the kind of do she was going to. Surely not. Surely not, these days. Why should she care?

The party she was going to was being given by one of the grandest (socially speaking) theatrical entrepreneurs in London. And there she was going to meet the hero of her childhood dreams. It was all quite romantic. His name was Howard Jago (quite the right sort of name, but people like that have that kind of name), and he was one of the biggest American writers of his generation. He had written plays that made her heart bleed when she was sixteen. They still, oddly enough, moved her profoundly.

She admired him more than she admired any other living writer. He hadn't kept up with the playwriting—she knew well enough that playwrights, compared with other writers, have a short working life—but he was now doing screenplays and also a certain amount of political journalism. He had published a couple of novels, which she had liked immensely: he seemed indefatigable.

When she was a child, she had wanted more than anything to meet him. She had even written him a fan letter telling him so. He did not reply. Probably it never reached him.

She had had several opportunities to meet him before, as he was quite often in Europe and was published by her publishers. But she had always declined.

Why had she declined? Was she afraid of being bored or disappointed? Afraid of not being disappointed? Was she afraid that he might not have heard of her (when, by the rules of the game, he should have done) or might find her boring? Combing her hair, now, looking at herself in the mirror, she wondered. Perhaps she had simply been too busy, on other occasions: or Dan had been at home and had not wanted to go. He didn't care for grand parties, and neither as a rule did she. They preferred to get very drunk quietly at home among friends: that was their favorite form of social life.

She couldn't work out why she hadn't wanted to meet him before: nor why, now, she had decided that she would.

She put him out of her mind, as she went downstairs and found herself a taxi. There would be plenty of other people there that she would know.

And so indeed there were. She knew nearly everybody, by sight or in person. She thought with some relief, as she looked round the massive house in Belgravia and its glittering inhabitants—film stars in outré garments, diplomats, writers, cabinet ministers, actors, actresses—she thought that at least she didn't have to feel nervous anymore. In a way that took some of the thrill away, but it was much pleasanter to be comfortable than thrilled. Being thrilled had always been so exhausting, and such a letdown in the end. Nowadays she sought and found more lasting pleasures. Nevertheless, she had been very different once. Ambitious she must have been, or she wouldn't have found herself here at all, would she? And, as she talked to a friend and kept an eye open for Howard Jago, she said to herself, If I'd known twenty years ago that I would ever find myself here, in a room like this, with people looking like this, I *would* have been delighted. A pity, really, that one couldn't have had that particular thrill then—the thrill of knowing. It wasn't worth much now.

The house was enormous. Tapestries hung on the walls and statues stood in corners. The paintings were by Francis Bacon and Bonnard and Matthew Smith and Braque.

After a while she saw her host approaching her. He was leading Howard Jago in her direction: Howard Jago was doing his rounds. He looked as she had imagined him: wild, heavy, irregular, a bit larger than life-size, the kind of man who looks even bigger than he looks on the television. (She had caught a glimpse or two of him on the television.)

"And this," said her host, "is one of the people you particularly asked to meet. This is Kathie Jones."

Kathie smiled, politely. Jago shook her hand.

"I enjoyed your play the other night," said Jago, politely. He looked as though he was being careful. He looked as though he might be a little drunk.

"That's very kind of you," said Kathie. "I must tell you how very much I have always admired your work."

"I've admired it . . ." and she was going to say, since I was a child, which would have been true, but had to stop herself because it might have been a rude reflection on his age, and went on with ". . . I've admired it ever since I first found it."

They looked at each other, with assessment, and smiled, civilly. Kathie couldn't think of anything else to say. She had remembered, suddenly, exactly why she hadn't wanted to meet him: she hadn't wanted to meet him because she knew he was a womanizer, she knew it from a friend of hers, an actress, who'd had a bad time with him in New York. He can't help it, her friend had said, he's a real sod, he hates women, you know, but he just has to get off with them, he can't let them alone. . . .

The memory paralyzed her. She wondered why she hadn't thought of it earlier. It was obvious, anyway, from his work, that he had a thing about women, that he didn't like them and had to have them. He was a great enough writer for it not to matter to her: it was a measure of his greatness, for she did care about such things considerably.

She thought with a sudden nice physical recollection of Dan, who liked women, and loved her in particular, to her great delight.

She stood there, and smiled, and said nothing. Or rather, she said, "And how long are you in London this time, Mr. Jago?"

And he replied, with equal banality. It's all right, she was saying to herself, it's safe. It doesn't matter. (What did she mean by that?)

And as she listened to him, she saw approaching a film actress, a lady of considerable glamour, approaching with some purpose. "Howard, Howard, *there* you are, I *lost* you," she wailed, throwing her arm around his neck, possessively, her bosom heaving, her necklace sparkling: she started to stroke his graying hair, passionately, as she turned to greet Kathie. "Why hello, *Kathie,*" she said, "what a surprise, I haven't seen you in *years.* Howard went to see your play, was he telling you? . . . Oh look, Howard, there's Martin—" and she marched him off: but Kathie Jones had already turned away. Well rid of him, she thought herself. He was drunk: he swayed slightly as Georgina grabbed him. Georgina was well away. She was a young lady with a will of iron. She was quite amusing on some occasions. Kathie wished them joy, and turned to look for a sympathetic friend, thinking as she went that the poor sixteen-year-old child she had been would have been shocked, shocked beyond anything, to have missed the opportunity to ask him, to hear him speak, even, of what he felt about, perhaps, the freedom of the will (one of his themes) and evolution (yet another). She smiled to herself and went and talked to some publishers. They were much more interesting than Howard Jago had had a chance to be.

It was a couple of hours before he came back to her. She had been enjoying herself. There was plenty to drink, and some very good buffet food, and some people she knew well and some she hadn't seen for ages: she had been drinking quite steadily and was sitting on a settee with an actress and her husband and another couple she'd never met before, laughing, very loudly, all of them, choking almost, over some anecdote about a play of hers, when he came back. He was looking more morose than before, and more obviously drunk. As he approached, Kathie made space for him on the settee by her, as he clearly intended to sit: they were still laughing over the story as he sat. "Hello again," she said, turning to him, secure now, expecting nothing, willing to include him in the circle. "Do you know Jenny, and Bob . . ."

"Yes, yes," he said crossly. "I know everyone, I've met everyone in this place. I want to get out."

"Why don't you go, then?" asked Kathie, politely, slightly at a loss: and even as she spoke, she saw Georgina bearing down on them. Jago saw her too, and flinched: he rose to his feet, pulling Kathie to hers.

"Come on," he said, "let's get out of here." She was thrilled. She had never heard anyone talk like that except in a movie. And Howard Jago turned his back on Georgina, with calculated offense, and marched Kathie across the room, gripping her elbow, again in a way that she had only seen in the movies.

He paused, as they reached the bar, having shaken off their pursuer.

"You're not alone, are you?" he then said, turning to her with an amazing predictable heavy old-world gallantry. "It's not possible that the best-looking and most intelligent woman in the room could have come here alone, is it?"

"Yes, I'm alone," said Kathie.

"Where's your man, then?"

"He's in Hungary," said Kathie.

"I've had enough of this party," said Howard Jago. "Let's get out of it, for Christ's sake."

"I don't know . . ." said Kathie. "I should say good-bye . . ."

"There's no need to say good-bye," he said. "Come on. Let's get out."

She hesitated.

He took her arm.

She went.

They went downstairs and looked for a taxi: they found one easily, as it was that kind of district. They got into it. Then he said, again as though in a play or a film written by some playwright infinitely inferior to either of them, "Where shall we go, to my place or yours?"

"Yours," she said. "But only for a little while. I have to get home. I've a script conference in the morning." She was lying.

"Jesus," he said, looking at her legs, actually moving the skirt of her dress so that he could look at her legs, "you've got a beautiful pair of legs."

"They're nothing special," she said, which was true.

They arrived at his hotel, just off Bond Street. They got out and went into the hotel and up to his room. He asked the night porter to bring them a drink.

The room was large and expensive. Kathie sat in a chair. So did he. They drank the drink, and talked about the party, and about the people at it—their host, and Georgina, and various other playwrights, and the actress he had made so unhappy in New York the year before. Kathie knew exactly what she was doing: nothing on earth would induce her to get into that bed. She made it clear, as one does make it clear. They laughed a lot, and rang for some more drinks and a sandwich, and talked a lot of nonsense. She felt him move away. He had sense, after all. And when she said she ought to go, he looked at her, and said, "Ah, I'm too old for you, you know."

But he can't have said this with much conviction, or she

wouldn't have responded with the awful line she then delivered (which she had said, years before, to an Italian actor in Rome), "You shouldn't try," she said, smiling falsely, "to seduce innocent girls from the country."

He laughed, also falsely. She kissed him: they parted.

She went down and got a taxi and was in bed and asleep in half an hour.

And that is the end of the story. They were to meet again, over the years, at similar parties, and he was to remark again upon her legs and her looks. They never had any serious conversation. But that isn't part of the story.

The point is, what did she think about this episode? She emerges not too badly from it, anyone would agree. She behaved coolly but not censoriously: she said some silly things, but who doesn't in such a silly situation? She had no regrets on her own behalf, though a few on behalf of that sixteen-year-old girl who had somehow just missed the opportunity of a lifetime. She had grown up so differently from what she had imagined. And she had some regrets about her image of the man. It was spoiled, she had to admit it (not quite forever, because oddly enough some years later she went to see one of his early plays and felt such waves of admiration flowing through her, drowning her resentments, as though his old self were still speaking, and she listening, in some other world without ages). But for years and years, she thought she was never going to be able to take his work seriously again, and when she described the evening to Dan, she was so rude about him and his boorish chauvinist masculine behavior that Dan, who usually sided with her and was as indignant as she was about such matters, actually began to feel quite sorry for Howard Jago, and to take his part. *Poor* Mr. Jago, he would say, fondly, whenever his name came up, *poor* Mr. Jago, he would say, lying safely between Kathie's legs, *what* a disappointing evening, I feel quite sorry for him, picking you, my love.

But that isn't all. It ought to be all, but it isn't. For Kathie, when she told the story to Dan, was lying. She tried to lie when she told it to herself, but she didn't quite succeed. She was an honest woman, and she knew perfectly well that she had received more of a thrill through being picked up by Howard Jago at a party, even picked up as she had been, casually, to annoy another woman—she had received more of a thrill from this than she would have got from any discussion, however profound, of his work and hers. She would trade the whole of his work, willingly, and all the lasting pleasure it had given, for that silly remark he had made about her legs. She would rather he fancied her, however casually, then talked to her. She would rather he liked her face than her plays.

It's an awful thing to say, but she thought of his face, looking at her, heavy, drunk, sexy, battered, knowing, and wanting her, however idly: and it gave her a permanent satisfaction that she'd been able to do that to him, that she'd been able to make a man like him look at her in that way. It was better than words, better than friendship.

It's an awful thing to say, but that's how some women are. Even nice, sensible, fulfilled, happy women like Kathie Jones. She would try to excuse herself, sometimes: she would say, I'm only like this because I was a plain child, I need reassurance. But she couldn't fool herself. Really, she knew that she was just a woman, and that's how some women are.

Some people are like that. Some men are like that, too. Howard Jago was exactly like that. People like admiration more than anything. Whatever can one do about it? Perhaps one shouldn't say this kind of thing. One ought not to have said such things, even five years ago, about a woman like Kathie Jones. The opposite case, for political reasons, had to be stated. (This is only a story, and Howard Jago didn't really hate women, any more than Kathie hated men.) But Kathie Jones is all right now. The situation is different, the case is made. We can say what we like about her now, because she's all right. I think.